Body Love

Body Love:

The Amazing Career
of
Bernarr Macfadden

William R. Hunt

Bowling Green State University Popular Press
Bowling Green, Ohio 43403

Copyright© 1989 by Bowling Green State University Popular Press

Library of Congress Catalogue Card No.: 89-051126

ISBN: 0-87972-463-3 Clothbound
      0-87972-464-1 Paperback

Cover design by Gary Dumm

To my strong sisters—
Celia, Florence, Martina, Ilene, and Stella

Acknowledgements

In 1985 I had the pleasure of working at the American Medical Association Library in Chicago and in the archives of Georgetown University. Micaela Sullivan of the AMA provided expert guidance on the Bureau of Investigation files on Bernarr Macfadden and other individuals. More recently Marguerite Fallucco has helped me there. Georgetown University has the papers of Macfadden's long-time editorial assistant, Fulton Oursler, and the help Nicholas B. Scheetz gave me there is appreciated.

As so often in the past I consulted the librarians in the manuscript division of the Library of Congress with good results. Among collections there useful to this book are the papers of the Society for the Suppression of Vice, Anthony Comstock's tool for keeping the nation pure. I got help at many other libraries, including the University of Washington, Texas Tech University, and the Seattle Public Library, where a long run of *Physical Culture* magazine is located.

Without detracting from expressions of gratitude to librarians I should point out that it is unfortunate that early on they decided that most popular magazines, like those Macfadden published, are not worthy of collection. In consequence it has become extremely difficult to find runs of many of his magazines. The loss is particularly acute where the detective magazines are concerned because the quality of reporting on true crime in these publications has maintained a high standard for decades. Librarians, unfortunately, judged the books by their covers.

My thanks to Robert Ernst for advice on the location of the Oursler papers, and to James Whorton, Jeanne Schaaf and Robert Werner, M.D., Marjorie Cole, and Terrence Cole for reading the manuscript. Terrence Cole edited each chapter of my penultimate draft and cheered me on to the finish.

Contents

Chapter 1
  Sex Appeal   1
Chapter 2
  Hard Knocks   6
Chapter 3
  Nuts and Berries   13
Chapter 4
  "Weakness is a Sin"   22
Chapter 5
  Indecent Exposure   36
Chapter 6
  Strong Beliefs   54
Chapter 7
  "I'm Ruined! I'm Ruined!"   80
Chapter 8
  Nemesis   92
Illustrations   111
Chapter 9
  "The New York Graphic"   135
Chapter 10
  Age of Macfadden   153
Chapter 11
  Presidential Timber   168
Chapter 12
  The Ardent Lover   184
Chapter 13
  Too Many Wives   196
Chapter 14
  Flamboyance   202
Notes   204
Bibliography   213
Index   219

Chapter 1
Sex Appeal

It was proposed to exhibit the forms of young women, denuded of their proper womanly apparel.

Anthony Comstock

New Yorkers, in their raucous, excitable way, milled about in front of Madison Square Garden, jeering at the police. Roundsman Gleason of the Tenderloin Station had called out the reserves after the Garden's doors were closed to 5,000 disappointed folks who wanted to see the show. Eventually the muttering crowd dispersed to seek other diversions, still a little mad that they were not among the lucky 15,000 spectators who had jammed into the Garden before firemen closed the doors. Bernarr Macfadden's second bid for the money and acclaim of New Yorkers in 1905 was a startling success, but no one predicted that his flamboyance would continue to amuse and annoy them for half a century.

Inside the Garden spectators of what Macfadden called the "Mammoth Physical Exhibition Show," and newspapers labeled the "beauty show,"[1] were not much happier than the throngs turned away at the door. The crowd, expecting to see some nude or near—nude posing, found the actual proceedings a little dull. For two hours they watched foot races by male members of various athletic clubs, two wrestling matches, a high jumper, a weight lifter, and a fifty yard dash by seven women in knickerbockers. After these warm-up events, the exhibition of fine looking men and women was staged. According to rumor some of the posers would show more of their bodies than the law allowed. Alas! The rumors were untrue. Standing sedately before a black curtain under spotlights the posers only showed their finely toned muscles and good posture. The women wore tights and other garments. No nudes. No erotic dances. Nothing titillating. All was just as it had been advertised.

What stirred the audience more than the athletes was the performance of an usher, a red-headed young woman of strength and purpose, who ranged the arena to keep order in the audience. She forcibly ejected gentlemen from reserved seats who held only general admission tickets and, confronting six men who insisted upon sitting upon the backs of their chairs, she jerked each one into a proper seating position. Cheers echoed after these Amazonian feats. "Who is she?"[2] shouted someone.

1

"Anthony Comstock" was the answer roared back from many throats—and the Garden rocked with laughter and cries of derision.

Anthony Comstock, present or not, was the villain of the show. His antics in days before the event accomplished far more than Macfadden's advertisements in creating the sensation that brought the crowd out. He had caused Macfadden's arrest and the tearing down of advertising posters around the city. Newspaper accounts of the arrest and Macfadden's protests sparked an excitable interest, leading to the lively rumors of what might be offered at the Garden. Macfadden's published, solemn assurances that the posing men would only show bare flesh above the waist while women would wear white tights or union suits with sashes around their waists were disregarded. People figured that Comstock expected something nasty at the Garden and resolved that they would see it too. Comstock, the anti-vice crusader and professional kill-joy, was well-known. What he banned signalled interest to those of a different persuasion.

Anthony Comstock contributed a word—his own name—to the language. "Comstockery," coined by George Bernard Shaw and popularized by Macfadden and others suggested a narrow, cold, intolerant viewpoint, one hinting of dark, physic malady within. Both Comstock and Macfadden filled significant places in the long censorship struggle that has been going on since time out of mind. Each saw himself as the champion of an enlightened, goodly cause, and saw the other as an arch-fiend. While he lived Comstock won most of his battles but his spiritual descendants have not fared well. Perhaps if the two old antagonists met today in the neighborhood of the new Garden to review some of the sex magazines on nearby newsstands they would be equally shocked. Surely Comstock would rage, "I told you so;" then, Macfadden, recovering his poise, would insist that generations of suppression of healthy instincts imposed by Comstock and his kind had finally exploded—"I warned you this would happen."

Comstock, born in New Canaan, Conn. in 1844, showed a deep consciousness of sin and a vigorous militancy from his youth. In his years of fame he liked to boast of a youthful exploit that foreshadowed his career. Seeing a mad dog running wild in the streets Comstock shot it dead. Subsequently, he broke into the dog owner's premises and poured out all his moonshine—a punishment for keeping such a dog and illegally trading moonshine for groceries. After Civil War service the stern-visaged reformer served as a store clerk, then a dry goods salesman in New York before embarking upon his true vocation. In support of the Young Men's Christian Association's campaign against obscene literature he confronted a publisher who slashed his face with a knife but did not dim his zeal. In 1873 he helped organize a committee for the Suppression of Vice which provided financial support for his work. His lobbying in

Washington led to the ban of obscene matter from the mails and his appointment as an unpaid special agent for the post office.

He hated obscene literature above all things yet also exposed frauds, quacks, gamblers, abortionists, lottery promoters, dishonest advertisers, patent medicine vendors, artists who depicted nude bodies, and liberals. His was a rich, full life, particularly rewarding when he grappled with a sensational case like that of Victoria C. Woodhill and Tennessee Claflin, two decidedly emancipated sisters whose periodical exposed the sexual indiscretions of the famous Rev. Henry Ward Beecher. Comstock also hounded the infamous Madame Restell, a wealthy abortionist and contraceptionist, to her suicide. She was, according to Comstock's boast, his fifteenth successful suicide; others followed.

Until the 1880s Comstock enjoyed the regard of most respectable citizens, although a few ridiculed his methods and choice of victims. Sterner opposition came from the National Liberal League, an enlightened, articulate group that tried to convince Americans that Comstock menaced democratic values. In lectures and books Comstock decried the liberals as libertines and quacks.

Shortly before the crusader brought about Macfadden's arrest he prevented the presentation of George Bernard Shaw's play, *Mrs. Warren's Profession*. New York gossips complained that Comstock's indignation at Shaw's introduction of the opprobrious word "comstockery" in the play motivated him as strongly as the drama's theme of prostitution. Through their persecutions by the anti-vice crusader, Shaw and Macfadden later became fast friends and mutual admirers. Shaw's much publicized devotion to a vegetable diet and his witty sallies at many conventions of the time provided moral support for some of Macfadden's causes.

With his portly figure, impressive side-whiskers linked to a thick, sweeping moustache, and his unhappy countenance, Comstock was the cartoonist's dream. He stood guard at "the sewer mouth" of society for forty years, secure in the conviction that God had commissioned his watchfulness. This certainty, and the support of influential Christian organizations, created controversial social confrontations and inhibited freedom of expression for decades. During his heyday other great reform currents swept the nation to achieve more democratic political processes and other advances we cherish, while Comstock's fulminations were reminders of the theocratic communities of colonial America.

When police arrested Macfadden on charges brought by the Society for the Suppression of Vice (SSV) he was in his office at 29 East Nineteenth Street where the *Physical Culture* magazine was published. The publisher wore sandals, a broad-brimmed hat, and, as the *New York Times* observed mischievously, "other clothes as well."[3] Reporters showed up to examine 500 pounds of exhibition posters, the most daring of which depicted a man in sandals and a leopard skin breech-cloth, and hear Macfadden's protests. "The purpose of the exhibition is to show how the spread of physical culture has improved the human body. Manifestly that cannot be done if the exhibitors are covered with clothing."

Comstock had heard too many excuses from men justifying their corruption of youth by exposing them to suggestive views of the human form to be impressed by Macfadden's bosh about physical culture. He had heard it all before from artists mumbling about artistic integrity in their glowing, provocative nudes and smut merchants selling dirty postcards. Nor could the anti-vice crusader be mollified by the physical culturist's moderate tone: "Comstock's intentions are good, no doubt, but he is going too far."[4] Macfadden went on to tell newsmen about the ages of antiquity when great artists and common people rejoiced innocently in the health and strength of their bodies. Comstock had heard this guff before too and had also heard about some of the unspeakable practices of ancient Greeks. He did not know much about art—or physical culture—but he knew much about Evil.

At the magistrate's court where Comstock appeared as prosecution witness against John Storm, accused of selling obscene postcard pictures, and at Macfadden's preliminary hearing which followed, he received rough treatment. Magistrate Pool did not see any obscenity in Storm's pictures or any need to be bullied by the crusader. Comstock raged and blustered until removed forcibly from the court. Reporters, pleased to observe that Comstock's face "took on a more roseate hue and his whiskers bristled," heard him mutter: "I'll have that man impeached yet!" Commenting on the Macfadden prosecution the *Times* derived some amusement at the removal of posters showing men and women clad "only in knit underwear" by Comstock, "who, as befits his specialty, is of a rather sweeping and indiscriminate temper towards all that invades it." The editor considered Macfadden well-named, "being a faddist and the son of a faddist." Judging from some of Comstock's performances, "it may well appear that the name of Mr. Comstock ought also to be Macfadden." While Comstock was a legendary figure in New York people were just beginning to learn about his latest victim. "We are reliably informed," said the editor, "that Mr. Macfadden is as honest a specialist in his kind as Mr. Comstock is in his, that he is really a fanatic of physical culture. He maintains with much plausibility that the physical charm of a human body cannot be judged when it is wrapped in a horse blanket or overlaid with an ulster." Looking forward to the later courtroom encounter of the two specialists the editor quoted Shakespeare: "Tis dangerous when the baser nature comes/Between the pass and fell incensed point of might opposites."

The records of the Society for the Suppression of Vice show that its case against Macfadden was not worth the effort. The specific charge was that "he sent vile pictures about the saloons and places of business downtown with complimentary tickets." Two magistrates had refused to issue a warrant; finally, a third, more sympathetic to the SSV was found. But even this friendly judge let the offender off with a suspended sentence.[5]

On this encounter Macfadden came out well. Later prosecutions would be more threatening. Over the decades of his life many critics were to question Macfadden's exploitation of sex. It seemed so wrong to him—and so silly. He was no sex fiend, no pervert, nor advocate of sexual license. He could never concede that he exploited sex to sell magazines or his theories. What others condemned as cheap and tawdry was a mere reflection of their prudish narrowness. Why should anyone complain just because he understood what people liked? And what they needed? Why pretend that sex does not exist? Was it not the clearest expression of human health and vitality?

Chapter 2
Hard Knocks

My life has at no time been a bed of roses.

Bernarr Macfadden

Making much of a hard youth is a tradition among "self-made" Americans. Birth in a log cabin is a preferred start but, failing that fortuitous happenstance, other rugged circumstances might infuse the humdrum with legend-making prospects. Politicians, seeking to establish their commonalty with voters, have been tempted to cheat a little, veiling the silver spoon reality in a cloud of imaginary hard knocks. Health faddists and professional strong men have even stronger motivations for showing their conquest of disease and puniness. As salesmen of health and strength it is persuasive to say: "I once looked as miserable as you. See now my manly vigor—and consider my remedy."

Bernarr Macfadden's infatuation with the moral tale of his youth was acute, and he never tired of stressing its meaning to biographers, interviewers, and readers. The sorrow, misery, and hardship he described was not exaggerated: young Bernarr did have an ugly start to life.

The boy saw his first light in the Ozarks of southeastern Missouri where his parents settled with other families in Greenwood Valley. Soon the green wood fell before the eagerness of residents to clear land for raising and training racehorses. William McFadden (the spelling of the family name before Bernarr changed his for greater typographical impact; changing the tame "Bernard" to the more dynamic "Bernarr" at the same time) loved racehorses and whiskey; the first kept him poor; the second cost him a marriage and hurried his death. Bernarr, born in 1868, was followed by two sisters, Mary in 1870 and Alma in 1873. After Alma's birth the parents separated and the children never saw their father again. Relatives raised the two girls while Mrs. McFadden moved with her son to Chicago where other relatives kept a hotel.

At age nine Bernarr knew the sad lot of poor, unwanted relations dependent upon those who resented them. Despite his hard work around the hotel he never knew a kindly smile. No one expected Bernarr to divert himself with school lessons when work needed doing. And conditions grew worse. His mother died of tuberculosis in 1879, leaving the sorrowing lad alone among hostile, ungracious folks. His chronic

6

cough worried him, especially after hearing someone say: "That brat o' hers is got it too."[1]

When his relatives sent him outside the city to earn his keep with a farmer he felt better. Hard, outdoor work, wood chopping and stock feeding, improved his health. All boys are gratified to see their muscles begin to bulge and feel their bodies gain strength, but for Bernarr the experience was transcendent—a veritable miracle of endless fascination. Little wonder that generations of magazine and newspaper readers would come to know his muscles better than their own: he never tired of having himself photographed in strong man poses. Mockery of his self-absorbed poses by jaded viewers never affected him. His body was a miracle and a great lesson for mankind!

Other farm experiences also left permanent stamps on his character. His employer, Robert Hunter, required church attendance. Hunter was a hard man, seemingly devoid of kindliness, sympathy, charity, or any of the other virtues Bernarr heard extolled by the preacher on Sundays. It seemed passing strange that old Hunter sitting there, could expose himself constantly to sound Christian teachings without being reached by them. After long consideration Bernarr concluded that Hunter and a lot of other Christians were hypocrites and that Christianity was a dismal failure. He never changed his mind about Christianity, yet saw enough value in organized religion to tentatively develop one of his own invention later on.

Two years of farm work were enough. After a brawl with Hunter over a seventy-five cent boot repair bill, Bernarr decamped for St. Louis where some relatives extended hospitality. He worked long hours at clerkish, indoor jobs and his health declined again. Unhealthy folks read newspaper ads praising patent medicines and buy them, as Bernarr did without gaining any relief. This disappointment engendered in the lad a hatred of doctors, genuine or quack, an obsession that lasted all his life.

In St. Louis Bernarr found the answer for everything in a pair of fifty cent dumbbells. It is too bad those dumbbells could not hang in a museum somewhere with Jesse James' gun and Harry Truman's piano (to name hallmarks of other distinguished Missourians). The dumbbells helped restore his health, gave him strength and relieved the tedium of clerical positions. And, eventually, they made him a celebrated prophet, health expert, and millionaire. All this for fifty cents!

So it was that a soaring life's course opened, one rich in promise of things that could hardly be imagined earlier. He started expanding at once, upgrading his dumbbells to larger models, taking longer and longer hikes, then carrying a weight to make his march harder. Finally he got enough money to visit a gymnasium frequently where he could use physical training equipment. Muscles developed at a great pace even if he could not do anything to gain in height once he reached full growth at five feet six inches—and his stumpiness always bothered him.

In 1885 he pulled up stakes again and moved to Kansas where a cousin who was a dentist needed a strong man to hold screaming patients in the chair. Dentists were a little slow in developing pain suppressors, which is one reason why our elders did not complain too much about their false teeth. Leaving the agonies of dental care he hoboed around Kansas doing farm work, always with his dumbbells near at hand for leisure amusements. Back in Missouri after he tired of Kansas he worked briefly in a coal mine, then returned to St. Louis for a variety of other jobs.

At age seventeen he was earning enough money as a bookkeeper to pay for membership in the Missouri Gym where he began daily training with great joy. Watching others work out on horizontal bars he devised his own system for acquiring the skills. Because he applied "scientific principles" to his training he was able to master the forward swing and somersaults in months, while other less studious fellows took years. Though not a bookish person he did search the public library for help and found William Blakie's *How to Get Strong*, a manual that became his bible until exhausting its possibilities. It was thrilling to discover that another man had experienced the same drives that had become his life's purpose—that he was not alone in his ambitious quest.

If Macfadden read any of the works of the Christian hygienists like Sylvester Graham or William Alcott at this time he did not record it. His own focus on commanding his body differed from that of the Christians who feared the body's propensity to evil. The reigning evil, as Macfadden began to perceive it, was a physically weak body. Yet, as he described his training routine there is an echo of the Christian hygienists: "Such a regime cleans the body of its impurities and releases deep-seated atavistic animal urges."[2]

Next Macfadden took up wrestling and soon was able to throw much heavier men with ease. Somewhere he had read about the advantages of a two-meal a day diet; he tried it and found an immediate gain in strength and endurance. The success of his first diet experiment marked his emergence as a hygienist or health faddist (the latter being the more pejorative term). His enthusiasm for experiments never ended. He tried meat abstinence and periods of total fasting, noting that his mental powers increased in both instances. Through thick and thin he never wavered from the belief that the mind's quickness, alertness, and sureness of judgment improved through dieting. When others praised his business triumphs he modestly attributed his mental superiority over rivals to his eating habits.

Eventually Macfadden discovered a means of uniting what he loved doing most with the necessity of earning a living—one of the chief keys to contentment for all individuals. He became a kinistherapist, a term he coined to describe a "healer of disease by use of movements." Today there are all kinds of specialists who teach, train, or administer forms of physical therapy, but in the 1890s Macfadden was far in advance of the boom. What a kinistherapist did for his clients would not have concerned the greater world if physical training had been its only purpose. But Macfadden presented himself as a "healer of disease," thus catching the attention of professional rivals in the healing arts—the doctors— who fancied that they alone possessed the proper credentials for healing.

Macfadden later claimed that his new service thrived from the start, then declined because his diet-exercise routines reduced him to a "depleted skeleton." He gave up dieting and his business to improve his literary skills. For some months editors had been rejecting his articles on aspects of physical culture because of his execrable writing. To remedy this impediment to the wider dissemination of his ideas he needed time to study so he took employment as gym instructor at the Bunker Hill Academy, a school in Illinois. For a year he worked, studied, ate three meals daily, and, at the end, suffered from a bad cold. It was time for a change! He limited his food to a little fruit for five days and was cured.

During this same period of time Macfadden took up professional wrestling. After winning the lightweight crown in St. Louis, he beat the welterweight champion, then challenged the heavyweight champ, who scoffed at the pretensions of a slight lad of 135 pounds. Readers can surely guess the outcome of the championship match. The champ fought desperately against the smaller man for ninety minutes but faded because of the other's supremacy in physical endurance. Thus did Macfadden become the holder of all the city's wrestling crowns.

When he was twenty-three years old Macfadden took a job as physical director at a military school near St. Louis. His high school wrestling team did well in city competition, as did his football team. Before becoming a coach he knew nothing about football, but as the game was not then taken too seriously he had time to pick up the rudiments and pass them along to his boys. Standards even permitted the coach to play quarterback so he really got his nose into the game.

During this school year Macfadden tested his literary powers by writing a novel which was entitled *The Athlete's Conquest*. For lack of grammar, plot, or structure a vanity press publisher in Chicago refused to publish the book. Much chagrined, the author revised the novel and found a less demanding publisher who was willing to produce a book. Perhaps his only readers at the time were the author's students. One student's enthusiasm even extended to reading it covertly after light's out, as the author liked to brag in later years. Readers of *Physical Culture* magazine also got a chance later to follow the adventures of the novel's hero through serialized episodes.

A young man like Macfadden, bursting with energy and ideas, will invariably find the opportunity to thrust towards his goals. Events can affect the timing of success and Macfadden's destiny was spurred by his participation in the Chicago World's Fair in 1893. The great fair enchanted numbers of visitors with its gleaming White City laid out amidst lagoons and fountains on the shores of Lake Michigan. Arriving at the fairgrounds by boat Macfadden landed at the Peristyle, a mock marble colonnade with lofty columns topped by an entabulature depicting, as with an ancient Greek temple, naked men and women posing heroically. Seeing all those muscular forms moved Macfadden deeply. They represented what he wished to achieve for his world—his contemporaries must come to aspire to such magnificent bodies and be willing to display them with dignity and honor. The sight of the entabulature was really all that he needed in the way of a classical education: it fixed forever his idealistic conception of classical times. In those old times civilization had reached a pinnacle in things artistic, political, and intellectual. Every school boy had some notion of these attainments of the ancients but what was less understood and appreciated, was that the leaders of that magnificent society celebrated the beauty and purity of the human form. Anyone who looked at classical art should, Macfadden believed, sorrow over the debasement of American ideals. Americans venerated progress, wealth, expansion, and engineering feats, but ignored their bodies. Was it shame? Or just ignorance? Now Macfadden understood more fully why he perceived the body in ways that were beyond the ken of his contemporaries. Although only a Missouri farm boy turned into a crude athlete, his appreciation of the true classical spirit had come naturally—not from book learning or language study but from deep intuition. Looking up at those prancing gods and goddesses on the entabulature he vowed to restore the verities to his own society; he would teach others to see the beauty in their bodies.

While these entrancing visions danced in his head, he took a job demonstrating a muscle exerciser an inventor-manufacturer was hawking at the fair. On off hours he wandered the fairgrounds and learned a little bit of showmanship, particularly at the shows of the great strong man, Eugene Sandow, who used a mirrored cabinet to make his huge muscles look even larger than they were.

When the fair ended Macfadden returned to St. Louis. But he was on fire with his expectations and found means to relocate in Boston, the nation's intellectual capital. Enroute he stopped to look over New York and realized immediately that it was the place he must conquer if he were to conquer America. Everywhere the hustling style was apparent. Folks talked and moved faster because they expected to go places and get something done. New York was the right place for him.

He had just $50 in capital. Rent for two rooms at 24 East 20th, near busy Broadway, came to $10 weekly. Soon placards exhibiting his compact, muscular body and inviting clients to learn from the professor the ways of strength and health, blanketed the city. Conquering New York caused some anxiety. Two weeks passed before his first physical culture client appeared. With the front money Macfadden received, he dashed out for the first square meal he had enjoyed in some time. Soon other clients followed but he still felt pinched enough to accept a demonstrator's job with Alexander Whitely, whose exerciser he had exhibited at the World's Fair. He only traveled for Whitely during the dull summer months when New Yorkers were less likely to feel energetic enough to engage his services. After his tour he had enough money to rent better quarters at 296-Fifth Avenue. Business was pretty good but fame eluded him and he really needed fame, both for his self-esteem and because it was essential to his mission of reforming the world.

Magazine and newspaper editors continued to frustrate him by rejecting the articles he offered on physical culture. They just did not think that readers would be interested. In hope of making more money Macfadden became an inventor, tinkering with Whitely's machine to improve its function. But a swing around such shops as sold sporting goods did not yield him many sales. Macfadden never doubted himself but it became clear to him that the times were out of joint. Americans were not alert enough. They did not want to patronize his physical culture studio and they did not want to buy his exerciser. All they wanted to talk about was the Spanish-American War. That people showed such intense excitement over international events greatly puzzled him. "His message," as a biographer later put it, "was a thousand-fold more important than the most sensational jingo utterance; but man is prone to shut his ear to truth, and gape it to noisy trifles."[3]

With this disgusting state of affairs slowing the course of destiny Macfadden resolved to try his fortunes in England. Surely the people of an older European civilization would be closer to classical ideals and hence more receptive to his reforms.

He booked passage on a Cunard liner, seeking opportunity. He hoped to get some capital by selling large numbers of his exercisers. The voyage to Liverpool occupied the most miserable week of his life. Sea-sickness reduced him to a quivering ruin by the time he stumbled ashore. Later he worked out a diet and some exercises that prevented sickness. Exercises included 20 miles of pacing the deck daily.

In England he found a sporting goods firm willing to manufacture his exerciser and booked a demonstration tour. The tour became a "triumphal march"[4] as Englishmen accepted his message and purchased his device with great enthusiasm. Before each lecture he posed in a cabinet against a stark background of black cloth, in imitation of Eugene Sandow. In the glare of a spotlight against the cabinet Macfadden looked about six inches taller and much more muscular all around. He posed, as was the custom, in imitation of classical statues like "The Boxer" and other wonderful treasures of Greek-Roman art which audiences were supposed to recognize. Whether the ordinary Englishman was any better informed about classical art than Macfadden is questionable but they knew about bulging muscles. Fellows wished to have such muscles, especially if their girl, who might be with them, oohed and aahed at Macfadden. After each posing Macfadden gave a lecture on health, then pitched for sales of his exerciser.

He made good money in England and success stirred his ambitions to return home. He had an idea that he could reach more people and make more money with a publication. If he could produce his own magazine and make it popular he could spread his health message to millions. Getting started might be difficult but once he got things rolling the momentum would revolutionize society.

Chapter 3
Nuts and Berries

Why they expect a man to live on nothing but food and water.

W.C. Fields

"Rape and murder may be due to constipation confused with sex passion," reflected Macfadden in his *Encyclopedia*,[1] that amazing compendium of his wisdom on physical culture. While his linking of waste elimination with extreme criminal violence and sexual perversity may seem absurd it had been introduced by earlier students of Christian physiology. It was Sylvester Graham, namesake of the flour and the cracker, who broke through the thicket of mystery surrounding human conduct early in the nineteenth century with a remarkably odd lot of Christian dogmas.

Macfadden's theories owed much to Graham, a Connecticut preacher born in 1794 who was America's first food reformer and deepest thinker on sex-diet relationships. A short list of evils abominated by the fluent, feisty clergyman dove-tails with those Macfadden scolded about—feather beds, white bread, meat, tobacco, condiments, corsets, and heavy clothing. In some ways their approaches differed: Graham hated feather beds because they encouraged copulation; Macfadden was against them because soft beds made people soft.

One need not be too deep nor too distrustful of human motivation to notice that Graham, like other Christian physiologists or hygienists, had serious reservations about the non-procreation values of sex. Macfadden, in sharp contrast, considered sex a healthy, joyful pursuit even if he never went so far as to suggest that sexual activity disassociated from procreation was something worth considering among life's interludes. Both men wrote marriage manuals, heavy with warnings about the dire consequences of too much sex and the wrong kind of sex, but even when their language seems similar differences in attitude can be detected. It is likely that some of Macfadden's aping of the Christian physiologists can be attributed to his fear of censorship rather than conviction.

Graham's lectures, "Advice to Young Men," were among the first given in the nation on the ticklish subject of sex. His boldness was rewarded with excellent lecture fees in the 1830s and high ranking as a Christian theologian. There were occasions, however, when he was hooted down by the mob and threatened. Some folks considered that bringing sex to the attention of women was the devil's work.

Although Graham was not among the more learned men of his day he could read Latin, Greek, and Hebrew texts of the Bible. Yet, he gloried in his ignorance, insisting that he had never read any other book other than the Scriptures. If this were true he could not be accused of plagiarizing his ideas from others, despite considerable evidence to the contrary.

Another reason for maintaining his innocence of book learning was to give preference to the source of his ideas—the mind of God. It was directly from God that he learned about the superiority of dark over white bread. Refiners of flour had begun to remove the bran from wheat, leaving a product that was prettier looking but distressfully unhealthy. When commercial bakers got hold of it they often made it worse by adulterating the flour with cheaper stuff. Graham urged everyone to do their own baking at home. He seemed to believe that dark bread, or Graham bread as it came to be called, was his particular discovery. That the ancient Greeks and others had also preferred dark bread was not anything that he cared to admit—if he knew. Intellectual arrogance is the mainspring of reform and Graham was as well equipped as a man could be. In defense of his modesty regarding his research it should be noted that diet experts rarely reveal a sense of history. Today's diet promoters are usually touting schemes that have been urged at other times under other names.

Whiskey was the starting point for Graham's reform campaigns. The heavy consumption of booze in those days did cry out for attention from reformers. His was one of several voices in the wilderness decrying the social consequences of too frequent imbibing, but he also worried about sex a good deal. His remarkable finding that a proper dark bread-vegetable diet solved both evils elevated him in one bound to the Pantheon of seminal thinkers on practical morality. In revealing that avoidance of meat and sex were demanded by human nature, he moved consideration of both activities to another plane.

Graham's discovery that one particular sexual sin outranked the others in nastiness was another singular breakthrough in theological history. Hitherto, adultery and fornication had always headed the lists of iniquities in the sexual line, but Graham revolutionized the traditional order of things by elevating masturbation to the leading spot. Graham also stepped outside Protestant tradition to extol virginity over the practice of legitimate marital sex. Since it had long been the custom to advise libertines to marry (better to marry than to sin, said St. Augustine), this was a new departure. But people listened to Graham's arguments because he was very persuasive.

What had tipped Graham off to the danger of any kind of sex was the intense agitation it excited in the body. "The brain, stomach, heart, lungs, liver, skin, and the other organs, feel it sweeping over them with the tremendous violence of a tornado," cried Graham. Then the tortured heart drove the fearfully congested blood to the visceral—"producing depression, irritation, debility, rupture, inflammation, and sometimes disorganization: and this violent paroxysm is generally succeeded by great exhaustion, relaxation, lassitude, and even prostration."[2] In short, sex was damnably unhealthy and must be avoided except for procreation, and that limited to once monthly for younger, more robust couples, and less frequently for the older and more delicate partners. Graham differed from earlier authorities on sexual hygiene who believed that frequent sex and frequent masturbation caused impotency. What excessive sex stimulated, he warned, was more excessive sex.

Incredibly enough, Graham's fantastic moral pronouncements influenced medical opinion. Doctors, without questioning the scientific basis of the preacher's theories or raising an eyebrow at a layman's intrusion into their garden of truths, accepted his nonsense because it had a forceful moral tone—and they were lazy. Doctors found it good to have certain mysteries clarified and doubly good to pass along advice reflecting advanced thought and social responsibility. In succumbing to Graham's conviction that masturbation caused insanity the medical men had encouragement from their scientific authorities as well. Insanity, like sex, was a troubling medical and social problem; linking the two vexations in a way to suggest the victim's guilt salved the social conscience and averted any temptation to question the Divine purpose.

Since Graham's anguish over what men poured down their throats had started his inquiries it is no surprise that he also looked at the food they ate to determine if it affected their drunkenness. Sure enough, he found a direct relationship. By now he was an expert in sensuality and could prove that the Serpent always lurked in a full pantry. The wrong food could turn people into sinners.

Food reform in the United States began in the 1830s when Sylvester Graham and others decided that the Bible stood against white bread and other common feeding habits. Their strictures against eating habits were far more fruitful of long-term change than those against sexual activities.

Graham looked with fearful scorn at the national diet. Americans ate like starving peasants who had suddenly found themselves unhampered in the landlord's pantry during a famine. Men and women ate too much and were inclined to wash food down with whiskey and beer. Huge breakfasts, including pies and salt fish, were common, as were dinners featuring salt pork and beans. Dyspepsia was the natural condition of folks who expected to dine, when prosperous, on several meats, gravies, pickles, vegetables, condiments, cheese, bread, and butter before finishing off with sweets, fruits, puddings, and cakes.

The problem of overstuffing was complemented by poor food preparation in many households where the frying pan served most cooking needs. Still another hazard to the internal organs was the national habit, much commented upon by European visitors, of wolfing food down as if in frantic competition. "Gobble, gulp, and go," characterized busy Americans who disdained lingering at table.

Poor people, of course, did not usually get too much to eat and what they got often lacked nutritional value. Staples varied from region to region but there was nothing about the diet of the poor anywhere to justify any nostalgia for "the good old days." Dr. John Kellogg, the Battle Creek food reformer, recalled that his childhood diet in rural Michigan had been corn-meal mush and little else. As a youth he contracted tuberculosis while his father suffered from chronic diarrhea and constant eye inflammation.

People who survived diet deficiencies and excessive eating made the fortunes of patent medicine manufacturers for whom the second half of the 19th century represented a "golden age." Pills, tonics, and other remedies urged on the unwell in heavy newspaper, magazine, and billboard advertising included a goodly share directed to digestive woes. Products too numerous to count included such popular items as Hostetter's Celebrated Stomach Bitters, Warner's Safe Cure, and Castoria.

Graham's diet reforms were much debated in his day and sometimes ridiculed by the unbelieving who found the causal connection between diet and eternal damnation hard to grasp. "The fiend Infidel is to be put out of the way," noted a New York newspaper, "by nothing less than some spare diet and a course of vegetables."[3] Why a preacher suddenly linked ungodliness with eating habits was not clear to everyone but, if they attended Graham's lectures or read his books, they could hardly miss the connection. He had already gained public renown by lecturing on masturbation, drawing heavily on S.A. Tissot, an 18th-century French writer.

With unabated zeal Graham embarked on a mission to bring about a hygienic millennium. From brown bread advocacy he went on to promotion of vegetarianism. He fought hard for the cause, never giving credit to any other authority—ancient or contemporary—for his ideas, and consistently overstating his case with bad science passionately expressed. He argued that condiments promoted depression and insanity; that meat eating inflamed the "baser propensities;" that tea drinking caused delirium tremens; or that chicken pie and excessive lewdness caused cholera morbus. He was sure that this was true.

For a time Graham Clubs and Graham eateries flourished as centers of civility and reform discussion (including talk of free love; abolition; and other radical notions) over beans, boiled rice, Graham bread, and puddings. Graham died in 1851 and the influence of his followers waned. Diet reform slumbered for some years until resurrected under the inspired leadership of the Seventh Day Adventists.

Without doubt Sylvester Graham has been one of the most influential Americans in history. He was one of the first hygienists to stress exercise for health and bathed in the cool waters of the Mill River which ran through his hometown of Northampton, Mass. As he took himself very seriously indeed he apologized to the world-at-large when he experienced an illness. Life was a battle for the contentious little man who was not much loved as a child or as a man, and not much honored by his wife. For some reason men predominated among converts to Grahamism and Mrs. Graham disdained her husband's theories. Scandalously she entertained with high style, offering dinner guests a bountiful fare of flesh and other foods, victuals that poor Sylvester had labeled "abominations."

Graham may not have known about the "Noble Savage" popularized by Rousseau and other savants of the European Enlightenment but he, too, made a giant contribution to an appreciation of nature's way. He showed the wonderful healing power of nature itself, thus challenging the assumption that civilized ways were superior. "Nature's way," became an oft heard cry through the land. Swiftly patent medicine manufacturers saw the appeal and advertised many contrived and artificial compounds as "nature's way" to relieve this or that. So the sincere true believers and the charlatans adopted nature's way with all the innocence and cunning they could muster. Bernarr Macfadden, when it came his time to be smitten, was one of the sincere believers and an extremist: he would teach that the natural way was the only way.

William Alcott, another Christian physiologist of the last century, who was a contemporary of Graham and a fellow citizen of Connecticut, influenced opinion along lines similar to Graham. Alcott did have more education in anatomy and physiology than the preacher although he chose education rather than medicine for his profession. The Connecticut educator produced a hundred books and articles on self-improvement before his death in 1859 but he was proudest of the *Young Man's Guide* and the *Physiology of Marriage,* treatises that delved into vexing sexual matters. Unlike Graham, Alcott saw no evil in natural sexual appetites, although he subscribed to the masturbation-insanity connection and considered that marriage mates should limit their copulation to once monthly.

Alcott and others concerned about health during the nation's first great reform did not limit their inquiries. They also decried women's corsets, a stifling fashion decreed by the demands of the fashionable hourglass figure with the support of New England's important whaling industry. And they spoke harshly against liquor and tobacco. Alcott urged folks who would be healthy to take more exercise and fresh air and to shun heavy eating.

Alcott's arguments against flesh eating resemble those of Graham against sexual activities. Meat eating gave one a feeling of strength yet the arousal of the bodily organs to vigorous digestive feats led to a wasteful expenditure of vital energy. Meat eating shortened life: "The system...is inevitably worn into a premature dissolution by the violent and unnatural heat of an over-stimulated and precipitate circulation."[4] A cool vegetable diet, Alcott observed, not only eliminated the ruinous effects of over-stimulation on the organs but "has a tendency to temper the passions."[5]

Like Graham, Alcott promulgated the oneness of morality and physiology: eating vegetables became a Christian duty. Health faddism reached its mid-nineteenth century high point when Alcott toasted fellow vegetarian banqueters with a glass of cold water, announcing: "a vegetable diet lies at the basis of all reform, whether civil, social, moral, or religious."[6]

While Alcott recommended physical exercise for health and even ran the mile from his home to the post office, the exercise for health mania only bloomed later in the century. George Winesap began lecturing on physical culture in the 1860s. He was the nation's first popularizer of weight lifting, a practice he started as a Harvard medical school student after a class bully humiliated him. As Winship progressed in his strength program he sought confirmation in his new passion in the writings of health authorities: "I read anew the works of Graham and Alcott," he said, "and conceiving that my strength had reached the stagnation point, I gave up meat."[7] Soon the five foot seven inch, 143 pound package of muscle was astounding the nation in lecture demonstrations. Folks were staggered by his strength and amazed that one who avoided meat could perform so heroically. A lifting fad swept the country as various inventors and manufacturers came forward with wonderful machines to test and expand the muscles. "Strength is Health!" cried Winship. "Amen!" answered his perspiring disciples. The cultural revolution wrought by Winship and the Christian physiologists was absolute and, although it faltered a bit when Winship put down his weights, it was permanent.

What were women supposed to do for strength? Dioclesian Lewis had the answer. Lewis, a medical graduate, earned his living as a lecturer and writer from the 1850s into the 1880s. Such books as *Chastity, or Our Secret Sin* and *Our Digestion; or My Jolly Friend's Secret* place

Lewis firmly in the Graham-Alcott tradition of linking morality and digestion. But Lewis did show some innovations in gymnastics where he introduced exercises suitable for women and for men who wished to be limber but not muscle-bound. Bean bag tossing, hoop catching, wand exercises, dancing, and marching led the list of prescribed activities. Lewis hectored the public relentlessly on the place of gymnastics in the schools. Physical education, he argued, was the indispensable foundation of all other education.

Adventists and Shakers, who combined principles of Grahamism with hydropathy or water treatment to achieve health kept the reform movement alive after Graham's passing. A particularly effective disciple, Dr. James Caleb Jackson, abolitionist, water-cure doctor, and lecturer, established a health resort at Dansville, NY. Dr. Harriet Austin, Jackson's associate, designed a bloomer-type women's outfit called the "American costume" which shocked some of the locals while pleasing men and women of reformist propensities. Patients at the sanitarium heard lectures from Jackson and Austin and from visitors like Mrs. Amelia Bloomer, the temperance and women's rights advocate. By chance Bloomer's name was given to the Turkish style costume that existed in many versions from mid-century although she was certainly not the originator of it.

Most patients took water cures and conformed to the Graham vegetable-based diet. Jackson also originated a food called Granula, a mixture of graham flour and water baked in sheets, then broken into bean size nuggets, then baked again, and ground down to smaller size bits. This dish, created in 1863, should have caused a great trembling on the planet on its first ingestion because it rang in a new and incredible fashion in eating. Granula was indigestible until milk was added. Soaking up lost moisture occupied some time but an overnight icebox sojourn produced a creamy mess which, when sugar (not yet an abomination) was added, made a palate pleasing start to the day. Many years and many travails would pass before inventors figured out how to work all their unnatural wonders on grains and finish with an instant breakfast food. John Harvey Kellogg and C.W. Post did eventually succeed in boxing some crunchy materials that created universal satisfaction.

Reformers of Dr. Jackson's day shared other ideas that were to pop up in Macfadden's canon of beliefs. The vegetarians tended to oppose compulsory vaccination as a particularly objectionable state-directed interference with nature's way. Other notions of wrong practices were more local and more ephemeral as with the ban on cotton bloomers at Bronson Alcott's Fruitland's Colony. Bloomers were made of linen because cotton was the product of slave labor.

Jackson passed the reform torch to the Adventists when they began coming to Dansville in the 1860s. Sister Ellen White was more than ready for the reform diet because she had discussed Graham crackers and the two-meal-a-day system with an angel. Such divine conversations were eventually to give the somewhat hysterical Mrs. White the leadership of the Adventists and she was influential in the church's move to Battle Creek in 1863 to establish a sanitarium like that of Jackson's.

Ellen White experienced many visions but her first on health reform occurred in 1863. The angel warned that meat eating inflamed "animal propensities," i.e., sexual desire, and a thirst for ardent spirits. Messages received by White while she was in a trance shaped Adventist doctrine and created uncomfortable practices of diet. Self-denial was not easy for Ellen White, a heavy eater, who frequently defected from the established, stern course of graham bread, fruits, vegetables, and water when emergencies demanded that she take butter, cream, and meat to fire up her energies. White also moved the Adventists along in dress reform, although rejecting the popular bloomers because the dress above the pantaloons was too short for her taste, and because it was worn by spiritualists and radicals, types of women she did not admire.

James White, Ellen's husband, became head of the new group of Adventists at Battle Creek, although her visions gave her effective authority. The Whites added "Seventh Day" to the Adventists' title to signify their finding that Saturday was the Sabbath. Originally the Adventists had been followers of farmer William Miller of Hampton, New York, a prophet who predicted Christ's return to earth in 1843.

At Battle Creek the Whites singled out a young parishioner, John Harvey Kellogg, for a medical education. After his studies Kellogg returned to become the colony's chief spokesman and medical expert. Kellogg, a genius in his own right, made the sanitarium a success, and, as Ellen White grew older and crankier, he took control from the church elders. The "san" became a secular institution and the best known health center in the nation under Kellogg's guidance. Other healers were drawn to Battle Creek to establish their own sanitariums.

From the teachings of these worthies emerged the health fanatic of the nineteenth and twentieth century, the man, as Mark Twain quipped, who eats what he doesn't want, drinks what he doesn't like, and does what he'd druther not, all the while smugly announcing himself to be energetic, joyful, and certain of long life, and exhorting his errant neighbor to reform. Hygiene demanded ceaseless vigilance.

Health faddists infuriated writer H.L. Mencken, not just because he loved his cigars and Pilsner, but because he was a fan of the health sciences and ever the critical reader of medical literature. It pained him that "hygiene is the corruption of medicine by morality." He grumbled that "it was impossible to find a hygienist who does not debase his theory of the healthful with a theory of the virtuous. The whole hygienic art, indeed, resolves itself into an ethical exhortation."[8] Mencken did not distinguish between secular and religious applications because the results were the same in either case. The religious cried that good health helped lead one to the Kingdom of God while the seculars urged good habits that would lead all to the Kingdom of Health. For both schools of thought a moral obligation was involved—either to God, race, nature, or to self. It follows that the leaders who appointed themselves in a secular capacity as advisors on such moral obligations take on an evangelical tone. The secular teachers are as certain as the religious ones that they know the truth and bear the burden of spreading the gospel of health.

Bernarr Macfadden exemplified the kind of health fanatic Twain and Mencken deplored. He was a secular reformer with a religious fervor who carried a nineteenth century cause into the modern era. Like others of his persuasion he was selective in the application of modern science.

Chapter 4
"Weakness is a Sin"

Shakespeare was a great Physical Culturist.

Bernarr Macfadden

The *Physical Culture* magazine was Macfadden's first publication and his first and last love among the many magazines he published. It gave him a sustained source of income that ended his dependence on selling exercise machines and giving physical training. More significantly, the magazine provided what he needed most—a strong voice to channel his message to the world.

While in England in 1898 he had published a brochure extolling the merits of his exercise device for distribution at his lecture demonstrations. Back in the states he conceived the notion of publishing his own magazine to promulgate his views on physical culture, but lacked the capital for anything much more pretentious than his exerciser brochure. The first issue in 1899 was small but brave. It proclaimed his health doctrines in terms expressing his unwitting kinship with the Graham school of Christian hygiene: "It is the Editor's firm and conscientious belief that weakness is a sin."[1] He liked the ring of the phrase, "weakness is a sin, don't be a sinner," and it subsequently appeared on every magazine cover.

Macfadden's slogan expressed the general sentiments of the school of muscular Christianity that had evolved in the nineteenth century. In 1869 writer Moses Coit Tyler defined muscular Christianity as "Christianity applied to the treatment and use of our bodies...he who neglects his body, who allows it to grow up puny, pale, sickly, mis-shapen, homely, commits a sin against the Giver of the body...Round shoulders and narrow chests are states of criminality. The dyspepsia is heresy. The headache is infidelity. It is as truly a man's moral duty to have a good digestion, and sweet breath, and strong arms, and stalwart legs, and erect bearing, as to read his Bible, or to say his prayers, or to love his neighbor as himself."[2] It was this message that had helped establish gyms throughout America, like the one in St. Louis that had changed young Macfadden's life. All that Macfadden had altered in the doctrines of muscular Christianity was his secular emphasis. A sin to him was not a violation of God's law but a violation of the body.

Initially, the new publication had to be used as the prototype he had published in England—for the promotion of his exerciser. But as subscriptions came in he could devote more space to articles and within six months established its uniquely successful formula. At first he wrote all the articles himself under various pen names because he could not pay writers. He discussed dieting as a means of improving the complexion; the best means of caring for the hair; the benefits of muscle building; and many of the other ideas on nature's way to health that teemed in his brain. It was a relief to eventually be able to pay writers and confine his own work to editorials, and the quality of the magazine improved. While many steady readers were folks with a very high consciousness of health, those sometimes called faddists, nuts, or cranks by their friends and relatives, the reading fare was broad enough to attract those less committed to the physical culture life. There were always two serials running, rousing stories that had little to do with health, and articles on provocative topics like marriage and sex education. Prosperity allowed the publisher to add illustrations, improve the paper quality, and gain distribution through newsstands—and, rather quickly, Macfadden became a man of some consequence.

The articles published in the magazine's first year tell what Macfadden's mission was all about:

The Development of Great Muscular Vigor.
Is Disease Necessarily an Accompaniment of Genius? Is Muscle Bad for the Brain?
Marriage of the Unfit.
Home Exercise for Little Tots.
Theodore Roosevelt, Rough Rider and Athlete.
Criminal Neglect in Our Educational Methods.
Can the Highest Degree of Attainable Physical Perfection Be Acquired, if Absolute Continence Be Observed?[3]

His was not the only health magazine, but he intended to go far beyond the scope and readership of his rivals. Somehow he knew that he could find ways of attracting readers away from other magazines. He did not expect to do it without talented help so he created a woman's department and put Dr. Ella A. Jennings, formerly editor of *Humanity and Health,* in charge. In many respects he was a bold, forthright man but dealing with many letters from women complaining of private matters could be embarrassing and it was good to turn it over to Jennings.

The magazine's first cover showed photographs of "Prof. B. Macfadden in Classical Poses." He found it right, fitting, and wholly satisfying that his own image should adorn the magazine that would carry his reforms to the nation. His poses were to appear again and again in articles and in advertisements for his other ventures. He enjoyed seeing himself and believed that others enjoyed it too.

Macfadden appreciated that controversy sold magazines, but it was also true that controversy was inevitable considering his cause of reform. Increasingly, as time went on, he attacked the medical profession and the American Medical Association. He did not do so in any playful, provoking spirit, but as one locked in a death struggle with a powerful, deadly antagonist. At first the A.M.A. did not even know he was there, but eventually his challenges annoyed very much. All advocates of holistic medicine or natural treatment naturally resented established doctors who interfered with natural processes in such terrible ways yet were the recognized authorities. And Macfadden was always very definite in his basic natural approach to health: "There is no disease without a cure, and if the cause is removed the body will cure itself,"[4] he assured readers.

On the cover of the September 1900 issue were two naked profile photographs of Macfadden, showing him before and after a seven day fast. Fasting, he argued, in the cover story, was the sovereign remedy, certain to "help and generally cure asthma, epilepsy, bronchitis, constipation, heart disease, insomnia, paralysis, obesity, diabetes, impotence, dyspepsia, kidney ailments, bladder trouble and much else."[5] Over the years in the magazine and in his *Encyclopedia* he would have much to say about fasting because in over fifty years of preoccupation with health he never wavered in his conviction that over-eating caused most woes. His mention of obesity as one of the health problems recognized the new tendency to treat obesity as a serious health problem, but it was not one that he put much emphasis on. After all, if a patient exercised and fasted to cure whatever it was that ailed him, any problem of obesity would be cleared up along the way.

Macfadden liked to blast any detractors of his theories, particularly if they were famous. Arthur Brisbane, William Randolph Hearst's best known journalistic pundit, drew the publisher's fire by arguing that muscle building hurt the brain. Macfadden's command of history was not based on much reading but he always had certain facts on hand, including the names of all past geniuses who had also been devoted physical culturists; and the list was an impressive one. Macfadden could never understand common jokes about the thick-headedness of strong men.

In those days Americans were infatuated with the image of the Venus de Milo, the toast of the Louvre in Paris. Macfadden wondered why she did not wear a corset—or rather why, if American women wanted a figure like hers, they wore corsets. "We hate the corset," he wrote, "because it comes in the guise of a friend and ends by being the most terrible enemy to health, to happiness, and to beauty that woman comes in contact with during her entire life."[6] The corset made women old while they were still in their prime and perpetuated the notion that maternity destroyed a woman's figure. "How a woman can wear a support for her bust from childhood and then have the incomprehensible audacity to expect it to remain round, firm...until advanced age is more than this writer can understand." Corsets crushed, deformed, and inhibited proper muscle development. "We intend to fight the corset curse to the bitter end, and if women will persist in debilitating their bodies and destroy their womanhood by its embrace, we will see that the man who marries their kind will know the kind of risk he is taking."

Macfadden and other critics of corsets won their battle as soon as manufacturers began featuring "health corsets," which were supposed to squeeze less and in healthy ways, but he continued firing away at the much riddled target long after it was dead. The corset was such a meaningful symbol of the struggle for health, the war that he was leading, that he was loath to give up abusing it. He also liked attacking corsets because, he had noticed, that any public mention of women's undergarments stimulated folks.

He considered himself a liberal and a reformer but rarely supported the causes of feminists beyond the matters of clothes and health. He was essentially a male supremacist, but was careful to obscure his deeply ingrained conservatism. His concern for women's health was genuine. He was quick to utilize the talents of women in his enterprises, but he believed that lacking the male's sexual parts limited them somewhat. Sometimes he would annoy his wife or other women with his evident satisfaction with the hegemony of the barnyard where the rooster preened in all his feathered glory and crowed of his prowess to the world. The submissive hens clucked around the base of the dunghill from which their sexual master reigned: it is nature's way, he reflected.

The first serial appearing in the new magazine was a favorite novel of the publisher's, *The Athlete's Conquest,* his own creation. Curiously enough, the corset is the villain of the novel. Young Harry Moore, a fellow whose triumph over weakness and disease was very much like that of Macfadden, is admired for his strength and health. Even shy, proper Victorian ladies cast glances at his manly form that suggest an innocent (or ignorant) appreciation of the male power he represents. "Oh hum!" says Harry to these gals. He wishes to marry but is repelled by the crippled, distorted figures of women who have been ensnared and deformed by corsets. Suddenly, one day, by golly, he sees a beautiful girl.

"Well, how strange! And what a beautiful thing she is! She doesn't wear a corset! Heavens! She has the features and figure of a goddess. I didn't think there was a woman living who could affect me like that! exclaimed Harry with a long drawn sigh as he remembered how the sight of her face affected him."[7] Harry wins this fine girl in the end after some twists and turnings of a conventional kind.

The magazine gained popularity because it was well presented, lively, and sharply focused. In the early years of the century Americans were getting concerned about health once more and supported a number of health magazines. The popular interest in health and in Macfadden's magazine increased from year to year, and accelerated notably when the nation became scandalized by the high rate of unfitness among young men drafted during World War I. There were cynics, though, who attributed the magazine's success to the emphasis on sexual hygiene and sexual education, and readers' expectation that a publisher once convicted under the obscenity laws would give them some smut.

Macfadden was more than willing to address himself to complaints that his concern with sexual hygiene and education was either unnecessary or too intense. In one editorial he addressed readers who thought he devoted too much space and attention to sexual matters. Usually "a spirit of hostility and misunderstanding" motivated critics but he conceded that "a few, honest, regular readers might wonder at the editor's belief in the importance of sexual discussion."[8] To these honest readers Macfadden confessed that his emphasis was costly to the magazine in prestige and numbers of readers, but his principles demanded that the fight for a rational sex education go on. If children and adults were properly educated they would appreciate that sex was for procreation and that enjoyment had nothing to do with it. With these truths firmly in mind the young would direct their former wayward curiosity to understanding the bodily functions. Understanding would establish responsibility in sexual activities and attitudes. "Well we know that since the day of the first man and woman the tendency of human creatures has been toward looking upon the sexual function as a sinful outburst of emotion, rather than as distinctively an important step in parenthood. It is unreasonable to suppose that we can overcome and dissipate these delusions and perverted conceptions within a few days, or a few years,"[9] but he would continue the fight on ignorance.

Such explanations may have convinced some dubious readers that the publisher was on the right track. Perhaps they could detect his sincerity but would they be likely to believe that once individuals knew sex was for procreation the old lure of enjoyment would vanish? Did Macfadden really believe this? We cannot give certain answers to these queries except by noting evidence that he sometimes coupled with women without any desire for procreation.

Even if some readers complained about the sexual hygiene articles it is clear that they were the attraction for most subscribers. With good reason people had become a little impatient with lingering Victorianism, the long established reticence surrounding any discussion of sex matters. They knew sex was important and refused to accept the prudes' insistence on veiling rational consideration of it. Regardless of what preachers said, their interest was inevitable, and readers wished to hear what the experts had to say. *Physical Culture* was far too daring for the tradition-bound and deeply religious, but there were plenty of others clamoring for freedom of expression. And certainly Macfadden's tone of presentation was pleasing enough to all but the wretchedly biased. No one could complain that sex was treated lewdly—or even lightly.

Macfadden was not the only one to notice the crying need for sex education. Concern among progressive era reformers in the first years of the century over prostitution and venereal diseases had led to many studies of the matter. Feminists were concerned too, arguing that the lack of economic opportunity for women turned some into whores. After attending an international conference on VD in Brussels, Dr. Prince Albert Morrow of New York published the first pertinent American text on these problems. His *Social Diseases and Marriage,* published in 1904, was followed by his establishment of what became the American Federation for Sex Hygiene. Macfadden did not notice that some doctors were in the forefront of this reform movement but he often reminded readers that the neglect of doctors had encouraged the spread of VD. He was accurate on this point. For many years many doctors had pretended that venereal disease did not exist to avoid offending the moral sensibilities of their communities. Since many practitioners would not even treat the disease, patients were driven into the welcoming embrace of a legion of quacks who offered multitudes of cures, including some deadly ones.

The heart of each issue of *Physical Culture* was its editorial page, entitled "The Editor's Viewpoint." Macfadden was no passive voice pretending a neutral point of view under an editorial "we." Readers knew who the editor was and what he stood for. They knew this after reading a few issues and did not know it much better after reading several hundred because the same theses were expressed again and again. Readers heard about the need for dieting, fasting, exercise, and fresh air and they heard about the perfidiousness of the AMA and prudes.

As the magazine continued to prosper the publisher could pay good prices for stories and sometimes featured popular authors. Jack London's *Burning Daylight* was serialized in 1914 and the distinguished George Bernard Shaw appeared several times as with "What's Wrong with Marriage?" in January 1917. For the most part, however, the topic was more important than the author. Macfadden did not enjoy paying for famous authors and used the lesser known routinely, thus with Mary Ballard writing on the corset; Alice Ludlow on looking young; Gwendoline Lent on childrens' left-handed tendencies; and others discussing the care of teeth, housecleaning, girl athletes, vibration techniques for health, or contributing short fiction or serials. Pseudonyms were commonly used to disguise the work of staff regulars.

Certain authors, like Horace Fletcher and Upton Sinclair, were great favorites of the publisher. Fletcher was singular among the hygiene reformers of the late nineteenth and early twentieth centuries in his wide range, personal charm, and good-humored optimism. This cheerful, attractive man, born in Lawrence, Mass. in 1849, traveled widely as a youthful sailor on whaling vessels before matriculating at Dartmouth. After leaving college he married and settled in San Francisco where he became rich by manufacturing ink and selling Japanese art to American collectors. His leisure hours were also profitable: he became an accomplished painter, a renowned rifle marksman, and an all-around athlete. Always restless, and loving travel, he moved to New Orleans in the 1890s to manage an opera company, then to Paris as art correspondent of the *New York Herald*. By 1898 he lived in a medieval palazzo on Venice's Grand Canal when he was not off lecturing or pursuing adventurous travels in distant places.

Fletcher did conform to the usual health reformer's pattern in one sense. He was "born again" at age forty upon noticing that his once trim, athletic figure had ballooned tremendously through the advance of years and his enthusiastic devotion to good food and drink. When a life insurance company refused him a policy Fletcher renounced his old ways. As he was currently enchanted with the positive thinking fad his first book, *Menticulture* (1895), expressed faith in one's ability to overcome obstacles. Anger and worry must be purged, he argued, then one was free to build a better world—one without greed, exploitation, wars, and other unpleasant excesses.

Fletcher's positive thinking dovetailed nicely with his discovery in 1898—from studying the books of earlier hygienists, William Alcott and Martin Holbrook—of the germ of his famed theory of mastication. In *The New Glutton* (1903) and other works Fletcher established himself as the new popular star among the proponents of holistic health treatment and laid down the law as he had determined it from Mother Nature. Overeating was wrong and the cause of many health problems, but it could be avoided by distinguishing the true appetite. One must only eat at the urging of appetite and stop when the urging is reduced. But since the taste of food is good it must be savored for as long as the flavor lasted. This meant that prolonged mastication of each mouthful of food was the necessary ideal. Food was only swallowed when every essence of flavor had been exhausted and this, sometimes, took a very long time. Believers in Fletcher's system were anything but quick shovelers and gulpers of food. How many times must each mouthful be chewed? Well, it all depended upon the food. Once he chewed 700 times on a green onion. When he finally swallowed it he was sure that it had no odor.

The results certainly benefited Fletcher's obesity: in mid-June 1898 he weighed 205 pounds with a 44-inch waistline; in mid-October the almost interminable chewing of his one daily meal reduced him to 163 pounds with a 37-inch waistline. And he felt great!

Soon "to fletcherize" became a new popular addition to the language and health faddists were boasting of their relentless chewing. It is not so easy to understand why this rather wearing method of eating caught on, but that could be said of many food fads promulgated by characters less charming than Fletcher.

Like other health faddists Fletcher was fascinated by the bodily process of waste elimination. Wonderfully enough he discovered that Mother Nature rewarded one durable enough "to fletcherize" his food thoroughly with a scanty, dry, almost sweet-smelling excreta. Since Mother Nature did not really like waste a careful eater would not need to defecate more than once over a six to ten day period—and the product would only amount to two to four ounces. Odorless stools were essential to Fletcher's sense of the correctness of his method. He worshipped cleanliness and hated the idea of unclean odors. It was just a matter of chewing well.

Fletcher's adherents included the novelist Henry James for a time. James lost his enthusiasm when an illness caused him to wonder if the benefits of mastication were worth the effort. Other disciples were more faithful, like Miss Palmer, a Chicago teacher who devoted twenty minutes daily to the serving and enjoying of a single cracker, and John Harvey Kellogg of the Battle Creek Sanitarium. One disciple wrote a song:

I choose to chew because I wish to do
The sort of thing that Nature had in view,
Before bad cooks invented sav'ry stew;
When the only way to eat was to chew! chew! chew!!![10]

It was one of the curiosities of Fletcher's beliefs that in emphasizing so artificial a custom as interminable chewing he was recapturing an earlier purer, barbaric day when "instincts reigned supreme."

Fletcher effectively demonstrated a commanding physical endurance on a number of tests he took to show the value of his dietary theories, but his lack of interest in physical training confused Macfadden. Otherwise it is obvious why, with his fame and adherence to Mother Nature, Fletcher attracted Macfadden's interest. Articles by Fletcher made frequent appearances in *Physical Culture* until the reformer died in 1919.

Upton Sinclair, another Macfadden favorite and a personal friend and disciple, wrote often for the magazine. Sinclair was a prolific and popular writer despite that his views tended far leftwards of the mainstream on political and social issues. His initial fame as a food reformer-rested on his sensational novel, *The Jungle*, a muck-raking exposure of conditions in the meat-packing industry. Americans were in the process of a somewhat hysterical discovery of germs when the insanitary horrors of the stockyards were revealed to them by Sinclair, who was primarily interested in reforming labor conditions. The book proved to be a powerful influence upon congressional passage of the first federal food and drug regulation in 1906.

Albert Edward Wiggam, a journalist whose articles on popular science were much in demand, was another Macfadden contributor. Wiggam and the publisher favored the same theories of eugenics, including a devotion to the superiority of Nordic peoples. Wiggam's "Should I Marry a Blond or Brunette," appeared in *Physical Culture* in July 1921 and made a great hit. Thousands of reprints were sold. Wiggam was one of the writers whose racist views influenced legislation restricting American immigration in the 1920s. Macfadden's major contribution to the eugenics theorizing was in offering to save the race through body building.

Features were important in the magazine. Readers' letters received a good play and each issue reviewed physical culture events around the world. And, of course, because of the publisher's obsession with circulation-building gimmicks, the magazine featured all kinds of contests, as one in 1915-16 for the "ideally proportioned woman." This contest provides valuable clues to the publisher's preference among feminine forms, although he expressed it in scientific measurement of height, weight, neck, bust, hips, calf, forearm, and other features and computed the result according to a complicated formula. Miss Nana Sterling of Houston won the first prize. She was a nineteen-year old beauty, five feet six inches, 130 pounds, with a thirty-eight inch bust and hips and twenty-six inch waist and twenty-two inch thighs. The runner-up was shorter but also had ample hips and bust. The winners, whose photographs were also examined, resembled Mrs. Mary Macfadden, the publisher's wife, in stature—an athletic woman who had won a similar contest earlier.

The magazine also had a "General Question Department" to which readers were encouraged to direct questions about health. Such questions were answered without any mincing of words, evasions, and certainly no one was ever advised to take up a tricky question of illness with the doctor. A reader asking about leukemia was told to "avoid drugs, take exercise, and keep his bowels regular."[11] One concerned with bow legs was told that "leg exercises should be used." A sufferer from varicose veins must "avoid constipation, bathe in cold water, exercise, and avoid elastic bands." A victim of epilepsy was warned that his "nervous system must be strengthened," and the way to do that was through fasting and an outdoor life.

Advertisements were plentiful once the magazine started attracting substantial readership. Macfadden gave plenty of space to notices of his own ventures, including his books and the Bernarr Macfadden Healthatorium in Chicago, a center housed in a handsome building that was pictured in the advertisements. "No one can put an adequate financial value on health," stated the ad. "To all those who are struggling for life's greatest gift, we have a message. We offer you health by the natural method. We have no mysteries to sell...The Healthatorium is in every sense of the word a health home, for it is the home of health for one and all regardless of their condition." The "natural method" of treatment for all diseases included diet, exercise, bathing and massage—a regime that gave "the natural forces the fullest scope by easy and thorough nutrition, increased flow of blood, and removal of obstructions to the excretory systems or the circulation in the tissues."[12]

Various Macfadden publications were advertised, including Macfadden's *Encyclopedia,* a work which held all of his health theories and treatments. Sales of the *Encyclopedia* received encouragement in editorials. An editorial noted the publication of the fifth volume of Macfadden's masterwork with heavy praise—"the most noteworthy undertaking ever achieved in the sphere of physical culture...the most comprehensive and complete work on health-building from the modern standpoint that the world has ever known."[13] It was the surpassing magnitude of the work that forced the editor to overcome his habitual reticence: "Rarely does this magazine comment editorially on books issued from its own press...[but] the work is a matter of such importance to physical culturists in general that it would be unfair to pass over its completion without remark."

"The big muscle boys," as the various strong men selling body-building courses were called by detractors, advertised heavily in *Physical Culture.* Because of this, and because Macfadden liked to be pictured with his own powerful muscles on display, some folks tended to lump Macfadden with other strong men. While such a mistaken comparison was understandable, it was something like confusing Harvard University with a Bronx Beauty College. Macfadden may have flexed his own muscles and sponsored the flexing of others but he looked far beyond muscle building to the perfection of society—and worked constantly at his long range goals. Muscle posing was a lure through which he gained converts to physical culture—just as sexy illustrations and exciting story blurbs in his confession magazines were ways to get across his moral lesson—and make money.

Of all the muscle men Charles Atlas was the best-known, and even achieved the distinction of a *New Yorker* magazine profile. Macfadden gave Atlas, then named Angelo Siciliano, his start in the 1920s by awarding him the *Physical Culture* contest prize as "The World's Most Perfectly

Developed Man." Other accolades attended the famous strong man's career, including his selection by a committee of artists at the 1939 World's Fair as the finest specimen of American manhood extant. The lead to all of Atlas' advertisements became as familiar as any ever set in type: "I was once a 97-pound weakling." This message and the revealing before and after photographs caught the eyes of many a boy and man who knew what it was to have beach sand kicked on them by a big bully showing off for a lovely lass each of the fellows craved. Who got the girl? It's obvious. But who got the revenge in time? Also obvious. The fantasies Atlas engendered were a cultural force. It is likely that the fantasy of bringing the bully to justice occupied as many American minds for a longer time than any other presented in ads. Statistics do not show what percentage of subscribers to the salesmanship of Atlas and the other professional avengers actually survived to knock down the beach bully. It was probably higher than the percentage of attainment in another favorite fantasy—buying the restaurant, shop, hotel, or whatever, to fire the staff member who had insulted you.

Lionel Strongfort was a muscle man with a pitch tied to sexual concerns. He went after men who were ill or thought they might be and those who worried about their sexual vitality. Since the belief that masturbation harmed health was so deeply rooted in popular consciousness Strongfort could appeal to general fears. "Strongfortism is a panacea for all habits that arise from physical weakness, as all bad habits do, because Strongfortism builds up strength that resists such habits."

The muscle man's promise of "vital energy" only differed from Macfadden's in being more blatant in sexual innuendo. Strongfortism improved "the inner muscles which control the vital organs, generating the Life Forces." At a small cost "the weakling is developed and inspired with the mastery of mental power and physical perfection—the glorious crown of MANHOOD."

Whatever Macfadden might have thought about the limited aspirations of the muscle men, their advertising contributed to a healthy income for the magazine. Most strong men and many patent medicine quacks promised "amazing secrets." Personally Macfadden scoffed at the notion of "secrets" but they were an essential part of the stock for many of his advertisers. Atlas' full page ads offered secrets for a mere $30: "My system is the last word in Health and Energy Building." He wanted students who were unwilling to disappoint their sweethearts and mothers, women who wanted protection and expected great things from their boy.

Other advertising strong men included Prof. L. W. Albizu, inventor of the Roller Dumb-Bells—"The World's Quickest Way to Strength." Albizu's secret was simple: one pushed the dumb-bells up and down the wall. Atlas' secret was even less complex: one pitted one muscle against another in a contest of "Dynamic Tension."[14]

Mr. Breibart's secret required purchase of a book and a Muscle Meter before learners could follow the master: "I support more weight than any other man. I drive heavy nails through many layers of oak and iron with my bare hands. I am able to bend heavy steel bars into carefully worked designs."

The publisher did not accept ads from Michael McFadden, the "Champion of Champions," who advertised his $8 exercise machine and even the *Michael McFadden Encyclopedia* in other magazines. Bernarr Macfadden was certain that the similarity of his own famous name and that of the strong man was not a coincidence but rather a blatant attempt to fool people.

Most of the strong man ads were innocent appeals to the infantile instincts of boys and men and any resultant sales probably did no harm to anything but the hopeful's pocketbook. But other advertising in *Physical Culture* on health treatments and patent medicines raised more serious questions about Macfadden's sincerity. Dr. Morris Fishbein's survey of the magazine's ads heralding Sargol, Absorbine, Jr., Murine, Sanatogen, Liquid Arvon, Ozomulsion, Cleartone, and other products convinced him that Macfadden was a quack—and was a hypocrite to boot. How could Macfadden, Fishbein asked, persistently announce himself to be a steadfast foe of drugs and still accept ads for Sargol, an obvious drug mixture despite its identification in ad copy as "a scientific assimilative agent." By any label, Sargol, which was laced with strychnine, was threatening to health and eventually its manufacturer was forced by the postal inspectors to stop advertising and had to pay heavy fines for violating earlier court orders. Absorbine, Jr., offered no perils although extravagant claims were made for the nostrum—"the only remedy known that positively cures varicose veins," which was also good for rheumatism, corns, headache, goiter, dandruff, and milk leg. Murine was another product that brought postal inspectors into action, as it advertised as "A Positive Cure for Sore Eyes." Other drugs Macfadden allowed space to included Liquid Arvon, a dandruff cure and Ozomulsion, marvelous for poor blood, chronic coughs, "or any wasting, weakening diseases."

Macfadden had often enough bragged to the world about how he cured his own hair loss through exercise—the vigorous tugging at the roots—with splendid results, as his much pictured pompadour-styled head of hair showed. Despite his insistence upon the efficacy of his treatment he saw no harm in earning a few dollars from the Alois Merke Institute. The Institute would grow "more hair for you in 30 days— or no cost." If their nostrum failed *Physical Culture* readers could, perhaps, recover their money and invest in a product offered by the Modern

Vacuum Cap Company. Put it on for a few minutes daily and the hair grew!

Dr. Benedict Lust also advertised in the magazine, pushing "a miracle of rejuvenation...a blood washing treatment...which will put a spring in your step and a flash in your eye." Yet, on closer examination, Lust did not wash the blood at all; he sold a water shower device that, perhaps, impacted the skin vigorously but fell short of being miraculous.

Yes, Macfadden urged fasting, but he did not refuse Dr. Walter's ads for rubber reducing garments which "dissolved the fat through perspiration." Readers should have known better because ads for Macfadden's *Encyclopedia* included the information that "fat cannot be sweated out." Arguably the publisher's inconsistency only showed his tolerance. He told folks the truth but, if they wished to experiment for themselves, they were free to do so. The only trouble with this rationalization was that it conflicted with the magazine's repeatedly stated editorial policy: "We stand back of our Advertisers—Say 'I saw it in *Physical Culture.*' "

The Cartilage Company of Rochester, NY, whose advertisements and testimonials promised *Physical Culture* readers a two to five inch increase in their height would appear to be hard to "stand back of." When federal authorities examined the advertised devices they concluded that no lad or man applying them had a ghost of a chance of growing into a six-footer. Macfadden's magazine backed its promise to support its advertisers. Among the material the Cartilage Company mailed to potential customers was a letter from O.J. Elder, *Physical Culture's* business manager, who answered an inquiry from someone in rather favorable terms. He did not "guarantee absolutely" the apparatus but did guarantee "beautiful results, the exercises that go with this system are excellent and well worth the price asked." Elder, of course, covered himself well, but it does seem that such questionable participation in an obvious fraud was a rather careless trading on the magazine's good repute.

Another great fraud, the New York Institute of Science, collected $1,500,000 from the gullible through magazine advertising, offering a correspondence course in gaining "magnetic influence" and "hypnotic power." If ad readers did not care to learn how to be magnetic, a rather expensive course, they could pay $5 for the Actina Appliance Company's device. This was a small, cyclindrical apparatus with an opening for application to the eye and another for holding at the nose. Some substance within the device stinked terribly of something like decayed onion and certainly made the nose run and the eyes water, but beyond that results were inconclusive so mailings were banned by federal authorities.

Macfadden often boasted that he warred on quackery before the cause became popular and was picked up by larger magazines like *Collier's*. It is true that a couple of early issues of his magazine featured exposures of quacks but his work did not compare to that of *Collier's* in comprehensiveness or impact. It is also true that he became most hospitable to quack advertising. He saw no harm in the ads of food expert G.H. Brinkler who pretended to cure any disease "by prescribing a particular diet," because he made pretty much the same claim himself. And he was an old hand at circumventing censors and federal bureaucrats so he suffered fewer setbacks from them than did Brinkler.

The magazine expressed the crank ideas and sympathy with quacks of its publisher, yet it effectively advocated sex education, wholesome diet, fresh air exercise, and other living practices of indisputable value to health. Its success revealed that the publishing world had a new figure to reckon with, a man of daring, keen business sense, and a genius in discerning the public taste.

Chapter 5
Indecent Exposure

I want women with hips and breasts.

Bernarr Macfadden

Health reformers who feared evil worldly influences on their disciples and wished to control the environment established sanitariums. In the nineteenth century Americans seeking health supported a great variety of spas and resorts catering to their needs. Some of these served the sick and were organized along the lines of hospitals, but others provided a setting—with varying levels of luxury—for supervised dieting, water treatments, physical conditioning, or other treatments dictated by the management. The medical profession generally encouraged sanitariums and, in fact, staffed many of them, although opposing those run by quacks and/or health faddists who crossed the line separating treatment from conditioning.

Macfadden first ventured into the sanitarium field in 1901 to test the several diets he had been featuring in *Physical Culture*. After leasing a farm near Kingston, New York, he announced treatment of selected patients at no cost. Flocks of suffering folks showed up pleading for a place but Macfadden weeded out the hypochondriacs and others unlikely to benefit under his care. Six lucky individuals survived the screening, including Mrs. Cole, bent almost double by rheumatism and hindered too by a paralyzed digestive tract; Mr. Tarbox, a longtime asthma sufferer; Mr. Axelson, a tuberculosis victim who also had a hernia; and three others whose conditions showed "general emaciation."[1]

Without wasting any time on diagnosis Macfadden put his patients on a strict diet—beet juice, carrot juice, honey, and rainwater constituted the only nourishment for the first few days. Later some solid foods were added but quantities were very small. After only a month Mrs. Cole could stand straight and could digest what little food she received; Mr. Tarbox was free of asthma; Mr. Axelson threw away his truss; and the others showed vast improvements. With such startling cures Macfadden might have claimed some super-human power but he did nothing of the kind, and did not express any surprise that he had been able to achieve such outstanding results. Public interest in the experiment was demonstrated by Tarbox's dilemma over his mail. Letters poured in and he threatened to deny his cure unless Macfadden provided a secretary.

With this success Macfadden resolved on bigger things, a sanitarium on Long Island at Lake Ronkonkoma. This time patients must pay for treatment and plenty were willing to do so. Unfortunately, Macfadden's management was faulty. Patients exceeded the building's housing capacity so Macfadden, unwilling to deny his benefits or reduce his income, housed the overflow in tents. As tent dwellers paid the same fees as the patients under a roof, much jealousy and bitterness ensued. Macfadden also erred in staff selection—a critical mistake as his absences attending to other business were frequent. Patients accused staffers of robbing them shamefully and neglecting them while indulging in loud, drunken parties. In disgust Macfadden shut the place down.

He was not accepting defeat, however, as it was never his custom to accept—or even admit—defeats. He was finished with Long Island and with the operation of a petty health home because visions of a far grander role stirred his volatile imagination. Let others have health homes, he declared, he would establish the world's first Physical Culture City! His city would draw multitudes of health enthusiasts and become the renowned, well-established headquarters of all his enterprises.

Readers of *Physical Culture* heard all about the planning for Physical Culture City, a place where the physical perfection of men and women could be attained. It would be the ideal community because the physical perfection of its citizens would flow over into other aspects of their beings. Crime, discord, and other unpleasantness familiar to ordinary communities would be unknown.

It is unlikely that Macfadden devoted any systematic study to the many problems that a unique community would face: he was confident that he could work things out. He had heard enough about the amazing town of Zion, Illinois founded by John Alexander Dowie to believe that he could do as well. Dowie's career impressed him mightily. "He is the greatest leader and the most remarkable reformer in a century,"[2] said Macfadden in 1903. Later he did not liked to be reminded that he had ever mentioned the man.

Dowie, a shining star among the unbroken line of religious gurus who have misled the faithful in America from colonial times, was much in the news in the early years of the century. He was born in England, emigrated to Australia, and ordained a Congregational minister in 1870. After some years of success achieved along conventional lines he discovered that he could heal diseases through prayer. He relocated in San Francisco in 1888, then moved to Chicago after a couple of quiet years. In Chicago he did much better because the ministers and doctors ganged up on him in 1895-96 by filing over 100 law suits charging the unlicensed practice of medicine. Dowie won them all and won also the admiration of

Macfadden and the worshipful obedience of a fast growing flock of followers. As a preacher Dowie was a huge success—a forerunner of Billy Sunday—with a peculiar style of American Billingsgate. Folks loved his vituperative, sensational attacks on others, and accepted his self-elevation to apostolic status readily. He looked like a prophet with his wide brow, big eyes, and long beard, and in his flowing robes might have served Michaelangelo as a model for paintings in the Sistine Chapel.

Macfadden probably heard some of Dowie's sermons in Chicago where the Divine Healer had three churches. Preacher Dowie, no mealy-mouthed apologist for God's work, demanded tithing of his congregation and violently castigated slow payers: "If you do not come up to the Standard of God's word, quit calling yourselves Christians. You are a pack of thieves and robbers, and I do not want to have anything to do with you in fellowship...You have a curse upon you, and you will curse the Church with your presence."[3]

Dowie called doctors sorcerers and scorned their advocacy of vaccination. Doctors wanted "a right to control humanity from the cradle to the grave."[4] The law defended their craze for inoculating: "Every kind of filthy disease can be injected into the blood and into the flesh of humanity. The result of that will be that humanity will rot! ROT! ROT!!! That is the Devil's trick to kill off the Church." To these tirades against doctors and vaccination Macfadden gave his full support, although he had to be more constrained in his editorial language than Dowie.

For his new Christian Catholic Church Dowie determined to build a new city, choosing a site forty-two miles from Chicago, called Zion City. Some 5,000 to 10,000 zealots moved to Zion, delighted to give up theatres, dance halls, secret lodges, drug stores, doctors, smoking, drinking, and pork eating—which were among the things Dowie banned. A prosperous silk factory was among the industries of the new city, which like the Zion City Bank, were totally controlled by Dowie.

Zion was doing fine until the prophet's megalomania induced him to tackle New York City's conversion. His "invasion" with 3,000 followers on ten special trains, followed by great rallies at Madison Square Garden in fall 1903 was not well received. New Yorkers laughed when the prophet had himself driven from the station to the Plaza Hotel in a magnificent carriage drawn by four horses while his followers walked behind. Soon everyone was singing:

> Hark! Hark! the dogs do bark!
> The Dowies have come to town.
> Some in rags, some in jags,
> But ONE in a velvet gown.[5]

The invasion was rumored to have cost $300,000 and only highlighted what Zion insiders had been suspecting for some time: that their leader had lost contact with reality. He battled against the rising debt burden and economic collapse of Zion and against disturbing rumors about his personal life—apparently he strayed from monogynous marriage—until felled by a stroke in 1905. While recuperating in Jamaica his reign was overthrown and he was suspended from the church for "polygamous teaching and other grave charges." Some months later he gave up the ghost.

Macfadden's great experiment began in 1906, the year before Dowie's death. Physical Culture City was only superficially modeled after Zion City as Macfadden had no ambition to control the minds, pocket books, and routes to eternal glory of his neighbors. He did not hope to attract nearly as many people as Dowie, who drew on his churches in America and abroad; Macfadden's appeal was to free spirits who were health fanatics.

The place was reasonably well located on a 2,000 acre tract bordering on the Pennsylvania Railroad. The railroad agreed to establish a station but refused to use Physical Culture City as the station's name. While the intransigence of railroad officials aggravated Macfadden it did not prevent trains from halting at the nameless station to drop off individuals and families ready to begin a new life.

Among the early arrivals at the mosquito-infested pine woods site in New Jersey was young Harry Kemp, later to be moderately famous as the "vagabond poet," who was a follower of the physical culture cult. He was eager for closer communion with other kindred souls and liked community life. Kemp had just stormed away from the Roycroft community at East Aurora because of his disenchantment with its leader, Elbert Hubbard.

Hubbard was another of those restless individuals who rejected the conventional society. He had cast off his place as a successful soap manufacturer to found a community dedicated to craftsmanship, along the lines of that established earlier in England by William Morris. At Roycroft artisans under Hubbard's direction produced beautiful leather-bound, handsomely illustrated books, furniture, pottery, rugs, stained-glass, and music. Hubbard also published an iconoclastic magazine, the *Philistine,* and a series of biographies, "Little Journeys to the Homes of the Great," which were widely read. Artists, writers, radicals, and scholars assembled at Roycroft to enjoy a unique cultural program of concerts, debates, and lectures when they were not crafting Roycroft's products. The inmates also scandalized their neighbors by indulging in nudism. Hubbard liked the attention of the public to his affairs. Like Macfadden he found exhibitionism fulfilling and profitable. Roycroft eventually folded when the resident artisans realized that Hubbard's once spiritual aims had swerved sharply to commercialism. Kemp's disenchantment had occurred earlier, after Hubbard published the lad's poem on Thoreau under his own name.

Kemp was eager to help build Physical Culture City. He was excited about the prospects of devoting himself to Macfadden's teachings and awed as the leader, "a pyramid of perfect muscles,"[6] led the daily exercises. After vigorous exercise to begin the day the volunteers, always scantily clad and sometimes nude, laid out the streets and building sites of the future city. More helpers arrived as the work progressed, including fanatics like Kemp and some so extreme that he labeled them "nuts." But many of the colonists could not help much with the work: they were the sick waiting for the birth of a place where they could regain their health.

Kemp lived in a tent lent him by a woman, a cancer patient, who defected after arguing with Macfadden over the natural cure he urged upon her. Each day was rapture for Kemp, starting with a naked plunge into the community lake and, later, eating the day's only meal, one recommended by the master: a dish of "whole wheat grains, soaked in water till they burst open to the white of the inside kernel."[7] He felt wonderful and, after a day's work, he relaxed in his tent, reading his beloved Shelley or Keats, or working over his own poems.

Macfadden welcomed all health nuts without discrimination. Among them was a little, shriveled woman who rarely touched solids and imbibed no fluid except that found in fruits. There was also a raw meat eater, a man from Philadelphia who would eat nothing else despite the eruptions all over his body—which, according to the gossip among the vegetarians, were caused by his diet. Vegetarians of all persuasions were far more common than eaters of flesh, raw or cooked. Two Italians argued loudly that cooked vegetables killed one as surely as flesh eating did. What all the residents had in common—except for those too feeble to indulge— was the belief in exercise. Of course, theories on the best and proper forms of exercise in body-building and health treatment varied widely and always provided citizens with lively discussions.

Gawkers from neighboring towns and rural areas routinely showed up on Sundays, watching from a safe distance the cavorting of the cultists. Some, no doubt, harbored hopes of glimpsing some nudity, but generally they saw only women swimming in men's reasonably decorous bathing suits, designed along the model of union suits, while the men bathed in trunks. Kemp liked to wear a daring gee-string costume but Macfadden asked him to avoid scandalizing the spectators.

In Kemp's fictionalized account of the colony Macfadden is described as "a strange, strong-minded, ignorant man,"[8] who lived according to his strenuous doctrines of exercise and fasting. As a fledgling author Kemp wondered how Macfadden achieved the writing style displayed in his magazine and the books that came later. It appeared that he was "hardly able to compose a sentence in correct English," but hired assistants for their grammatical insight, "while he supplied the initiative and original ideas."

Kemp did not care for Macfadden's second wife Marquerite, whom the publisher married in 1903 and would divorce in 1911. Marguerite, a nurse, had helped her husband out with the health home and knew something about management. But, according to Kemp, the colonists disliked the "fussy Canadian woman who interfered in everyone's affairs beyond endurable measure."[9] The colonists were amused by her efforts to improve Bernarr's personal appearance by hiding his old clothes and laying out proper-looking suits. But it was no use. Macfadden's need for exercise might come on him at any time and sternly pressed garments restricted him. When he became famous he could sometimes manage a necktie when news photographers called, but he cared no more for such haberdashery than for corsets. Besides that he did not like to spend money for clothes.

Disciples at the new city gossiped about Marguerite because she appeared pompous and patronizing to them and obviously favored people of social distinction. Residents believed that she doubted Bernarr's sexual fidelity—and with good reason. They sympathized with Bernarr in his obvious infatuation with his secretary, "a beautiful, gentle, large-eyed girl...wholly feminine."[10] When the couple went off for a long walk all eyes in the camp were upon them, approving Macfadden's escape "from the nagging of his wife, from her blatancy and utter lack of sympathy with any of his projects." Marguerite made a great fuss over their baby daughter, but Macfadden, who had not yet become obsessed with the "perfect family" scheme, seemed little interested.

The founder's thoughts on life in the new city were a little vague on some critical aspects of life for the residents. Some industries or other means of earning an income were certainly desirable, but little attention had been given to practical necessities. Bee-keeping was considered a very good thing by Macfadden, but even that form of cottage industry had not been well planned. Perhaps Macfadden did not anticipate the emergence of anything like a conventional city with conventional needs in the early stages of the project because residents were separated into two categories: students and patients. Students worked toward their diplomas attesting to their physical superiority but were required to provide labor on various community projects. Patients were required to pay for their board and room at the sanitarium so their fees contributed to the support of the whole venture. But the students began complaining at the hardness of their lot. For ten hours daily labor on bee culture, farming, or carpentry they only received fifteen cents a day and a little— a very little—nourishing health food. Early escape from a rather unjust tuition seemed impossible as the diploma program called for a commitment of five and one half years. Macfadden might have found some way of dealing with students' complaints but, unfortunately, patients started complaining too. Why, they asked, are we paying $18 weekly for board when the sanitarium regime began with an immediate fast of several days and, in most cases, called for the renewal of the fast at regular intervals?

The colony's neighbors began protesting too, either because they saw too much or too little nudity. As Macfadden bustled around trying to appease dissidents he got a terrible shock. The *New York World* sniffed out the news value of the new community's distress and dispatched a reporter to make a secret investigation. Poor Macfadden, always so eager for publicity, was now humiliated by the exposure of the scandal. He had given his all to his dream, his vision of a physical cultural utopia, and now all the wiseacres in New York were smirking and laughing at his discomfort. It was a bitter time for him.

In his outrage he sued the *World* for libel, asking $50,000 damages. Whatever his own views on any mischief among his students might have been he realized that a sex scandal was the kiss of death for the new colony. He certainly found the reporter's sly comments odious: "The city was all work,"[11] the newsman said, "and no study and the contract provisions were arranged that graduation was virtually impossible." But, he added, if there was no time for study there was time, as the city's neighbors had suspected, for "intimate physical research" among the young men and women. Libel cases are hard to win and Macfadden had no luck as the judge concluded there had been no wrong in the journalist's reporting of what he observed. Macfadden was sore and remained sore; the incident was a topic he never discussed with his many biographers.

As devastating as all this was to the dream of Physical Culture City, the impact of it was trivial compared to the post office's attack on *Physical Culture,* which was then being published at the new community. It is conceivable that but for this assault Macfadden might have come to see his tilt with Comstock over the 1905 Madison Square Garden show in an amusing light. But to have criminal charges filed against him two years later fixed him in the martyr's role for the rest of his life. And one can hardly wonder at his rage and despair over the snooping of a government department over public morals rather than timely delivery of the mails.

The trouble erupted over a novel serialized in *Physical Culture.* Macfadden, concerned over the high incidence of venereal disease among Physical Culture City colonists, had brooded over means of alerting the nation to its danger. The disease spread because it was not respectable to talk about the problem and Macfadden was out to change this ostrich attitude. Of course, the post office did not realize that its prosecution of the publisher of the novel, *Wild Oats,* set back Macfadden's mission of sex education. Officers sincerely believed they were ridding the nation of smut.

In retrospect *Wild Oats* does not seem like such hot stuff. It was not one of the better efforts of John Coryell, the prolific writer who turned out prodigious amounts of copy for Macfadden and others. The title page did not deceive except in obscuring Coryell's hand and crediting a medical doctor:

WILD OATS
—Sowing and Reaping

The Confessions of a Lost Soul. Shedding Light on the Road to Ruin and Death. Immorality Brings Weakness of Body, Mind, and Soul. 'The Wages of Sin is Death.'[12]
Edited by Robert H. Welford, M.D.

The plot of *Wild Oats* was certainly straight-forward. It concerned the life of Reginard Barnes-Carter who was born with the taint of venereal disease and was also unfortunate because his parents did not want to raise children. Much on his own Reginard depended upon the wisdom stable grooms, boarding school inmates, and nasty books for his sex education. At age sixteen he seduced a half-witted kitchen maid but is protected from shame by his mother's payment of $100 hush money. Reginard goes from bad to deplorable, what with drinking, smoking, gambling, and traffic with a diseased whore. Foolishly he brags about the freshly raging nastiness within him because he and his low-brow cronies see disease as a badge of manliness.

We could almost guess the rest of the story. Enter innocence—a young girl, infatuated with Reginard because he helped her family out of a scrap, allows him to make love to her. She becomes pregnant and the young scoundrel goes through a fake marriage with her. She agonizes at his neglect and the illness of her tainted baby who dies after two troubled months of life.

Reginard, undaunted, is betrothed to a society girl whose moral sense is much like his. He meets the sweet young thing he so misused in a saloon. She is now a drunkard and, after further contact with him, ends up in a sanitarium. Before Reginard can marry the society girl both families hear all about his misuse of the other girl. Yet, for muddled reasons, the marriage is allowed to proceed. This time Reginard is the victim. He becomes insane and arranges to have himself burned to ashes.

Macfadden believed that anyone responsible for presenting the nation with the powerful moral message of *Wild Oats* deserved honors. Instead he was arrested on a federal criminal warrant, charging him with sending lewd and obscene matter through the mails. He was apparently not too alarmed as he assumed that any judge would see the matter as he did.

At trial the federal prosecutor made it clear that the government was out for blood, and Judge Lanning of the district court shared the view of the prosecutor. He fined Macfadden $2,000 and sentenced him to two years in prison.

Now the publisher gave all his attention to staying out of jail. His next magazine editorial declared his resolve: "With this penalty staring me in the face, which, to my mind, is a disgrace to the nation, I am going out among the people, among my friends and my enemies. I am going out to preach the gospel that stands for manhood and womanhood, that stands for the clean minds and clean morals. I am going to put my case before the people. I am willing that my verdict should rest with the people. I am willing that my life and my work shall be submitted to any tests that may be brought to bear upon them."[13]

As he appealed to the Circuit Court of Appeals, the publisher took to the road, lecturing in Boston, Cincinnati, Baltimore, and other cities, where he asked audiences to make their displeasure known to Washington. The Circuit Court refused to reverse the conviction and the U.S. Supreme Court did not recognize a constitutional issue that would justify their consideration. The appeal process took two years yet all the anxiety and expense had achieved nothing to save Macfadden from jail.

Fortunately, the case had received a great deal of publicity and ardent physical culturists were not alone in believing that the court's judgment had been unfair. Over this period the Department of Justice had received a heavy mail favoring Macfadden's cause and Attorney General George Wickersham advised President William Taft that a pardon was justified. There may have been some wags who were amused that our greatest president, in terms of girth, was the one to save the Father of Physical Culture, who did not look kindly on the obese. It might have been more expected that Taft's predecessor, Teddy Roosevelt, would have come to the rescue had he been in office, because Roosevelt, as Macfadden noted more than once in *Physical Culture,* was a born again health and strength addict himself. Taft, however, did come to Macfadden's rescue, and thus in the nick of time the publisher avoided jail, but it annoyed him that the government refused to pay back his $2,000 fine. The overall effect of the prosecution was disastrous. As a biographer put it, "the experiment [of Physical Culture City] had cost him a hundred thousand dollars; and the city had slumped back into a shiftless village. The small fortune he had piled up was gone. This was what his fight against prudery and the conspiracy of silence regarding love and venereal disease had cost him."[14]

Macfadden turned to other schemes. He opened a Penny Restaurant near the Bowery in New York. On the basement level a diner could have a bowl of hot soup for one cent and a hunk of bread for a cent more. A dish of beans or cabbage and other victuals also cost a cent.

Upstairs one dined with more style where dishes cost five cents each. The self-service system foreshadowed the popular automats of later years. As competitors rushed into the new field Macfadden left the restaurant management to others, although he returned to the field during the depression.

Besides editing the magazine Macfadden wrote books on special health and sex hygiene topics and worked on his encyclopedia of health. He also established the Physical Culture Training School at 112 West 18th Street.[15]

Macfadden wanted another sanitarium to replace that abandoned at Physical Culture City and decided to invade the mecca for natural health treatment at Battle Creek, Michigan. Dr. John Harvey Kellogg, probably the most famous physician in America, had his sanitarium at Battle Creek and numbers of other health establishments abounded there. Battle Creek, thanks to Dr. Kellogg and his brother, Will, and Charles Post, was also the famed center of breakfast cereal production. Macfadden had hopes of developing his cereal food, Strengtho, into a rival to the cornflakes of Kellogg and the toasties of Post. Post, after a spirited race with the Kelloggs for breakfast food supremacy, had withdrawn from Battle Creek to found a new city in West Texas. Macfadden leased the grand mansion Post had built in Battle Creek and got busy, although he had to travel to New York often for magazine business.

Dr. Kellogg, in the course of making the Battle Creek Sanitarium world famous, had broken with the Seventh Day Adventist Church. For many years he had walked a perilous tightrope between Adventist fundamentalism and modern science. Evolution came to make more sense to him than the divinity of Ellen White but he tried to be discreet. As a power in the church and undisputed master at the "san," he benefited from exploitation of church members willing to labor hard in caring for patients for small returns. Eventually, the Adventists expelled him but the division did not affect his reign at the "san" or its prosperity. Kellogg was an amazing character, short, plump, bearded, fiercely ambitious, and terribly loath to share credit for his attainments with others. He drove himself relentlessly, working long hours, and only reluctantly taking time off. His medical education had been conventional and distinguished, particularly in surgical studies. Early on he had broken away from the Adventists' passion for water treatment. He was a vegetarian but during the early years of the san he offered meat to guests unwilling to forego it—until Ellen White halted such compromises with principle. Some of his health theories were not regarded as orthodox by other medical men but none ever termed the distinguished physician a quack.

Kellogg's adherence to the autointoxication theory illustrated one of the oddities he shared with Macfadden. Of course, Kellogg would have been insulted by any linking of his name with Macfadden's, a man he considered a crank and opportunist. The good doctor was simply fascinated by the colon, "that most despised and neglected portion of the body,"[16] that some experts had declared "useless and unworthy." With facile pen, light touch, and easy wit the doctor straightened the world out on his favorite organ in a 300 page book, *Colon Hygiene*, which sold 18,000 copies in 1915-16.

For forty years Kellogg had studied the colon and concluded that it must be reckoned with in "the treatment of every chronic disease, and most acute maladies."[17] Constipation was the menace because it caused autointoxication. Herrmann Senator, a German doctor, was the first to spread the alarm in the late 19th century. He alleged that toxic substances were produced in the putrefactive decomposition of intestinal proteins. With constipation the toxins permeated the intestinal and colonic linings, poisoning the system with terrible results. For Kellogg and Macfadden autointoxication was a wonderful discovery because it confirmed their fixed theories about bodily malfunctions and certain favorite treatments.

Kellogg developed a celebrated surgical remedy to the colon's problem but insisted that most cases could be cured by the proper diet. He did not approve of the eminent British surgeon, Sir William Arbuthnot Lane, who liked to remove portions of the colon to cure epilepsy and nervous ailments. Despite Lane's cutting skills a high percentage of his patients died in surgery.

Quacks stirred up many lucrative ventures in response to the theory that constipation could cause disease. People worried a lot every time they experienced constipation and, as most could not afford either Lane or Battle Creek, they purchased pills, tonics, or enema devices like the Cascade marketed by Tyrell's Hygienic Institute. Medical research in 1919-22 showed conclusively that autointoxication was an imaginary ailment but its long run as a menace did not suddenly stop. Kellogg was forced to back away from his colon dedication but Macfadden continued to warn of constipation and advise fasting. Kellogg had always ridiculed fasting as a remedy: "It is sometimes prescribed as a remedial measure but necessarily leads to constipation unless some preventive method is adopted."[18]

Kellogg's sanitarium had a tremendous effect on Macfadden. It was as if he felt the necessity of legitimizing his health theories by establishing an institution of comparable renown. Once he had found success as a publisher he had neither the need nor the time to devote to sanitarium management yet he persisted in Chicago and elsewhere throughout his life.

Macfadden's effort to develop Strengtho as a health food was a direct emulation of Kellogg and Charles Post as was his move to Battle Creek. While Macfadden had much in common with Dr. Kellogg as an expert in health he was more the personality twin of Post. Post was a singular character who sought treatment for his health at Battle Creek at age 36 after varied hard work and commercial adventures in Illinois, Kansas, and Texas. He arrived at Battle Creek in a wheelchair, broken in health and finances by reverses in manufacturing farm machinery and fabrics. Post and his wife could not afford rooms at the san but received treatments there. He also attended lectures on diet, nutrition, health foods, and mental suggestion—subjects that stimulated his inquiring mind. Kellogg could not cure him but a Christian Science healer did better. Post recovered his health and became a mental healer himself in 1892. He practiced at the La Vita Inn, a wing of which held Post's small factory making suspenders, directing exercises, music, and mind games for other Kellogg drop-outs.

In 1893 Post published *I Am Well, The Modern Practice of Natural Suggestion as Distinct from Hypnotic or Unnatural Influence*. In this and another book published in 1895 Post set down what folks needed to convince themselves that they were healthy. He suggested that just reading the books would turn the trick for diligent readers.

Post might have gone on to great things in mental healing if he had stuck to it, but other more surely profitable ventures lured him to manufacturing. Dr. Kellogg had developed Caramel Cereal Coffee for Adventists and others who despised coffee. After some study of the situation Post began making something very similar from bran and molasses. In 1894 he borrowed enough money to start manufacturing Postum. Later he added lines of Grape Nuts and Post Toasties. That these products succeeded beyond all imagination needs no telling but the reasons for Post's triumph are sometimes forgotten. It was not the essential goodness of Postum, nor the flavorful, fully satisfying, health-stimulating properties of the cereals that made Post a millionaire, it was his daring in teaching folks about goodness and flavor. Post possessed the same genius in advertising that Macfadden had in creating popular magazines. The former mental healer knew what consumers wanted with their breakfast—vibrant health, so he promised it. He had a happy gift for the right phrase for products such as Grape Nuts: "It Makes Blood Red." Who could resist the sales pitch? No one, as it turned out, except the churlish. *Collier's* magazine refused to take Post's advertisements because his copy resembled that of the most blatant vendors of patent medicines but other publications felt no scruples. Post attacked *Collier's* in other advertisements because he was pugnacious—"all cat, part wild and not quite safe to cuddle," as a friend put it.

Post created another great slogan for Grape Nuts: "There's a Reason." Who knows how many individuals pondered this cereal advertisement on the package while munching those gritty nuggets, longing to know the reason. Post never told them.

You can sell just about anything if you find the right way to give the consumer a good feeling about his health. It is not easy and others failed where they succeeded. Will Kellogg, the doctor's brother who was in charge of the health food end of things at the san, also launched an all out advertising campaign with his cereals. Will made a huge fortune and fought off the doctor's law suits repeatedly. Dr. John Kellogg did not really care for money but he hated to see his kid brother capitalize on something that he no longer controlled, even though Will's purchase of the doctor's patents had been on the square.

Post died in 1914 at age 60. Over his last years he expended his considerable energies fighting organized labor through a national organization which he hoped would replace labor unions. He also occupied himself establishing a model city and cloth factories in West Texas. His penultimate battle was against nature. He resolved to bring rain to the region through the detonation of tons of high explosives in assaults on moisture-bearing clouds. As a rain-maker his attainments were modest. Post's last battles for life and health were news-makers. After an appendicitis attack he chartered a special train for a cross-country dash from California to the Mayo Clinic in Rochester. He won that race but, on returning to his winter home in Santa Barbara, could not conquer his depression. He died by his own hand.[19]

By the time Macfadden entered the cereal sweepstakes the Battle Creek landscape was littered with the remains of manufacturers who had challenged Kellogg and Post. Niel S. Phelps, owner of a printing and publishing business, backed Malta Vita flakes, the first commercially successful flaked breakfast food produced at Battle Creek. Malta Vita flakes, nicely curled and crinkled, were sweetened wheat flakes that owed much to Dr. Kellogg's invention of Granose Flakes and Post's introduction of the malting process in his factory.

Competition among cereal makers was intense and the planting of spies in rivals' factories or otherwise ferreting out trade secrets was commonplace. In all some forty-four breakfast-food concerns started up in Battle Creek in the early 1900s. Some were cottage industries—mom and pop efforts—lacking the necessary capital and machinery; others were substantial factories producing Cero-Fruto, Mapl-Flakes, Norka Malted Oats, Tryabita, and many other wonderful, health-giving products. All the cereal makers understood that they were trading on a special mystique concerning Battle Creek and its religious-health traditions established by the Seventh Day Adventists. Some taboos had to be observed, however, as Charles Post learned when he over-reached in Biblical reference. He called one of his early versions of corn flakes, Elijah's Manna, and marketed it in a box showing the prophet feeding a raven from his hand. Preachers decried his sacrilege from their pulpits and its sale was prohibited by law in England. Post, who was usually too clever to make major mistakes, quickly came up with a fetching, non-controversial, and highly commemorative name, Post Toasties.

Cereals were not the only health products produced in Battle Creek. Following the lead of Dr. Kellogg, whose inventive brain had teemed with ideas on making the largely vegetable diet at the san more attractive to his fussy guests, juices of all kinds of fruits and vegetables flowed in drinks of a bewildering variety, and were surely adequate to replace unhealthy coffee and tea. From ovens, dehydrators, steamers, and cooking vats cunning fellows worked up marvelous foods from grains, nuts, dairy products, and vegetables. None of their creations had the impact of the breakfast cereals; few even survived, except in reinvented form in more recent eras of health food mania—except one, a nut butter originated by Dr. Kellogg, and tinkered with by Booker T. Washington and others until we got peanut butter.

Competitors existed in the sanitarium business too. It was very difficult to approach the appeal and magnificence of the san, which after suffering a serious fire in 1902, perhaps lit by one of Ellen White's Adventist loyalists, was reconstructed on a grandiose scale. Advertisements for the san in all the leading magazines hinted that guests seeking better health would not languish in wretched discomfort. "You can enjoy the luxury of a 'Florida' climate in 7 acres of perfectly warmed and perfectly ventilated INDOORS," promised a large advertisement in *Collier's*. "Here, in the beautiful palm garden, sun parlors, glass enclosed porches, separate swimming pools for men and women, great cheer-inspiring dining room, luxurious parlors and foyers, entertainment halls and notable gymnasium, you can find a new kind—the real kind—of Rest, Recreation and Health-Building." Dr. Kellogg, who always appeared in his natty white suit at his special Monday evening question and answer sessions so that all his hundreds of guests gained the impression of having received his personal attention, respected the social amenities. He took care to let the world know that the great men of American industry, politics, and other endeavors came to Battle Creek. His advertisements suggested opportunities for conversing with guests who just might be cabinet officers and business tycoons. "You will have an opportunity to talk with hundreds of interesting people from all parts of the world who are steadily and undeniably improving in health. Their enthusiasm and progress will give you new courage, new hope and a new spirit of 'fighting for health'—which is more than half the battle." Battle Creek was not for those "half-hearted, hope-diminishing travelers from one climate to another," but rather for the "enthusiastic, determined seeker after health." One went to Battle Creek to learn about the restoration of natural functions by natural means, "such as, a delightful, satisfying diet prescribed in definite calorie values and prepared by expert medicochefs; all forms of massage, electricity, mechanotherapy, medical gymnastics, hydrotherapy, phototherapy, etc."[20]

Kellogg offered a great program. You did not need to be sick to enjoy benefits. Whether sick or well you could either be examined on arrival so that you "know your exact physical condition" or you could skip the examination so that neither you nor the staff had more than a fuzzy focus on it.

Rivals of the san tended to be more modest in their establishments although Niel S. Phelps, of Malta Vita fame, made a substantial challenge in the late nineteenth century with the Phelps Medical and Surgical Sanitarium. Phelps built a large, stone, colonial building very near Kellogg's place. Its splendid rooms, furnished in Flemish oak, presented an elegant setting for those who did not foreswear luxuries in their quest for health. Lovely nurses in pink and white uniforms saw to the needs of guests. Entertainment was provided by the Phelps Orchestra and by other musicians and lecturers. Phelps fully intended to put Dr. Kellogg out of business. He was sure that people did not really prefer health foods, vegetable diets, and restrictions on smoking. He offered the good life, lots of meat at table, and fine smoking rooms. One need not feel guilty in his enjoyment of creature comforts at Phelps Sanitarium.

According to Battle Creek legend Kellogg watched carpenters raise the imposing edifice, then sniffed to friends "Later I will buy the place." And later he did. But not before Charles Post, a man he disliked far more than Phelps, bought it as a residence when the Phelps Sanitarium failed. Its challenge to Kellogg only lasted four years. When Post established other residences in Washington D.C., Santa Barbara, and in Texas, he leased the place to others. Macfadden was one such lessee.

Every sanitarium operator bragged about its distinguished clientele, but Macfadden did better than most Kellogg rivals by attracting a writer who became a good publicist for his theories. Upton Sinclair's poor health and his reading of *Physical Culture* magazine induced him to write Macfadden in 1909 about his Battle Creek sanitarium. Although Macfadden was no reader he knew Sinclair's fame and invited the notable "muckraker" and his family, promising to give personal attention to his ailments. Sinclair regarded Macfadden as one of the nation's more colorful characters as athlete, showman, lecturer, publisher, and health experimenter, and had earlier considered writing an article about him. He realized that "high-brows"[21] considered Macfadden "a symbol of the vulgarity and cheapness of America," which was in many ways an apt depiction. But Sinclair took a lot of hard knocks from the intelligentsia himself so he did not look down on a man who did not let the scorn of society check his ventures. And Sinclair was very fed up with doctors after paying thousands of dollars and receiving no substantial help for the fatigue and inertia that slowed him down. Like so many other folks he also deplored the fee gouging some doctors practiced and was curious about the claims of natural healers.

In matters of health as in other problem areas Sinclair's inquisitive mind led him to sharpen issues and pose key questions. Doctors did not talk about preventive medicine in those days and he wondered why they did not. "How can I keep well,"[22] he asked doctors? They were too preoccupied with curing ailments to address this question. Only a few individuals outside the medical establishment were concerned with keeping well: "the secrets of natural living were the property of a little group of adventurous persons known as 'health cranks.' " Later it seemed to Sinclair as if increasingly the "cranks" provided inspirations to medical authorities. Why did Dr. Augeste Rollier of Switzerland, for example, get credit for discovering the benefits of the sun cure for many ills when "the semi-lunatics of Physical Culture City were going around in breech cloths, men and women getting themselves arrested by rural constables, before even the word *Nacktkultur* was imported."

Arriving at Battle Creek Sinclair, an eccentric of world class himself, found congenial surroundings at the sanitarium. There were some 100 patients, all trying different things. One 300 pound man completed a ninety day fast; another did forty-five days attempting a cure for *locomotor ataxia;* but most tried shorter fasts. Initially, Sinclair fasted, then joined the milk diet group because they seemed livelier and talked more than the fasters. Soon he had reached the recommended intake of eight quarts daily, then came off milk to try vegetables, then sour milk and figs. He bloomed under these conditions and did not even complain when he smelled beefsteak cooking in Macfadden's private quarters, although he did not believe the leader's claim of an "experimentation."

After a ten day fast and a three week milk diet Sinclair felt great. So did his wife, Meta. They departed Battle Creek praising Macfadden and later Sinclair wrote a book, *The Fasting Cure*. As a satisfied patient rather than the exponent of his own theory, Sinclair's experiences were convincing. Doctors had generally opposed fasts as unnecessarily severe means of reducing eating that could do some harm. Why not just eat less, they asked—and still ask? Sinclair believed that light eating was better than hearty eating in the cure of disease, but he subscribed to Macfadden's insistence that a cure could not be expected "of a severe acute disease, or a long standing chronic one, by such half-hearted and temporizing measures."[23] Sinclair, who was not a dedicated self-sacrificer like Macfadden, saw the matter in practical terms: fasting for long periods was easier than light eating or fasting for two-three days at frequent intervals. "I find it very much harder to do that, because all the trouble in the fast occurs during the first two or three days. It is during those days that you are hungry, and if you begin to eat just when your hunger is ceasing, you have wasted your efforts."[24] He had always failed efforts to eat lightly: "The light meals are just enough to keep me ravenously hungry, and inevitably I find myself eating more and more. And it does me no good to get mad and call myself names about this."

Sinclair had been a patient at Kelloggs before trying Macfadden. Dr. Kellogg recommended that Sinclair eat nothing but a moderate quantity of fruit for several days. This diet not only failed to give him any relief from his general malaise, but also robbed him of his strength: "I would get so weak that I could not stand up—far weaker than I have ever become on an out and out fast."[25]

A friend, the poet Harry Kemp, who had been at Physical Culture City earlier, had contributed to Meta Sinclair's well-being at Battle Creek by seducing her. A highly publicized divorce scandal resulted in 1911, one which gave "artist bohemians" like Sinclair a rather bad name. On the brighter side Upton met a young lady from Mississippi who was staying at the Kellogg institution with older relatives. Eventually, Mary Craig Kimbrough became his wife.

Macfadden did not want Sinclair's money for his treatment but he did want his testimonial to use in advertisements. Sinclair's fame as the author of *The Jungle* and other books was considerable and it was to increase with time. Authors in those days were far greater celebrities than at present when they rank well below entertainers.

The writer's endorsement did not keep Macfadden's sanitarium from failing after a couple of years but over the years Macfadden bought numerous articles by Sinclair for *Physical Culture* and his other magazines. Sinclair became the country's best known socialist but Macfadden, a deep-dyed political conservative, was not receptive to articles exposing the iniquities of the capitalistic system. The free market worked well enough for the publisher except in the areas of health and censorship, although the workers seemed to get more uppity all the time. Macfadden was not too keen on Sinclair's advocacy of womens' rights either, which the author declaimed with great force. The two friends were one, however, on venereal disease and other health matters. Together they saw the opening American performance of Eugene Brieux's *Les Avaries*, a scandalous exposure of the effects of syphilis. Sinclair rewrote the play as a novel, *Damaged Goods*, which was serialized in *Physical Culture* before publication as a book in 1914. Later Sinclair wrote *Sylvia*, a novel describing a wife's infection with venereal disease by her husband and the birth of a blind child. Needless to say, Sinclair championed the cause of sex education.

It may have been Sinclair's concern for venereal disease that allowed him to be duped by Dr. Albert Abrams. After a friend of his boasted of the syphilis cure gained from Abrams, Sinclair went out to San Francisco and observed the doctor's use of his magic box, the oscilloclast, for diagnosing illness from blood samples. Sinclair planned to write a book about Abrams and wrote a spirited defense of the doctor to the AMA.[26]

Sinclair's friendship with Macfadden and through him with Fulton Oursler, gave Oursler a good contact with the progressive element of the literary world. Like pacifist David Starr Jordan, suffragist and settlement worker Jane Addams, Socialist Scott Nearing, and conservationist Gifford Pinchot, Sinclair represented the large group of lively, forward-lookers of the post-World War I years.

H.L. Mencken was a friend of Sinclair's but could not forebear mocking him for his zeal of uplifting humanity. Mencken's regard for the masses' collective wisdom was not high enough to make him optimistic about bettering the society. To Sinclair's advocacy of the initiative and referendum, birth control, Fletcherism, fasting, sexual hygiene, free trade, and osteopathy the caustic sage of Baltimore moaned: "He believes in every one of them, however daring and fantoddish; he grasps and gobbles all the new ones the instant they are announced. But the man simply cannot think right. He is wrong on politics, on economics, and on theology."[27] Mencken had little regard for Macfadden, although he acknowledged the physical culturist's sincerity, but he did not believe any more in the essential perfection of nature's cures than in the essential goodness of man. Sinclair and Macfadden's disdain of doctors did not bother him but their airy dismissal of science did. Although Mencken liked to use the terms "doctors" and "quacks" interchangeably, he was an avid reader of the medical literature. He might make fun of "a faith in science," but would not prefer a trust in nature or the multitudes of natural healers who claimed to understand how good health should be maintained. As for fasting, well, such absolute self-denial and romantic expectation of rejuvenation was typical of the grim coupling of religious fervor with the health quest. Besides, he liked his eats and drinks.

Chapter 6
Strong Beliefs

I have no set and immovable theories to defend.

Bernarr Macfadden

After failing with his city and Battle Creek sanitarium Macfadden wanted a fresh start. Despite his dread of seasickness he voyaged to England in 1912, hoping to make money. He believed that the English were likely to be more receptive to his health theories than Americans had been and resolved to remain abroad long enough to establish himself. He would also have the pleasure of visiting George Bernard Shaw for exchanges of wisdom on health and mutual compliments. He left the publication of *Physical Culture* in the hands of Charles Desgrey, a trusted editor.

His first commercial venture was the establishment of a health resort at Chesham. When this did not thrive he planned another sanitarium at Brighton, which seemed a better location. Meanwhile, he staged a contest for "Great Britain's Perfect Woman," and gained a huge amount of publicity from the lively British press, always keen to rise to the popular appeal of such themes.

As Bernarr had been recently divorced from Marguerite it is probable that he was looking for a third wife. He was only forty-five years old and his vital forces, as he often explained to clients and magazine readers, were wonderfully dynamic. Besides, he had another scheme in mind to demonstrate the veracity of his health theories: he wanted to propagate a beautiful, healthy family whose vitality would confirm his own.

Finding a bride was not too difficult for a famous man. He certainly liked the looks of Mary Williamson, a champion swimmer and all around athlete who had the kind of figure he admired—breasts and hips and 142 sturdy, muscular pounds. Her bust-waist-hip measurements were 38 and 1/2, 25, and 39 inches. Mary, in fact, was very close in size to Macfadden. She was just an inch shorter at five feet five inches and virtually the same weight, although his varied with the timing of his fasts. Mary won the contest as "Great Britain's Perfect Woman" and, soon after, accepted Bernarr's proposal. She was 19 years old.

Mary wrote a very entertaining memoir of her life with Bernarr Macfadden entitled *Dumbbells and Carrot Strips*. Unfortunately, neither her memory nor her good intentions can be taken without question in a book published in 1953. By then her feelings towards Bernarr lacked warmth.

As a bride Mary loved Bernarr and believed in his work. She appreciated that he was a bit different from the common run of men in many ways and that he had a number of foibles. Some were amusing, as his wearing of hats with ventilation holes of his own devise (later he would swear off wearing hats entirely), and his vast discomfort whenever he was required to wear a collar and tie. She enjoyed many of his favorite expressions, particularly those that betrayed the uncertainty of his ear: "She is making a laughing stork of herself;" "There's always a flea in the ointment;" "I'm not going to buy a pork in a poke;" "At heart I'm just a Huckleberry Flynn."[1] What she deplored was his lack of sentiment, as with the purchase of her wedding ring from a pawnshop, and his dogmatic decision—making relating to all family and household matters bearing on the principles of physical culture. Since the principles of physical culture, as interpreted by the man who liked to be called the Father of Physical Culture, touched on virtually all matters small and large from the domestic through international politics to cosmic concerns, he laid down the law over a wide range.

Winning the perfect woman contest and her marriage opened a new, unfamiliar world to the young woman who had held a menial laboring job in a Halifax carpet mill. Suddenly every mail brought proposals of marriage and declarations of undying affection from strangers who responded to the publicity about her. The mail and encounters on the street with ardent men did not turn her head and she understood why these things upset Bernarr. She was not quite as clear on why he seemed to resent her popularity with fans once they started their tour of British cities or why he was so annoyed that she was a better swimmer than he. But they got along. She thought it was funny that he tried to improve his remarkably poor speaking voice by going to the zoo, listening intently to the lions' roar, then trying to imitate their powerful sounds.

Meeting George Bernard Shaw was a treat for Macfadden who admired his stand on vegetarianism. "Barney Shaw," Bernarr told Mary, "has a physical culture brain. He'll be turning out stuff when he's a hundred years old, long after his whiskey-drinking and meat-eating competitors are dead!"[2] Bernarr was not, of course, a big reader of Shaw's works, other than the pieces the author let him have for *Physical Culture* at no cost. In fact, Macfadden rarely read anything except in the needs of his business. Even newspapers did not interest him much unless one was reporting on his activities. And he often warned his young wife that the reading of novels or any other reading done strictly for pleasure was a dangerous pursuit.

Mary readily shared Bernarr's belief that he was a Man of Destiny, one certain to gain recognition as the prophet of healthy living. His frequent fasts helped give him second sight. The ancient prophets had been able to see the future after fasting and he was getting closer to developing the same ability. Food and exercise were his obsessions— thinking about and researching food, not eating it. He dug deep into Biblical and modern lore on vegetarianism. He championed the vegetable diet but was not consistent in following it because he felt stronger after eating meat. For some strange reason he feared poisoning and sometimes asked Mary to taste his food before he tried any. Years later he concluded that the AMA was trying to poison him, but in England his fears were much vaguer and rarely detracted from his ebullience regarding his mission in life. He felt sure that he had made monumental discoveries about health and was on the way to others. Earth magnetism was one of these. He believed that one should remain in direct contact with the earth as much as possible in order that the earth's energy flow could enter the body. Eventually he would take up bare foot hiking and sleeping on the floor in order to accomplish this.

Yes, it could be said that Macfadden was different in his beliefs, his expectations, and sometimes in the way that he regarded other people. The French, for example, were not among his favorites. After spending some time in France arranging a lecture tour that had to be cancelled he carried away a distinct impression that France and Frenchmen were wrong. He added a stinging rebuke to his arsenal of rebukes. "A man who would do (say, or believe) that," he would comment of anyone who did, said, or believed anything he disapproved of, "has been to Paris."[3]

It was not the language that bothered him because he could come up with a few phrases, but that "these Frenchmen run everything in a crazy way." He did not like their excited gestures, their preoccupation with food and drink of unwholesome kinds, nor their emphasis on sex. The French were not too much taken with him either and newspapers ridiculed his dedication to muscularity. He might have saved them, however, if circumstances had permitted, but World War I broke out while the Macfaddens were in northern France where Bernarr was writing his memoirs. Hurriedly they returned to England, then voyaged on the *Lusitania* to New York, arriving in November 1914.

Bernarr liked England but had recovered his confidence in his ability to achieve greatness in America. He had brought the best part of England home with him, a young wife with a baby daughter—strong components of the fast developing "perfect family." Mary would be a great help to him and he warned her not to read about the suffragettes who were causing such a stir in London just before the couple had gone over to France. "What those frustrated females need is babies,"[4] he assured her, "I've a mind to tell 'em to go home and have babies. That's what women are for! If this suffrage business ever got started God knows what would happen! It might sweep to the States. We've got enough crackpots over there to grab this thing and start a lot of trouble. Can you imagine women in Congress making laws for men?" He had been very angry when the women stormed the National Gallery and defaced the "pink posterior" of Velasquez's "Venus." Bernarr knew this famous painting because he had used a photograph of it in *Physical Culture* and he did not like the implications of the womens' point of attack. He assured Mary "That Spaniard painted it the way it should be...Those hellions! Where the hell was Scotland Yard? Are they afraid of women?"

But he could forget all that back in the States. On the voyage he had written his manifesto for publication as an editorial in *Physical Culture*. He announced his return and his notion that revolution was in the air: "Reforms of all kinds are vehemently demanding recognition!"[5] But only one of these reforms was important to him: "The value of strength cannot be exaggerated. It represents a capital that is stable and fundamental. It is essential to life regardless of what your activities may be." He had been enthusiastically received in England but America, always quicker to change, was ripe for his message. France was fifteen years behind: "They have no physical culture literature." But all nations would benefit from the propagation of physical culture and eventually the movement would play a role in politics. "Political contests in which the opponents derive their support through advocating physical culture reforms will...become a reality in the not far distant future." Our principles, as "definitely and emphatically advocated in the first issues of this magazine" would, he hoped, be accepted and taught in "minute detail in every home and school in the world!"

Macfadden's "principles" and his understanding of human physiology and matters of health were incorporated in his multi-volumed *Encyclopedia,* published 1911-14. Its format was not all that unusual for the time when many households depended upon particular books for health guidance. What made Macfadden's singular was its wide scope in theorizing on health matters affecting individuals and society. He did not ask readers to use his remedies on the basis of any faith in him but made it clear that all the remedies he suggested proceeded from a particular understanding of physiology and health.

He termed his method of treatment Physcultopathy and it rested in firm opinions about diseases and their causes. Diseases were caused by heredity, mental influences, contagion, improper diet, overstrain or understrain, physical causes, mechanical causes, and chemical causes.

He made some good points as, for example, warning that fear and other mental distress were injurious. Other theories were a little odd and were perhaps a reflection of certain traumatic experiences in his own life, as, for example, his insistence that prudery caused disease. He distinguished prudery from true modesty. "One may be ever so modest, and yet consider and discuss the subject of sex in every detail, in a pure-minded, wholesome manner."[6] But the prude is a hypocrite and a liar and likely to be prurient. He counsels ignorance about sex, hence ugly things occur.

In presenting his great work as "the final culmination of a dominating ambition to free the human race from slavery to drugs,"[7] Macfadden credited his experience and the literature research of himself and his staff. "It will perhaps not be exaggerating to say that at least a half million or more people have sought advice from me, either through my literature or various schools and other institutions that I have conducted at different times." He claimed his conclusions were based on facts garnered from thousands of cases examined: "I have proven time after time that the science of health building through physical culture methods is definite and accurate. You can depend absolutely upon the principles advocated."

In essence he believed that impurity of the blood was the only disease and that it should be cured through natural methods rather than by drugs. Of the germ theory that had been so much popularized since the discoveries of Louis Pasteur (to whom he always referred to privately as "that French quack") he had serious misgivings. He did not quite deny that germs existed but certainly derided them as perils to health. Doctors created a climate of fear with all their talk about germs and fear was a greater killer than any so-called "disease germs." In fact a healthy person had no reason to worry about germs at all because his body would usually repel their attacks. Any such signs of disease as did appear were actually beneficial because the symptoms warned of an irregularity within the system that should be remedied. He believed further that "most manifestations of disease are curable...and it does not require drugs, special nostrums, great learning or superior intelligence. All it requires is common sense, persistence, energy, belief in the body that it is doing the best it can for itself, and that if helped, not hindered, in its efforts, it will bring itself to a healthful condition."[8] He knew this to be true because thousands of people who suffered from every disease known to man had written him to explain that after exhausting "every method known to medical science" without results they followed his "simple suggestions" and recovered their health.

His simple suggestions centered on diet and exercising. He favored vegetarianism, milk diets, and, most of all, fasting. The originator of the fast as a means of retaining health was a sixteenth century Italian,

Luigi Cornaro, who cured himself of gout and stomach disorders caused by gluttony. Cornaro threw away all the medicines that had been given him, reduced his eating and drinking, and went on to live to a great age while taking time to warn his countrymen: "O wretched, miserable Italy! Dost not thou plainly see, that Gluttony deprives thee of more Souls yearly, than either a War, or the plague itself could have done?"[9] Macfadden thrilled to the Italian's early discovery that "every Man...might become his own Physician" by watching his appetite, "which indeed ought to be every one's Chief Business and Concern." Cornaro had been a great influence on Jacksonian America's burst of health reform and his writings were translated by America's champion reformer, Sylvester Graham. The Italian taught wonderful truths: rejuvenation and longevity could be achieved once one made an inner change that resulted in permanent rewards.

Macfadden has a good deal to say about fasting in the *Encyclopedia* and pays his respects to disciples like Upton Sinclair, whom he quotes generously, and others who advanced similar ideas like Dr. H.S. Tanner and Linda Hazzard. He was tolerant enough to point out a disagreement with the well-known writer, Sinclair, in regard to periodic fasting. Sinclair advised against periodic or habitual fasting. It should not be necessary to fast, Sinclair argued, if one's life habits and eating practices were correct. But Macfadden saw a need for a yearly fast, at least: "Just as the early day Catholics used to fast for religious reasons, so would I urge upon people today to fast for the physical, mental and spiritual benefits that would arise therefrom...If it did nothing more, it would be a good thing annually to remind the appetite that it is not the master of your life."[10]

Macfadden could become somewhat lyrical on the benefits of a fast: "The breath becomes sweet and clean. Abnormal craving for food will disappear and in its place will come the natural desire for some wholesome article of food." And there was nothing to fear: "Reader, if you are suffering from either an acute or chronic disease of which you wish to rid yourself, the first and best thing you can do (unless your body is too enfeebled) is to understandingly lead your mind to see the rationality and wisdom of fasting and then as quickly as possible begin the actual experience of the fast. It is a natural method of cure. Nothing natural can be injurious. The experiences of thousands who have fasted from one to ninety days have demonstrated that there is nothing to be afraid of. Master your fears, resolutely control your abnormal appetite, summon your will, be a man, a woman, and fast."[11]

The distinction he made between appetite and hunger was very important in the views of Macfadden and other fasters. Babies cried and adults ate all too often in disregard of any genuine hunger but because compelled by unhealthy appetites. Consequently babies were fed too much—and suffered accordingly, and adults ate too much and made themselves easy victims of disease. Linda Hazzard, a leading disciple of Macfadden in the Pacific Northwest, always gave the same answer when patients or the curious demanded to know how long a fast should last or how she knew when it should be ended: "It is evident when one's hunger returns."[12] This answer sometimes puzzled those who could not quite grasp the distinction between appetite and hunger. Those who professed to believe that all that was natural was good had learned early to make such distinctions.

Macfadden often praised the fasting theories and practices of Dr. Henry S. Tanner who had amused New York in 1880 with a public fast. Tanner, a practitioner of the eclectic school of medicine which was then jousting with the medical establishment over matters of certification, had lectured in several eastern cities on the merits of fasting. Regular doctors abused him and newspapers made sport of his theories. It was often said that his wife, "a good feeder,"[13] left him because she was not given enough to eat. She complained that her husband expected her to live on air. When asked about her charges by newsmen Doc Tanner was forced to admit that his wife was a gross eater whom he tried to rescue from gluttony. He had been zealous about fasting benefits for three years—ever since he fasted for forty-two days to cure himself of asthma, rheumatism, and heart disease.

Scoffers always turned out at Tanner's lectures to cast doubts on his claim of surviving a forty-two day fast. In order to convert the unbelievers Dr. Tanner announced a forty day public fast. Doctors were outraged, "Bosh,"[14] said the Surgeon General of the U.S. Army. "He is either a fraud or a lunatic," cried the *New York Times*.

Tanner hired the Clarendon Hall on West Thirteenth Street and arranged to start his fast at noon on June 28, 1880. Official watchers, selected from among regular physicians, were designated. The public was allowed into the hall early to inspect Tanner's rocking chair, iron cot, mattress, and writing stand. At noon the short, roly-poly, sparsely gray-haired, fifty-one year old man allowed himself to be searched for hidden food by the watchers. A watcher blew the starting whistle and began his scheduled six-hour watching shift. Tanner sighed, scratched his head, then sat to begin rocking vigorously. While Tanner's performance was rather static public interest was high. Doctors journeyed to New York from other cities. Visitors crowded into the hall most hours of the day and night, paying twenty-five cents admission after the first ten days of free entry. On Sundays, ministers who perceived some threat to divine laws denounced Tanner, while others came forward with various reflections upon the event's meaning.

Newspaper coverage was extensive. The Doc received lots of fan mail, some 300-500 letters daily. Some writers praised the doctor; some were obscenely threatening; and some wrote to tempt him with tantalizing descriptions of food. Tanner rocked during the day, slept at night, and sometimes took supervised rides about the city. At first he drank no water but began drinking after he began feeling weak. Taking a drink of water after two weeks had been a tonic to Tanner because he had just challenged a young, vigorous reporter to a foot race. The reporter had been insisting that the Doc's strength must have faded away. The older man showed the scoffer his heels: "The doctor so speedily and easily outran his competitor, and the reporter so labored, puffing and blowing in distress, that everyone saw the absurdity of continuing the race further,"[15] reported the *Times*.

On the tenth day the rivalry between the eclectic and regular (allopathic) schools of medicine erupted with violent charges of fraud. Allopathic watchers protested when Tanner's eclectic supporters gave him a sponge. "Stop. The sponge may be filled with soup,"[16] cried a suspicious doctor. The uproar subsided when Tanner and his followers submitted written denials that the sponge held soup. At day thirty Tanner showed a weight loss of twenty-five pounds. He felt fine and continued to day forty with ease, losing eleven pounds more.

Linda Hazzard of Seattle was a disciple of Doc Tanner and of Macfadden and her persecution as a "starvation specialist" went far beyond anything suffered by the senior fast advocates. Macfadden invariably argued that fasting never harmed anyone, yet in 1912 the Kitsap County, Washington prosecutor charged Hazzard with killing a woman by starving her to death. The victim and her sister had been patients at a sanitarium Hazzard operated near Seattle. As the medical society had been trying to have her place closed down for years she took care to identify herself as a diet specialist rather than a healer but she did not employ a staff physician.

The sisters in question were two wealthy Englishwomen who had been on a world tour. While visiting Victoria, the quaint capital of British Columbia, they had heard about the famous Linda Hazzard. As they were health faddists of long standing they may have read about her in *Physical Culture* or Macfadden's *Encyclopedia* because he often made reference to her work and had included her portrait in the *Encyclopedia*. After a ferry ride from Victoria to Seattle the sisters, Claire and Dorothea Williamson, called on Hazzard. The "starvation specialist" did not need to give the women a physical examination to recognize that they needed a diet and supervision as out-patients. After four weeks Hazzard, alarmed at their condition, ordered them to move to her sanitarium.

Their removal to the sanitarium made conditions ideal for fasting, yet the treatment did not seem to help. Claire was so taken with Hazzard's solicitude that she ordered her Seattle banker to pay any checks on her account drawn by Hazzard. She also altered her will to provide a small endowment to the sanitarium. Dorothea resisted Hazzard's influence a little more strongly but she did allow her protector to manage her finances.

Claire went downhill fast. She showed signs of mental instability so Hazzard applied for a court appointment as guardian and executor of her will. Just a month after reaching the sanitarium Claire died. She only weighed fifty pounds at the end—down from the 126 she carried on arrival in Seattle. Dorothea was probably saved because a relative visited the sanitarium after Claire's death and took her away. She weighed forty-eight pounds at the time.

Puget Sound newspapers made much of the murder trial which did nothing to advance the fasting cure favored by Hazzard and Macfadden. Jurors agreed with the prosecutor that Hazzard's willingness to manage the sisters' finances was very suspicious, although they could only agree on a conviction of manslaughter.

While her appeal was pending Hazzard sought to swing public opinion to her favor by holding a public fast. A newspaper, the *Seattle Star,* sponsored the event. She did not know how long she would fast; it would perhaps be thirty days before "the return of hunger."[17]

The event attracted general excitement. Old Doc Tanner, then 82, came out from the east to give moral support. "Nothing to it,"[18] he told reporters in reference to his own fasts, "fasting is a picnic. When I feel run-down I quit eating for three or four days." But Seattle's doctors warned about long fasts, predicting that Hazzard would be dead after thirteen or fourteen days. Not that they minded. Over the years they had been aggravated often by Mrs. Hazzard. She was a tough bird and knew what they were thinking: "If I die that means one less quack in the world."[19]

Hazzard carried on for several weeks under the supervision of the *Seattle Star's* vigilant committee which "watched her day and night." She was seen often in town, taking long walks, or giving lectures in the theatres. The *Star* filled in accounts of her daily condition and activities with stories about Tanner and his good friend, Bernarr Macfadden of Chicago, "the vegetarian physical culturist who keeps fit by fasting when not dining on lettuce and nuts. He has the physique of Hercules and appetite of a wren."[20]

Hazzard reached the thirty day mark in good form to announce that her "hunger had not yet returned." She figured that she might need fifteen more days to complete her fast. She actually quit a few days later, feeling that she had made her point, and somewhat annoyed because the *Star* had neglected her for stories about the sinking of the *Titanic.*

After serving two years in prison Hazzard was pardoned by the governor. On release she was refused a license for a hospital but she continued to practice without one. In 1925 a man died of tuberculosis after an 85 day fast under her supervision but the county prosecutor, after reviewing the evidence, did not file criminal charges. She died at age 70 during a fast intended to clear up her pneumonia.

Macfadden did not publicize his favorite's downfall. He knew that newspapers were quick to blame non-establishment practitioners for the deaths of their patients even if the treatment had no bearing upon it. In 1914 *Physical Culture* published a letter from June Oakes, a Seattle nurse, who described the many failures of doctors she had worked for and her accidental discovery of dieting as a cure. She had learned all about fasting from Dr. Linda Hazzard and recommended her book on the subject to readers of the magazine.

Even Macfadden's bitter enemies among doctors had no quarrel with the attention he paid to the value of fresh air. He applauded the use of sleeping porches and the increasing use being made of patios in sunnier parts of the nation. His enthusiasm for fresh air carried him into an advocacy of deep breathing. "The Hindus," he observed, "the most intelligent race the world has ever known,"[21] had long practiced deep breathing. He praised the written treatises by Yogis on the subject but warned against some charlatan representatives of Hindu scholarship in this country. He also acknowledged the contributions to breathing theories by Sylvester Graham, Dio Lewis, Martin Luther Holbrook, and other hygienists.

It is intriguing in reading Macfadden's praise of such respected figures as breathing advocates to come upon a tribute to Thomas Lake Harris, the famous spiritualist. Macfadden does not get into the particulars of Lake's rather spotted career but his admiration was not limited to Lake's wisdom on breathing. Perhaps he was really intrigued by Lake and the equally bizarre and suspect community leader, John Alexander Dowie, because they had imposed their wills on followers and founded their own communities. Harris and Dowie were great showman.

Harris and two partners founded the Garden of Eden at Mt. Cove, Virginia for 100 members anxious to avoid world destroying convulsions forecast by Harris. The partners accepted whatever wealth the members possessed "in trust for God." Soon the partners disagreed on policies and broke up. Harris took his share of the Lord's money to Salem on Lake Erie in New York state where he established another utopian colony. Harris resembled some Old Testament figure with his thick, gray-streaked hair, heavy brow, full beard, flashing eyes and a most remarkable voice. Actually he had two voices: his "near" voice was big and booming, while his "far off" voice seemed to originate from some spiritual source. With two such suggestive, intimidating voices he made an impressive orator.

Certain complexities make it difficult to define Harris' teachings, but the major tenet concerned the supposed dual-sex of God and men. Men were not necessarily to achieve their bi-sexual nature until they gained Eternal Life, but they were to seek it on earth all the same. The great goal was to find one's complementary half and it was very likely that his presence could be experienced while one was in the arms of a earthly lover. Harris, a very vigorous man, may have set an example for his followers, although a recent biographer has insisted that he practiced celibacy. His heavenly counterpart was called Lily Queen, and she was adept at comforting women who bedded down with Harris. Only superficially was fornication involved in this effort to bring the consolations of Lily Queen to his feminine disciples—though it was observed that only young, attractive women were privileged to share in the experience.

Harris' community was destroyed by a law suit won by Laurence Oliphant and his wife. Oliphant, a noted English writer and diplomat, was completely dominated by Harris. Oliphant joined the colony with his bride who was induced to turn over her large fortune to Harris. The leader counseled the Oliphants to avoid sexual relations and saw that Mrs. Oliphant received the attention of Lily Queen often. Eventually the couple concluded that they were being used and sued for the recovery of money given to Harris.

Harris died in 1906 with his reputation in tatters, yet in 1911 Macfadden recalled him as "the greatest mystic that America has yet produced," and described his volume on "The breath of God in Man" as "one of the most eloquent and beautiful presentations of the subject that it has been our good fortune to read."[22] It is hard to imagine down-to-earth Bernarr reading any of Harris' mystical tomes.

Among the fringe practitioners popular at the time were osteopaths and chiropractors. Macfadden was not too hard on them because they were drugless healers who were persecuted by the established medical profession. But, as their usual treatment involved manipulation of the body, they encroached upon his own special field of physcultopathy. "We do not altogether believe in the bone-breaking treatment advocated by some classes of drugless physicians."[23] He believed spinal adjustment could be maintained by the strength of the muscles and ligaments and that adjustment should be achieved through exercise rather than "the bone-breaking method (or what often seems to the patient to be such)." Macfadden's Mechanical Physcultopathy was infinitely superior to osteopathy yet he believed "there is everything to be gained in the choice of the Osteopath as against the regular physician."[24] He could not accept the osteopaths' belief that all ailments were spinal in origin because he knew that all ailments were caused by impurities of blood. "Even the lesions of the spine which are credited with being the direct cause of disease are in most cases themselves the result of vicious habits, errors of diet, lack of activity and various unwholesome conditions."

Osteopathy intrigued him because its success showed "the failure of the medical profession"[25] and because its founder's dynamic personality inspired him. Andrew Taylor Still originated osteopathy after a colorful career on the Kansas frontier in the 1860s as a healer of Indians. His father had been a quack but Still claimed an incomplete course of studies at the Kansas City School of Physicians and Surgeons before serving in the Civil War. After the war he desired to help drug and alcohol addicts who were largely ignored by regular doctors. He lost three of his children in an epidemic of cerebrospinal menigitis. Subsequently he grew curious about human anatomy and studied the cadavers of diseased patients and old bones he disinterred from local burial places. Eventually he arrived at certain conclusions. Evolutionists had suggested that man had not always walked upright; it appeared that the human spine was poorly engineered for the new posture of humans. From this he determined that man's upright posture was the source of all his ailments, thus osteopathy ("bone suffering") was born. All illness was due to malpositions or subluxations of the joints in the spine and every disease could be cured by manipulation of the spine.

Still was excited to discover that lung fever was caused by disturbances of the vertebrae on the upper neck and that typhoid, dysentery, appendicitis, cancer and most "female complaints" were produced by woes of the lower vertebrae. Later, in an article for the *Ladies' Home Journal,* he specified his findings: "I do not believe that there are such diseases as Fever, Typhoid, Typhus, Rheumatism, Sciatica, Gout, Colic, Liver diseases, or Croup."[26] When folks suffered from ailments resembling these it was "because their nerves and vessels are interfered with in the spinal columns and on the way up."

In his late years Still believed that God had given him healing powers. His attacks on doctors were hard-hitting: "Shame on the knife that cuts a woman like a Christmas hog. Almost one-half the women of today bear a knife-mark, and I tell you, God's intelligence is reproached by it. An Osteopath stands firm in the belief that God knew what to arm the world with, and follows His principles. And he who so far forgets God's teachings as to use drugs, forfeits the respect of this school and its teachings. God is the Father of Osteopathy, and I am not ashamed of the child of His mind."[27]

Initially, Still's theories aroused a chorus of ridicule but, as he continued to practice in Kansas, he was able to spread the good word of osteopathy. In 1892 with the help of three sons, a daughter, a reformed quack pile doctor, and a former vendor of lightning-rods he established the American School of Osteopathy in Kirksville, Mo. The school thrived and continued on after Still's death in 1917. Several other schools also turned out osteopaths despite the opposition of the AMA. Modern osteopaths have not followed the notions of the founder and have attained respectability by upgrading their training and through effective lobbying with state legislatures to protect their licenses to practice.[28]

Chiropractic was also created in the quack-favoring clime of the Mid-West. Daniel David Palmer, a Canadian-born grocer, settled in Iowa where in the late nineteenth century he studied spiritualism, phrenology, osteopathy, and magnetic healing. After curing a janitor of deafness by adjusting a misaligned vertebrae and saving a heart disease victim with similar nimbleness of fingers he was off and running with a new science of health treatment. Chiropractic, which was called "Osteopathy's skeleton in the cupboard,"[29] by a critic, fared even better than osteopathy in attracting practitioners and patients, although it encountered a severe crisis when Iowa authorities jailed Palmer for practicing medicine without a license. Palmer sold the school to his son, Bartlett Joshua, who carried on the tradition for fifty years. Young Palmer, perhaps inspired by Dr. Albert Abrams, the Californian who made a fortune with a "black box" full of electrical wires, invented one of his own in the 1920s. His "neurocalometer" consisted of two simple thermopiles which were placed on either side of a patient's spine. Wires attached to a galvanometer gave readings of significance to the specialist. Like Abrams, Palmer would lease but not sell his machine to assure higher profits. He invented another diagnostic machine that was not too successful, perhaps because its name, Electroencephaloneuromentimpograph, put folks off.

The AMA fought hard to relegate chiropractors to illicit back-alley dens but lost the struggle throughout the states as legislators, ever keen to support cost-cutting competition in the healing arts, sanctioned licensed practice.

Chiropractors have harbored pretenses for their arts that make those of the osteopaths appear modest. The New Jersey law governing practice lobbied through by chiropractors in the 1920s proclaimed their science to be "the study and application of a universal philosophy of biology, theology, theosophy, health, disease, and death." Palmer's original School of Chiropractic in Davenport, Iowa was truly democratic: there were no academic admission requirements; anyone with a few hundred dollars for tuition was warmly welcomed. It was not the strange origin nor dubious practice of osteopathy and chiropractic that made Macfadden disrespectful of them but their indifference to fasting. His own discipline of Physcultopathy, a school of Naturopathy, could not be traced to either an ancient or modern founder and varied widely in its forms. Nature's way of healing was, the key—but how was nature to be utilized? Most Naturopaths like Macfadden stressed fasting. "In its best known form," an English critic observed, "it consists of elegant and expensive fasting—

the physical equivalent of the spiritual retreat, a penance which some men and women are willing to suffer gladly once a year."[30]

The core of Macfadden's teachings on exercise are found in a chapter of the *Encyclopedia* entitled "The Simplicity and Certainty of Physcultopathy." After giving some credit to Christian Scientists "because at least they do not directly interfere with and impede the curative efforts of the body itself," and damning the doctors who introduce "poisonous, nauseating drugs, and other contrary methods"[31] to thwart nature's healing, he expanded on exercise. He cautioned desk workers about the "fatigue-poisons" that accumulated in the body over a day's brain work. This poison could only be carried away by the quick use of his muscles; lung and blood circulation activity would then flush every tissue and carry away all the wastes. He confessed he did not know how these things were done but knew that they were done and found the system "very ingenious, complex, and wonderful, and yet, at the same time...very simple."[32]

Macfadden professed to share the belief of the early Christian hygienists who advocated vegetarianism for moral as well as physical reasons. He had himself established through his own physical tests that the vegetarian has as much strength and endurance as any meat eater—and often more. Some things were not so responsive to testing as the performances of athletes in races, wrestling bouts, weight lifting and the like, yet Macfadden, following the vegetarians' traditional medical and theological views, expressed himself strongly and positively. "Experience has also demonstrated the following facts in regard to the relative merit of the two diets. Meat-eaters are more often addicted to the use of alcohol than vegetarians; they are more apt to be sensual and gross in their lives; they are more easily subject to disease; they are harder to cure when diseased, and in order to hasten their recovery, the first and wisest step is to put them on a vegetarian diet."[33] These were certainly remarkable advantages for the vegetarians, but there were others more remarkable still: the vegetarian is not as inclined to be "combatively aggressive as his meat-eating brother, but is physically his superior, has a clearer mentality, is less liable to the temptations of the flesh, and need not always be worrying himself lest he contract this, that or the other disease."

Macfadden considered the physical development of women as carefully as that of men. He liked certain physical attributes in women like a large bust: "A faultless bust is to be desired not only because of its aesthetic and artistic value, but for the far deeper and biological reason that it is so intimately related to the very fountain of life."[34]

Flat chested women were a disgrace and a danger to themselves: "The lack of bust development is an evidence of lack of vitality and health. It is true that one may have the health, so-called, which permits her to be on her feet and to walk around, but she is not a complete woman or in perfect health if she is lacking in this respect. A flat-busted, flat-chested condition may not indicate absolute sterility in a woman, but it indicates a condition of health in which approaching sterility may be a possibility...The full and perfect bust makes a woman attractive because it indicates her fitness for motherhood, which also to a very large extent explains her magnetic quality."[35]

Macfadden did not think that large size in busts was the ideal as much as firmness and perfect shape. He included photographs of classical and modern sculptures to show what artists believed the ideal bust to be. "I would call attention to the works of art everywhere to corroborate what is here said upon this point."[36]

The *Encyclopedia* even included an original musical composition by Macfadden, who claimed that Beethoven's "Creation" stimulated him to the creation of a physical culture song. He included the music and the words with the hope that his disciples would sing it and other songs in order to exercise their vocal chords, a matter of great importance that was often neglected. "The song...has not the jingle that would perhaps gain it popularity; it has not been written for that purpose. Rather it is intended for those who have given considerable time to vocal culture and who can put unusual feeling into their vocal efforts."[37] The song was called "Manhood Glorified:"

> "The world re—sounds demand——————ing human glory
> The cry for health prevails throughout the land
> While groveling through life's mire
> Seeth not the strength, grace and poise offered to all men.
> Thy head hold up, and claim thy divine kingship,
> For thrortes of mighty strength await thee
> Claim thine heritage, tingling with power.
> And like a roaring lion fight,
> For manhood's great rewards."

Throughout the five volume work harsh words for doctors abound, but the chapter entitled "Medicine, The Science of Guessing" gives a focus. Plainly Macfadden found as many absurdities in the medical literature as his doctor readers found in his.

"Guesswork has been the history of the medical profession from time immemorial,"[38] he wrote. "It has never done anything of which it was absolutely certain except that it was 'certain' of some of its most foolish and erroneous 'guesses.'" The practice of medicine has historically been "utterly devoid of scientific principles." A review of medical history revealed much that was astounding, including "childish, foolish, mad and fantastic theories without end, based upon nothing but the crazy vagaries of superstition." And if the persistence of such crazy schemes for healing was not enough there seemed to have been efforts to provoke "the most dangerous and murderous methods" of healing.

Macfadden compiled a long list of horrors to make his point. Consumptives were treated with alcoholic beverages and shut up in rooms without sunlight or fresh air. Physicians loved to bleed their patients regardless of what was wrong with them and the treatment had more victims than could be counted, including George Washington. In an eighteenth century medical manual Macfadden found a case of headache treatment described. The doctor applied leeches to nose and forehead and opened veins in the arms. While the doctor felt right about the timeliness and good sense of his treatment he was forced to report that "notwithstanding these precautions,"[39] the patient died. Mark Twain, coming on the same account, figured that the ancient physician probably would have disemboweled a patient who complained of a stomach-ache.

The medical literature held many examples of recipes for medicines. One included mandrake, pepper, berries, weeds, parsley, gold, silver, pearls, stag's heart, wheat, and honey. It was good "for raising Flatulence in the stomach."[40] Macfadden agreed that "such a medicine ought to raise enough Flatulency to blow a gale."

Macfadden cited other curiosities and the viewpoints of modern doctors who plainly admitted that their predecessors had labored under many delusions. Some of the shifts in treatment made in recent times, as in the treatment of consumptives, had Macfadden's hearty approval, as did the "wonderful progress that has been made in aseptic surgery."[41] He reserved his highest praise for recent adopting of "principles of rational living, called hygiene, that the hydropathists and physical culture schools have been urging for generations."[42]

The big problem with the profession, in Macfadden's view, was that doctors in their commercial greed turned away from the principles of Hippocrates. Hippocrates found diseases in the fluids of the body—as did Macfadden. One cannot improve on Hippocrates. "When you have a disease...you rectify and change the blood—the fluids in the body—until you fill it full of the elements that nourish."[43]

Throughout the *Encyclopedia* Macfadden expressed his particular expertise and passionate commitment to matters of sexual hygiene. He considered himself a Messiah, a fully enlightened sage, anxious to lead the masses out of darkness and ignorance. Unfortunately, his views comprised a curious mixture of advanced and retrogressive theories. "Sexual passion," he asserts, "is the expression of race instinct, and the force through which, in its culmination, is accomplished that union of parental or germinal cells which marks the inception of new life."[44] It followed that the study of sexual hygiene was of surpassing importance because it aimed to prevent any dissipation of "the most vital force in life." Young and old must be guided by intelligent instruction. Even many old married folks were not "conversant with the very first and most fundamental of the physiological laws of sex."

Macfadden called for "perfect sexuality," by which he meant the vigorous employment of the love instinct by a married couple, yet he also expressed the moral dread of "offensive sex," that had been traditionally expounded by Christian hygienists of the nineteenth century. He was concerned that city life was not healthy enough to keep sexual vitality high. Yet he was worried about constrictive clothing of women that had a way of "inducing sexual excitement."[45] He favored cold baths for stimulating sexual vigor yet opposed anyone lingering in bed in the morning or retiring unless they were ready to fall asleep immediately. And diet, of course, was a major worry. "The average diet of today is altogether too stimulating in character, and if we could get back to the simplicity and wholesomeness of the diet of pioneer life, it would be better for the entire world. Much of the depravity and crime that arise from distorted, over-stimulated, one might say diseased sexual instincts, would be unknown if the average food supply"[46] were reduced one-half and restricted. "Pepper, condiments, hot sauces, tea, coffee, alcoholic beverages, white flour, and many other articles commonly found on the ordinary table are inclined to excite the sexual passions and should be avoided if one desires a life of high aims and refinement of character."[47] He also asserted that "meat is particularly stimulating and should be avoided as much as possible."[48]

What appears to be an inconsistency in Macfadden's attitude is rather a trick of our expectations. We do not expect someone worrying about pepper's effects on passion to be too keen on sexual vigor generally, but Macfadden makes his notion clear: He wishes people to control their passion and sexual power but not to lessen it—"which indeed would be undesirable."[49]

What he writes of the love instinct does not suggest the puritan: "Love, which is the higher interpretation of the sex instinct, represents the most powerful force in human character...Normal and well-developed men and women have an instinctive power of 'sensing' each other's sexual adaptation and responsiveness."[50] But it is as if he pulls back to a safe position when he reaches a certain point: "When we exalt the sex instinct to the highest and purest human function and no longer degrade it into mere beastly passion, the evils of unhappy marriage will vanish in nearly all cases." Procreation, he insists, is the only desirable reason for sex.

Among Macfadden's call for double beds and urgent warnings against sex during pregnancy or while a woman is nursing, and his kind words for the practice of continence in marriage—all traditional marriage manual theories, Macfadden does introduce one divergent view: "There is one school of teachers which believes that sexual intercourse is calculated to develop themselves and augment their happiness independent of all considerations of offspring. They assert that their principles controvert the prevailing ideas of baseness and degradation associated with the sexual nature and they believe that their teachings will lead individuals to purer lives, to better understanding and appreciation of the sex functions, to intelligent control of propagation, and finally, through right adjustment in most sacred relations, to the ideal marriage. They contend that their methods avoid the opposite evil of asceticism and self-indulgence, and do more than anything else to make marriage a perpetual courtship."[51] By slipping these comments rather inappropriately within his section on continence in marriage Macfadden indicated that there were some modern ideas abroad. And, significantly, he does not condemn the view that contradicts virtually everything else he has expressed.

Why should Macfadden, the agnostic, body-loving champion of "manly vigor" warn about "free indulgence" in sex? "It does not matter," he stated solemnly, "whether the waste of energy takes the form of excesses legally practiced within the bonds of marriage, or unsanctified gratification elsewhere, for the drain on the nervous system and the general vital exhaustion are just the same."[52]

Macfadden insisted that "the world is full of men who are nothing short of physical wrecks because of this sexual intemperance. We see them on every side, men who are not more than half men, and sometimes not even that—gaunt, nervous or nerveless, their limbs shrunken and weakened and their strength not that of a normal child." Certainly Macfadden, as he bounded through the streets of New York, could see plenty of such men as he described—weak-looking, unhealthy types. But what, in the name of either Venus or Apollo, directed his conclusion that these weaklings grew weak through excessive sexual indulgence? Surely a busy sexual performer requires health and stamina and was as cocky as a barnyard rooster (Macfadden's favorite animal). How could such miserable specimens as he described summon up strength enough to be excessive? Were they all once imposing sex athletes who came to ruin through over-indulgence or were they sexually active only out of unhealthy nervousness?

Macfadden is hardly more liberal than old sex-hating Sylvester Graham in recommending sex frequency. Intercourse twice a week, Macfadden believed, might overtax "even the strongest,"[53] so the average man should confine himself to intercourse three or four times a month. The young, old, and otherwise weak, should not risk so frequent an indulgence. As Macfadden knew himself to be an extremely virile man, he undoubtedly exempted himself from such moderating restrictions. He did not confess to readers that his physical conditioning put him on a higher plain, far beyond the need for cautions. We cannot know what sexual frequency he liked but the two wives who wrote books about him complained of his ardor.

Macfadden's difficulty in presenting a lucid and consistent slant on sexual hygiene can be traced to the peculiar biases of his authorities on the subject. Doctors and preachers had long taught that women were naturally indifferent to sex. This odd notion originated with William Acton, the author of *Functions and Disorders of the Reproductive System* (1857), a study based on the physician-author's countless hours of private consultation with his patients. Only out of fear that they would be deserted by their husbands for prostitutes did women over-ride their own inclinations and submit to their husbands' advances according to Dr. Acton. The theory appealed for a number of reasons. Male virility had become the center of attention and it was understood that mens' vital energies could be overly expended by sex. Women would not demand too much from men because they did not enjoy what he had to offer anyway. Men were advised to perform swiftly to save themselves and not worry about their partners' needs. As Acton put it: "The majority of women (happily for society) are not very much troubled with sexual feeling of any kind. What men are habitually, women are only exceptionally...There can be no doubt that sexual feeling in the female is in the majority of cases in abeyance, and that it requires positive and considerable excitement to be aroused at all: and even if roused (which in many instances it never can be) it is very moderate compared with that of the male."[54] In this context of belief the term "loose woman" had a strong meaning. Prostitutes, and other low and vulgar women, gave young men a false impression of the sensuousness of their sex. Good women express their passion in their love of home, family, and domestic duties.

Some protests were made against Acton's conclusions. Elizabeth Blackwell, a physician herself, argued that womens' repugnance for sexual passion resulted from fear of childbirth and, sometimes, earlier, unpleasant sex experiences. Dr. Frederick R. Sturgis of New York attributed female frigidity to womens' belief that the sexual act was solely for the pleasure and relief of men. Since it was not generally known that clitoris stimulation was necessary to womens' arousal, men disengaged before their partners could feel any pleasure.

But these few protests were swallowed up in the tide of prudery from the 1870s which was expressed in Victorian marriage manuals. Purity authors, who dominated the literary field, decreed that frigidity in women was a virtue. Women took to this notion because it elevated them and because it allowed them a means of resisting male dominance without defying convention. It is ironic that as women struggled to gain a more equitable legal status they were supporting a moral code that restricted their sexuality. To gain some dignity in marriage they accepted a convenient stereotype—a freedom to deny themselves pleasure.

The manuals incorporated much that Graham, Acton and other hygienists had taught. Sex was the basest human tendency and its abuse was invariably punished by anguish and disease. At the same time the manuals planted middle class ideals—romantic notions and pretensions that gave aspiring readers a sense of superiority over lower class transgressors of the purity code. Certain things had to be avoided like touching one's sexual organs and reading romantic novels. Most purity authors named the romantic novel as the leading cause of sexual neurasthenia, hysteria, and other illnesses. Novels tempted readers to impurity and the emotional stimulation tended "to develop the passions prematurely, and to turn the thoughts into a channel which leads in the direction of the formation of vicious habits."[55] Reading romantic stories sent the blood coursing to sexual organs, causing excessive excitement and disease. Dr. John Kellogg of the Battle Creek Sanitarium made the perils clear: "We wish to put ourselves upon record as believing firmly that the practice of novel reading is one of the greatest causes of uterine disease in young women. There is no doubt but that the influence of the mind upon the sexual organs and functions is such that disease may be produced in this way...Reading of a character to stimulate the emotions and rouse the passions may produce or increase a tendency to uterine congestion, which may in turn give rise to a great variety of maladies, including all the different forms of womb displacement, the presence of which is indicated by weak backs, painful menstruations, etc."[56]

Manuals advised married couples to have separate bedrooms or, if that was not possible, separate beds. This arrangement reduced temptations to have sex too often. Sex was for procreation alone and coition should be reserved for occasions when the couple wished to conceive a child. Any temptations to "gratify the lower nature"[57] by having sex without procreation in mind must be resisted. The vital energy a man saved by not expending his sperm recklessly was more properly directed to other channels. It was nature's law that sex activity be limited to procreation and violations of it would be punished in one way or another.

There is no reason to be suspicious of Macfadden's sincerity when the particular matter of sexual excessiveness was masturbation. On this subject he was not at war with his own energetic nature or with modern ideas that allured him. "The self-handling of genitals," he argued, "is not only one of the most destructive and devitalizing of all practices, but one of the most common among young persons...it is sometimes taught to young children by vicious nurses or depraved older children."[58] Macfadden's strident adherence to this established tenant of Victorian medical belief is a little odd for one so generally antagonistic to medical opinion. Since he did not believe that disease had any other cause than blood impurity he might have questioned what theologians and doctors had claimed for the "solitary vice." Of all the sexual activities deemed sins by Christian teachers only masturbation was identified as the chief cause of disease.

An anonymous eighteenth century pamphlet called *Onania* popularized the masturbation theories that prevailed for the next 200 years. Its author's only authority seemed to be the Scriptures where the "Sin of Onian" was described. The discovery of a vice more destructive than whoredom and adultery pleased readers. Some nineteen editions of *Onania* were published in the eighteenth century and the text expanded from the original sixty pages to one hundred and forty-two. The expansion consisted of letters from sufferers and repentant sinners confirming the author's thesis.[59]

Other writers hopped on the best-selling bandwagon to further entrench the basically preposterous medical views. While our literary history is rich with influential books espousing truths and untruths with fervor and skill the place of *Onian* and its most popular successor, *L'Onanisme*, published by Samuel Tissot in the mid-eighteenth century, is remarkable. Tissot was still being published in several languages as late as 1905, perhaps because he contributed a scientific basis with "medical proofs."

Tissot went beyond Biblical authority to call upon classical authors in support of his theories. Unfortunately, the ancients had ignored masturbation but Tissot, a researcher without conscience, used their censures against excessive copulation, debauchery, and lust as if masturbation had been their concern. Tissot argued that all ancient and modern authorities agreed that masturbation caused impotence, weakened the digestive system, sparked excessive appetites, produced vomiting, indigestion, the breakdown of the whole respiratory system and did severe harm to the nervous system. Milder effects included general lassitude, pallor, debility, and a slow-down of mental processes. Females suffered from all these hurts and more, including hysteria, incurable jaundice, stomach cramps, prolapse and ulceration of the womb, and clitoral rashes.

Masturbation caused these bad effects because of the excessive and unnatural loss of seminal fluid which debilitated the body; and the expenditure of excessive nervous energy which damaged the brain. The orgasm was a compulsive spasm which upset the delicate mechanism of the body's digestion, respiration, nervous system, and the brain. While the author of *Onania* had not done much to either show why masturbation produced bad effects or offer any advice about spiritual remedies, Tissot explained causation fully and described remedies: quinine and iron water, strengthening medicines, cold baths, health living, exercise, regularity of bowels, clean thoughts, and moderate sleep.

In the nineteenth century some physicians came to doubt Tissot's insistence that masturbation caused physical disease. Such skepticism hardly penetrated popular opinion because medical writers hesitated to mention masturbation. Writing in 1851 William Acton complained at the lack of reputable books on the problem: "By the neglect of the profession," he argued, "the subject has become the domain of the veriest quacks."[60] Yet Acton's adherence to the masturbation stereotype was absolute. He described the typical masturbator as a sallow youth, solitary and unclean in habits who was likely to "end in becoming a drivelling idiot or a peevish valetudinarian."

Advances in responsible medical opinion by the late nineteenth century limited the physical effects of masturbation to "degeneration," without defining the term's meaning very precisely. But masturbation's reign as a devastating force for ill health did not decline; it was just that the emphasis shifted from physical to mental effects. Medical textbook writers focused on "permanent damage [to the brain] from the constant irritation to which it has been exposed by the habit."[61] General paralysis was also a high risk and masturbation certainly accelerated the course of insanity among those prone to it.

Laymen generally accepted the brain damage theories without abandoning the popular conviction, still fervently pushed by preachers, that masturbation caused a multitude of physical and moral ills. Orson Fowler, the celebrated phrenologist, writing in the 1870s, described "personal fornication the worst" among sexual vices: "It not only poisons your body, destroys your rosy cheeks, breaks down your nerves, impairs your digestion, and paralyses your whole system; but it also corrupts your morals, creates thoughts and feelings the vilest and worse possible, and endangers your very soul's salvation! No words can describe the miseries it afflicts throughout your whole life down to death. But its ravages do not stop there. They follow and prey on you forever!"[62]

Dr. John Kellogg, attacked masturbation in the 1880s with virtual evangelical fervor: "The sin of self-pollution is one of the vilest, the basest, and the most degrading that a human being can commit. It is worse than beastly. Those who commit it place themselves far below the meanest brute that breathes. The most loathsome reptile, rolling in the slush and slime of its stagnant pool, would not demean himself thus."[63]

Doctors agreed generally that "wasting seed" wasted life and came forward with countless case histories to support their arguments. Overall the long sustained anti-onanist movement resembled a medieval witch craze. It was a belief that commanded universal adherence despite its shocking lack of sense or scientific proof, a long perpetuated myth that cause incalculable anguish to sensitive souls. It also made the fortunes of many quacks.

Coming to Macfadden's views we find an orthodoxy up to a point. "Manhood is the first requirement of a man," he declared. "If he is lacking in virility, then he also lacks in the physical energy and force of character which are necessary for any real achievement."[64] Vitality is associated with reproductive powers and good health. Anyone impotent was likely to be generally unhealthy and, obviously, anything like self-abuse, that, in Macfadden's opinion, caused impotence, was a willful destruction of one's vital forces.

Macfadden acknowledged that authorities differed on the question of seminal secretions and their effects on well-being. He favored the old opinion that undischarged seminal secretion was reabsorbed by the body for constitutional purposes. No one should waste their seed because it represented energy that could otherwise be employed for good purposes. He liked the estimate given in *Onian* that one ounce of seminal fluid was equal to forty or even sixty ounces of blood in its energy capacity: "We know positively that this life-bearing fluid is the richest secretion of the entire body, and that it is indispensable to the development and maintenance of all the essential elements of perfect manhood."[65]

Macfadden might have consulted more enlightened medical opinion of his day for a more sensible position on masturbation, but the theory fit his conception of virility very nicely. The body was as wonderful to him as to any Christian, something almost sacred in its own right— and not to be defiled or weakened. A masturbator fouled the temple of his body in a loathsome way. And, of course, he suffered in the worst possible way for violating his own virility: he became even less virile and would eventually hit rock bottom in Macfadden's canon of physical disasters: sexual impotency.

Perhaps another reason for Macfadden's infatuation with such hoary medical and theological views was in the connection he discovered with prudery. It was prudery that prevented doctors and parents from warning the young about the perils of self-abuse. If the young were fully informed about the detriment to health they would be less inclined to the vice.

Macfadden was not a prude, but neither was he the eager inquirer after truth where masturbation theories were concerned. As a fanatic he was not open to a consideration of whether the perils of masturbation had been heavily misrepresented. The cunning of the anti-onanist doctrinaires, who tied their moral resentment to curious conclusions on bodily strength, suited him fine.

The anti-onanist dogmas were also fulfilling to Macfadden as to orthodox Christians because of their expression of the historic Christian infatuation with the cycle of sin, confession, punishment or penance, and redemption. Doctors in the nineteenth century sometimes treated masturbators with sadistic cures, including cauterization of the urethra. Since fornicators and other sexual transgressors of the medieval era sometimes purged themselves through flagellation and other self-inflicted tortures to gain mastery of their lusts, the severe doctors were within tradition. Macfadden did not advise such severities but he recommended physical training for this as for every other ailment—exercises that must have struck some reluctant patients as the equivalent of flagellation or— in the truer meaning of the phrase—self-abuse.

A man like Macfadden does not shed deep-seated Christian beliefs by renouncing organized religion as he did as a young man. The cycle of sin, confession, punishment, and redemption was embedded deeply in his consciousness. As we know, his attachment to the sin cycle extended beyond health to encompass his exploitation of emotions in confession magazines.

To read Macfadden on masturbation is to discover a fanaticism worthy of Graham, Fowler, or Kellogg: "Both mind and body," he said, "suffer severely from the effects of frequent and long continued masturbation, and it is a question as to which endures the greater injury. Certainly the practice robs one of his manhood and makes him unfit for the duties of his life, ending in complete nervous and physical weakness if persisted in. It causes over-sensitiveness of all the sexual parts...a general weakening of the nerves, muscles and all of the structures associated with the generative system. The ultimate result is a condition marked by prematurity or impotence, either partial or complete. The constitutional and mental results are equally disastrous. The eyes are sunken, the skin is pasty, sallow and subject to an excess of pimples, the hand is clammy and grips without energy, the appetite fails, stomach and bowels lose their functional power, dyspepsia and constipation ensue."[66]

Macfadden was not sure about the repair of damages even among those who followed his treatment of exercise, diet, and cold baths; "Remember that the physical culture methods are wonderfully efficacious, and that although one may not be able to make himself quite the man that he might have been had he not thus abused himself, if he has carried the habit very far, nevertheless by a persistent and faithful struggle to regain his manhood, fighting for months and years for all that is worthwhile in human life, he will by these physical culture methods be able to develop and retain a satisfactory degree of vitality."[67]

Since Macfadden throughout his career ranked prudes as the greatest enemies of mankind his relation of prudery to sexual hygiene is interesting. "This gigantic evil of prudery," he wrote, must be unmasked "for the quintessence of prudery is pruriency." What were they saying, these prudes, these self-appointed censors, who spoke of decency and modesty—these hypocrites? Did they really represent the virtues they shouted about? By no means, Macfadden stated, "deep down beneath the hideous pretense of morality, we know that we would find the very soul of nastiness and immodesty, which it is the main purpose of the prude to hide." The prude's attitude towards life was nasty-minded; they placed a vulgar and degrading interpretation upon life itself. "It is not that there is anything in life that is obscene or impure, but only that the contemplating mind regards it as being so." The human body is the Temple of God, "through which human life is perpetuated and should be regarded with the utmost reverence and respect."[68]

Of all nasty things prudery was the worse. It "has sent more victims to an early grave" than war, famine, pestilence, and liquor combined. It has constantly wrecked lives and marriages while stalking the land, "parading the white garments of innocence while its hideous form is one mass of loathsome and evil corruption."[69]

How did prudes get that way? Macfadden believed that the situation of the excessive drinker could be compared. The drink evoked self-disgust in the drinker, and excessive sex and secret vices turned individuals into prudes. "It is a fact that can be readily verified that the most licentious and immoral people are invariably the most prudish. The most conspicuous in advertising their pretensions of modesty."[70] It comes from crying "Shame, shame!" at one's own body.

What exasperated Macfadden was the acceptance by the public of salacious novels, erotic plays, and—in particular company—smutty stories, while any serious, scientific discussions of sex were suppressed. Pious hypocrites in vice suppression societies, the Comstocks, were leaders in such suppressions and enemies of sensible sex education. Prudery caused the modern physical, mental and moral degeneracy everywhere to be seen. Because of ignorance of sex the race cannot be improved and millions of unhappy marriages result. "The beautiful, perfect ideal of the prude," is to send a girl into marriage "without knowing one solitary thing about what marriage means."[71] And there was New York City as a great example of what prudes had accomplished. It held 50,000 prostitutes. Venereal disease was widespread. And prudes made it possible.

The entire canon of Macfadden's teachings cannot be fairly summed up in just a few pages but it is possible to catch the drift of his mind. Many of his critics considered him an ignoramus and certainly there were gaps in his knowledge as well as an evident refusal to put all his theorems to a stern test. But to call him ignorant is unjust considering his construction of an intellectual edifice of some substance. The weighty *Encyclopedia* was not as magnificent as he considered it, nor so dismal a performance as his detractors thought it. It showed some appreciation of the medical literature even if his use of it was selective and personal. Overall the construction was not too shabby considering the weakness

of its underpinnings and the determination of the builder to win all
the arguments.

Chapter 7
"I'm Ruined! I'm Ruined!"

It was a short step from the nudist industry to the confessions industry.

Alva Johnston

"And I let Joe talk me into making the biggest mistake of my life," wrote the young, regretful woman. She did not give many details of her "mistake" but one could guess what was involved. She was less discreet on the anguish that followed her unfortunate affair, the heart-throbbing emotional wringer she was put through again and again. Readers had to go through something of her anguish as well, and they realized that she had brought her sufferings upon herself. Readers could also enjoy the sexual titillation offered. It was not much by today's standards but it was exciting without being nasty because the story was true and had a high moral purpose.

The first issue of the justly celebrated, long enduring, and amazingly popular *True Story* magazine appeared in May 1919. Its cover featured a man-and-woman tableau with the caption, "And their love turned to hatred." Also featured on the cover with the name was the slogan, "Truth is Stranger Than Fiction," and a call upon readers for more stories: "We Offer $1,000 for Your Life Romance." Within were stories titled "A Wife Who Awoke in Time," "My Battle with John Barleycorn," "An Ex-Convict's Climb to Millions, How a Man Won Out Against Prejudice," "How I learned to Hate my Parents," and "'Dearie'—The Lesson that Bullies Learned from Him—a True West Point Story."[1] The stories were illustrated with posed photographs and interspersed with a number of chatty interviews with stage and screen stars: Douglas Fairbanks, Billie Burke, William Farnum, and Dorothy Gish. Among its 96-pages advertising only accounted for 13 pages, mostly featuring patent medicines, correspondence courses, and self-improvement books.

Macfadden had a good idea when he conceived the new magazine. There was no other like it on the newsstands, yet it soon became apparent that hoards of folks had been hungering for just such reading fare. How did Bernarr Macfadden know about this public? How did this austere, devoutly disciplined, whiplash of a man know that the world yearned for true confessions from ordinary people? In the answer lies the genius of Macfadden—his sure sense of the popular mind.

Detractors came forward to abuse the publisher's achievement, sometimes betraying a strong sense of class: "No other publisher," wrote one critic, "has so adroitly pandered to the servant girl, bootblack, factory worker public."[2] Little Macfadden cared about such comments. Criticisms from the pulpit and the forces of vice fighters were another matter. He bore the scars of losses to the Comstocks and wanted no trouble that he could avoid. He was certain that his stories were not salacious and lewd as some critics charged but he also knew that the prudes would gang up on him if they could. A wonderful idea came to him: why not establish a lightning rod against moral censor by having a minister approve all the stories in advance? The Rev. Lee M. Hainer, who had recently resigned from the Baptist ministry, performed admirably. Later, to gain even more moral ascendancy, the publisher established an editorial board for the same purpose, including a rabbi and a priest, as well as a Methodist, Presbyterian, and Congregationalist. The priest quit after his bishop got wind of his association but the survivors looked after submissions to good effect. John S. Sumner, Comstock's successor at the Society for the Suppression of Vice, could not complain when ministers of national repute found the stories to be above reproach. Neither could the notorious Watch and Ward Society of Boston effectively cry down the new magazine.

Circulation rises came so fast in the first several years of publication that some income was lost. Advertisement rates were fixed at a current circulation that soared up before rates could be increased but the long-term exuberant health of sales offset any set-backs. It pleased Macfadden to see his creation on the newsstand beside the prestigious, well-produced *Cosmopolitan,* the flagship of W.R. Hearst's publications, a magazine featuring big-name authors like Fannie Hurst, Zane Grey, and Edna Ferber, and a cover painted by some well-known artist. By contrast, as Fulton Oursler once noted ruefully, the *True Story* cover featured a "coarse blown-up chromo of a Hollywood blonde,"[3] while its authors were unknowns and its story illustrations were tawdry posed photographs rather than elegant line drawings. But the comparatively cheap-looking newcomer sold far more copies than its august rival because its stories were readable and more pleasing. It had been quite a chore for girls and women of limited education to read the stories in Hearst's magazine but in Macfadden's they did not find a word that stumped them. Hearst did get a benefit from Macfadden, however, in the $14,000 full-page ads Macfadden purchased in Hearst's popular newspaper supplement, the *American Weekly*. With earnings from his new magazine of $10,000 daily Macfadden could afford some ads.

No one involved with Macfadden Publication Company questioned the extent of the publisher's participation in daily business. At times he could be deceptively genial and receptive to pleas from advertising managers keen to improve the tone of the magazine. He allowed editors to hire new artists, plan new layouts, contact famed authors, and envision the bright, new product of their dreams. Then, in his wisdom and impatience with artful novelties, he would dismiss the innovations in favor of the established format. Bickering over the amount of flesh to show in illustrations never ceased. When an editor or ad manager cried "too much," Macfadden would order the flesh to vanish. Sales would decline and a circulation manager would cry to the boss, showing him the impudent eroticism of a rival magazine while appealing for a little more flesh exposure. While the publisher moved with the pressure, he knew that answering cries for "good taste" invariably reduced sales. It was not his mission to improve taste.

Bad-mouthing critics might call Macfadden a panderer and other bad things but he had his own way of answering such misinformed insults. Usually a loyalist could be counted upon to rush to his defense, as with the accolade uttered by a minister on his censorship board, a statement that rang so true to the publisher that he quoted it in advertisements. "I think," the minister said, "*True Story* is a great magazine. In fact, anything that has the stamp of Bernarr Macfadden upon it is helpful, elevating and of God."[4] Another man might have been overwhelmed by such heady praise but Macfadden was rich, famous, confident, and—as always—surpassingly sure of himself so he could handle the tribute without succumbing to the sin of pride. Reflecting on this praise and other generous words received over the years he recalled harder days and believed any comments upon his success, regardless of their effusiveness, to be just and truthful. A man of vision moved along in response to his inner urges. Call him a "pander" or "God-like," or what you will—but nothing could make him swerve from his course. He had saved himself from weakness and dedicated his life to saving others. Making big bucks along the way did no harm.

Macfadden "confessed" that his inspiration for *True Story*, which was "the outstanding publishing achievement of the century" in his view (and one that was confirmed by other authorities in the field of publishing) came from letters sent by readers of *Physical Culture*. Men and women seeking relief from all manner of troubles—physical, mental, and spiritual—had written him over the years, telling their life stories. He marvelled in reading such poignant confessions, so fresh and true, and so meaningful to the tellers and, perhaps, to other folks as well. His correspondents did not dress up their feelings in fine or purple prose in the way of novelists: they told about incidents in simple, direct terms that, by their very starkness, gave deep meaning to their story. So he decided to solicit stories for a magazine that would focus on true stories of personal experiences of emotional portent. It proved to be a brilliant idea. Klondike gold prospectors dreamed often of the "mother lode," the great mountain of gold from which thin streaks of paydirt had emerged to form widely scattered pockets in some streambeds. The publisher's "mother lode" was an inexhaustible source of stories expressing universal themes, themes that touched the hearts of inexhaustible numbers of magazine buyers. Other publishers before and since have had inspirations but his idea did as well and has held up as long as any other. Other great American magazines were created in the 1920s, the *New Yorker*, *Time*, and *Readers Digest* come to mind. Each had its imitators yet thrived because, like *True Story*, it was the best in its field.

"Outrageous," cried the critics when the magazine appeared, "pernicious use of sex," "Satan's work," "base vulgarism." But Macfadden, knowing the world and the always lurking Comstock-like censors, took some counter measures and walked a careful line along acceptable standards of sex discussion and pictorial representation. He would be a little ahead of his time but not too much. Besides, it was the beauty of the story material that its sex appeal was less important than its emotional appeal. Readers did not demand, or even desire, explicit sex scenes. They wanted to run the gambit of emotional ranges with the confessors, to join in their longings, their expectations of romance and love, their sorrowful disappointments, and the crushing blows of betrayals. Readers wished to have it confirmed that others, too, had been tempted and proved weak. Readers could only sympathize up to a point: the confessors who did wrong must suffer for their sins. Retribution, as Macfadden knew, was an essential element in successful stories.

Oh, anyone could have stumbled upon this formula and made a success of it, cried some scoffers who could not stand to acknowledge Macfadden's genius.[5] It was a bit like Columbus showing others how to stand an egg on end. Once they saw how he did it they could do it just as well. But not quite. Other publishers certainly did jump into the confession trade with great dispatch and some did well, but none had quite the success of the master and innovator. It is odd that some critics have dismissed Macfadden's achievements as mere sex exploitation. After all, publishers had been exploiting the popular appeal of sex— and of emotional stories—almost from the time of the invention of printing. It makes sense to recognize that Macfadden had indeed discovered something that was novel and brilliant, and a smashing commercial success. Whether the publication was as uplifting and moral as Macfadden believed is quite another question.

The publisher overthrew two cardinal principles of magazine publishing with his story magazine: (1) Readers buy magazines to read stories written by "big names;" (2) A magazine's prosperity depended upon the astute selection of material by a professional and gifted editor. "No," cried Macfadden to both of these established "truths." Little people have wonderful stories to tell that will be appreciated by readers who are charmed by the sincerity and lack of artifice in the telling. Who needs the artful, established writer who is something of a phoney in most instances and, besides that, wants a lot of money for his stories? As for gifted, professional editors—why should they be needed? Why can't the authors be judged by their peers rather than by professional editors, men and women who were better able to appreciate the sentiments of the writers? And so Macfadden set up a system to accomplish his new order of things. John Brennan, editor of *Physical Culture*, would take over the new magazine but the choice of stories would not be in his hands. This important function would be given to a corps of readers, men and women of varied occupation and indifferent education presumed to be innocent of editorial knowledge or higher learning of any kind. Macfadden would hire readers after an interview determined that they really enjoyed reading magazines and could distinguish good from dull stories. Readers would only consider the interest level of submissions and ignore all other considerations. If they gave a grade of 95% or better to a story it was passed along for further review. Editor Brennan and others associated with the magazine were dismayed by the installation of this quaint and revolutionary system until the steady rise in circulation proved its reliability.

All stories submitted had to be represented as true, were generally told in the first person by a writer whose name was not usually given, and must teach a moral lesson. How many submissions actually came from truthful amateurs is a vexing question. Hungry free-lance writers did not mind trying their hand at the new market. Both Fulton Oursler and Emile Gauvreau, later to be editors for Macfadden, sold stories to the magazine before they joined the team. The rates were good: Gauvreau considered the $150 paid him well worth the effort of writing what was basically a simple story that could be knocked off fast after one got the knack of it. Even amateurs were capable of passing fiction off as truth and it is likely that many story submissions did not meet the standard of veracity Macfadden wanted. He did all that could reasonably be done to protect his goal. Contributors had to submit an affidavit and names of character references who would verify their general reputation for honesty. But, as Macfadden was not in the private detective business, he did not really want to be involved in the expensive chore of detecting frauds—especially if their stories were good. Rival publishers, of course, charged that Macfadden had a crew of staff writers hacking away at all times to produce just the right kind of copy. They were among the cynics who found it hard to accept that offerings from the woman-or-man-on-the-street could make a publisher's fortune.

Brennan and other editors had to see that the magazine came out on time and that the illustrations were suitable. It was Brennan's suggestion that they give up the conventional story drawings and use photographs to lend a greater air of reality to the stories. This proved a great touch—and a daring one at the time. The first models were members of Brennan's family; eventually Macfadden established his own studio and a stable of 300 part-time models.

The serial was a feature of the magazine that received a good deal of attention. Macfadden was ever a great believer in the power of serials in drawing buyers to the magazine. Quite reluctantly he agreed with his staff that amateurs lacked the talent to sustain a long-running sob-story with cunning enough to compel readers to the newsstands. Initially, the prolific John R. Coryell was the answer; he based serial stories on "actual happenings" so the thrust of real life experiences would not be disturbed too much.

Stories came and came in a ceaseless flow and it was not really necessary for Macfadden to sponsor prize contests to encourage writers as he did in his first issue. Out in the cold world there were apparently numbers of men and women—especially women—who were hurting and longed to tell all about it. Staff readers waded through up to 100,000 stories each year—tons of anguish from which to select the most heart-wrenching entries of the lot. Staffers did not look hard at stories rich in vocabulary, or too clever or sophisticated in their treatment.

After 1926, when William Jordan Rapp took over editorship from Brennan there were some policy shifts. The writing got a little better as editors took a heavier hand to copy. Rapp reasoned that public education was improving the standards of literacy all the time so that it did not do to present stories as crudely written as those of the early issues. The sex emphasis changed too. Seduction stories were not as much used as earlier. It is not clear that there were fewer seducers at work as the 1920s advanced, or that the more liberated lives folks seemed to be living made seductions unnecessary. Rapp simply determined that his readers wanted more novelties in the pattern of confessional life. Many readers were growing older and were less thrilled by seductions than formerly. Maturity had increased their awareness of life's emotional vicissitudes, particularly the strain of remaining virtuous in a swarming sea of temptation. Following the drum-beat measured by heart-throbs tapped out by newer confessors they devoured stories featuring marital problems in preference to those treating the perils of courtship. Eventually Macfadden sorted out the generation gap problem by targeting each of his several confession magazines at a particular age group. As time passed and folks were swept up by Depression and World War problems there were other shifts to meet the new awareness of readers. Social problems were noted and after World War II features appeared on homemaking, child care, medicine, and—wonder of wonders—national affairs. But such shifts and diversions from the original plan as may be observed in time's passing never altered the essence of Macfadden's original inspiration: the confession still ruled.

After the contemptuous editors in other magazine publishing houses finished hooting and sneering at the new magazine's simplistic vulgarity and improbable editorial direction they waited for it to die. When the story magazine showed every sign of bountiful health rival publishers hurled themselves at the "intimate," "secret," "personal," and "revealing" aspects of life with magazines imitating Macfadden's. Magazine buyers bought the imitations too. Who could resist stories like "That First Sin," "Slave of Desire," "Because I Was Easy," and "My Dude Ranch Love Affair?" Magazines like *Modern Romance* (Dell), *True Confessions* (Fawcett) and *My Story* (Dell) steamed up newsstands. Dell, fearful that buyers might miss the point of its other titles, called one short-lived magazine, *I Confess*. Macfadden's rivals did not make any fuss over authenticity in accepting submissions from writers. It was a good thing too that the other publishers were happy enough to buy the works of regular hackers because if the nation's housewives, clerks, and factory workers took more time from apple pie-making and jobs to fill all the new magazines with their stories the national economy might have ground to a halt.

Macfadden competed with the pack of *True Story* imitators by publishing other confession magazines, including *True Experiences* (1922), *Love and Romance* (1923), *True Marriage Stories* (1924), *True Love Stories* (1924), *Secrets* (1936), *Personal Romances* (1937), *Intimate Stories* (1948), and *Revealing Romances* (1949). Each magazine was slanted for a particular class or age group of readers. *True Experiences* and *Love and Romance* kept an unblushing eye on seduction and courtship, leaving anxieties over more mature emotional passages to their stable mates.

True Romances, was, according to Fulton Oursler the only magazine in history to sell out its first issue. While we can not be sure of Oursler's research into the matter it is plain that a magazine selling half a million copies by the end of its first year of publication was doing very well. The editors had designed the new magazine for younger readers, those who desired true tales of young love, and apparently there were plenty of them. According to Oursler, Macfadden did not continue coming forward with new magazines solely to make money: it seemed important to forestall rivals whose imitations of *True Story* sullied the purity of the publisher's original concept. Oursler believed that the public easily distinguished between the "sex-coy" imitators and the originals: "The public knew exactly what it wanted, and Macfadden was giving it to them."[6] Oursler insisted, against the evidence, that "the imitations have never made more than the most mediocre progress," and complained that their "cheap nastiness" caused misunderstanding among those who could not distinguish the titles of the better class Macfadden magazines from the others. "Their titles were similar so *True Story* was often accused of all the seven deadly sins of its unscrupulous rivals."

Readers certainly did not disdain either Dell's *Modern Romances* (1930) or Fawcett's *True Confessions* (1922). The latter magazine held second place to *True Story* for years, reaching a sale of over 1,000,000 by the mid-thirties.

Macfadden and his biographers told the story of the inspiration for the new magazine again and again, but Mary Macfadden put forward a conflicting version of events. Mary, who bore seven of Macfadden's children, separated from Bernarr in 1933. Mary tried hard to establish in court that she had given her husband the *True Story* idea. Obviously, she had much to gain in a property settlement if her argument prevailed.

Mary described the couple's situation in 1919. Expenses were heavy in a household of four children and Bernarr was keen to expand his health home and vegetarian restaurants. But he lacked capital. In what must have been an unusual moment of humility for him he beseeched Mary's help—"Can't you dig an idea from your mind that will pull us out of this hole." Mary rose to the occasion. She had long been the reader for *Physical Culture* and had noted that contributors and readers had more to tell about than their piano lifting prowess and their ability to hold their breath for four minutes. "Many gentlemen wrote in about how disappointed they had been in love after they bought fifteen-dollar Macfadden exercisers, and used them to put on wonderful muscles, and look like Greek gods,"[7] Mary said. She concluded that they had suffered disappointments because the right girls disdained their muscles. Mary was not surprised because over the years of her marriage she had grown a little weary of muscle men herself, but it interested her that the unhappy men could relate unhappy, interesting love stories. Women wrote in too, insisting that they were fallen women, after making one particular mistake. Many were more positive about muscle building because they took it up after their mistake and it seemed to accelerate the progress of self-forgiveness. The stories of their fall and of subsequent events, usually a marriage with an understanding man whose regard for them bridged a great tension on wedding nights, surely held great interest.

Like a good wife Mary handed this million dollar idea to her husband on a platter, including the new magazine's name. Amazingly, Bernarr resisted the scheme for a time. While he brooded over its practicality she became more and more convinced that she had opened up a gold mine. "Bernarr couldn't keep me living like a slave if he hit the jackpot. I was not yet twenty-five. I was still young enough to go places."[8] Soon Bernarr succumbed, announcing to her in one of his favorite expressions that he was "off to the races" with her idea. The first cover of the new magazine pleased Mary very much. It showed a man and woman exchanging longing looks over a caption that warned: "And Their Love Turned to Hatred." Mary's expectations turned sour too. Bernarr took full credit for the magazine and did not reward her brilliance with better treatment and a nicer life. She just got more children because of his commitment to building his "perfect family" as an advertisement for his health theories.

Regardless of its origin the new magazine rolled on into the twenties, that marvelous decade that was so outstanding from several perspectives. It was a time of incredible energy and diversity in American popular culture, the arts, social and economic movements. We often look back to the twenties with wonder and appreciation at its verve. And with good reason because life seemed to glitter then with prospects and the public stage was peopled by so many intriguing characters like Jimmy Walker, Billy Sunday, W.R. Hearst, Henry Ford, and countless others. *True Story* was a part of the twenties. By 1928 circulation had climbed past the 2,000,000 mark and advertising revenue reached $3,000,000. As we know, many things altered in the depression years but the popularity of *True Story* was not among them. Circulation in 1937 was 2,200,000 with an advertising revenue of $4,000,000.

The popular confession magazines probably affected manners and morals although it was not easy to determine the changes. In 1926 Frank Kent, an enterprising journalist, made a tour from coast to coast for the *Atlantic Monthly* and concluded that results had been ugly: small towns, influenced by the popular magazines and the movies, "seem literally saturated with sex."[9] Journalist Oscar Garrison Villard, who was not a Macfadden fan, nonetheless defended the place of the confession magazines. The magazines had succeeded "because there was a real need of simple, straightforward...melodramatic stories" like those that had been popular in the 1880s. "In a sense it is a readers' revolt against the conventional and sophisticated story which ornaments the pages of the more sedate and conservative magazines. People who led restricted lives want a kind of dream world that includes thrills, emotions, and the chance to sympathize with the unfortunate, or to rejoice in the misfortune of the very rich and of the villains they love to hiss at the movies." They did not object to the serious, moral tone, conventional endings, and conventional preaching. "If the career of *True Story* should come to an early end one wonders whether some sort of improved substitute ought to be offered."

Novelist Agnes Repplier had a sharper reply to Kent's conclusions that small American towns were "saturated with sex." Her memory of small towns was that they had never been saturated with anything, "but presented an air of general aridity." She was willing to believe that a current of sentiment might be felt "but not a tidal wave of sex."[10] Repplier questioned all the fuss over the Macfadden magazines which treat women "who part with their virtue in exchange for a firmer understanding, a greater and truer insight into life." Such frank disclosures "would be reprehensible if there were still left readers of any age who are unfamiliar with such themes." With William Jordan Rapp's editorship in the thirties the magazine still used serious, true to life, first person narrations in simple language, realistic stories that taught a strong moral lesson. When questioned Rapp insisted that there was no undue emphasis on sex in the magazine: "Our stories have only the normal amount of sex you'll find in anyone's life. They're written in a common idiom, that's all. And you've got to remember that with people of low incomes, there's a close relation between morality and economics." Liquor, immorality, and gambling destroy a wage-earner's home more quickly than those of the higher income groups, and if a husband runs around with another woman, "the security of his home is menaced economically as well as emotionally. Security—that's their chief concern, not sex."

It appears that even severe moralists had become accustomed to sex as presented in *True Story* by the thirties. The magazine had not become more daring over time and there were many truly lurid pictorial magazines on the newsstands that drew the fire of censors away from any Macfadden publications. *True Story* had its place in helping to expand the revolution in morals that occurred earlier and had set a certain respectable literary standard for the expression of it in magazines.

True Story was often called a pulp magazine by those who failed to distinguish among magazines of different prices and quality. Macfadden had, in fact, planned the magazine as a pulp, then changed his mind. His boldness in offering a twenty-five cent, smooth paper magazine opened the way for middle-class sales. When the lady of the house and her housemaid both laid down their quarters for *True Story* its success was assured. The nice paper and relatively sedate cover attracted readers but did not fool them: they knew that the magazine was a pulp at heart—a pulp in the sense of its rough democratic appeal to basic emotions.

Pulps provided fictional romance and adventure, wonderful means of escaping from reality. *True Story* also provided means of escaping from reality. In penetrating the dark secrets of his neighbor's home readers were not voyeurs. They had been invited to see what went wrong and to find satisfaction in the retribution that attended those things that went wrong. They were witnesses to domestic disasters that might well have caught them—or perhaps did. The ordinary people who confess their woes are highly plausible and their deceivers are the kinds of villains who invite hissing. Eventually the deceived, or even the deceiver, will be regenerated to walk from darkness into light after heart-throbbing adventures. Those deserving of further punishment are certain to get what is coming to them, just as those who found moral courage will reap their reward. The story plots were as stylized as fiction because the confessors see their lives along the formal, traditional lines of melodrama; they would not want it any other way.

Yes, there was some artfulness, some editorial help in the presentation of the plain words of plain people. But Macfadden did not want fiction. He never read fiction—despised it heartily. Fiction was not truth and he believed in truth. Fiction was phoney. Art that enhanced the plain, truthful words of plain people was permissible: real photographs to accompany the stories, though posed, were more truthful than drawings. Most of the rest of the editorial art involved was in protecting the plain words and, of course, getting the magazine out on time.

Harold Hershey, a pulp publisher himself, who worked briefly as executive editor for Macfadden, respected his uniqueness: "He had the common touch...he was the leader of a cause...he could not be content with anything but reality when it came to the matters of the average heart and mind."[11] Other publishers could not imitate him successfully, no matter how hard they tried, because Macfadden's products were personal. "He is not a romanticist deceived by the illusion of reality, but a realist undeceived by the illusion of romance, yet one who uses it as a sculptor does his clay: to mold these magazine images of himself as symbols of a simple faith."

Hershey's description of the editorial offices catch the spirit of the enterprise. On his first day of work Hershey met the publisher, then age sixty, after his "twenty-mile stroll down the Hudson River, most of the way in his bare feet." Outside Hershey's office there was a sea of desks where an army of staffers worked after the Father of Physical Culture led them through setting-up exercises. Macfadden made all the decisions and his executive editor realized that if he were not sympathetic "with the cause" he had better go elsewhere. Activity was intense from morning to night and conferences never ended over the mountains of manuscripts pouring in. Hershey was in the middle of many conflicts, as writers and department heads struggled against each other for preferment. Occasionally there was some reward amidst the pressure as when Hershey joined the boss and a motorcycle police escort to a ceremony at City Hall where Mayor Jimmy Walker gave Macfadden the key to New York. It was not clear to Hershey how Macfadden could handle all his enterprises and still express "warm, human, lovable" qualities, but he did not doubt that the publisher was "one of the most remarkable men of our times." Macfadden was never too busy at editorial conferences to tell the story of his life, explaining how his triumph over weakness had inspired every endeavor he had been involved in since his youth.

Hershey's account of the publishing enterprise is particularly interesting because, unlike Fulton Oursler and other long-time Macfadden apologists, he had no strong commitment to the boss—and no reason to be uncritical. He sat in on meetings with the board of ministers and discovered that they did what they were supposed to do with dispatch. Although he hated all censorship he was impressed because "they did not split hairs" but busied themselves eliminating or changing phrases in copy that might have caused the company trouble.

Hershey did not doubt that amateurs telling their own stories contributed most of the magazine's copy but admitted, as did others with the company, that serials were the responsibility of professionals.

It was no surprise to Hershey that Macfadden was able to get the kind of stories he wanted from confessors. The writers were not ashamed of their emotions any more than the publisher was ashamed to thrust them forth or readers were ashamed to find pleasure in reading them. The titles of the stories and the blurbs describing them were all important. Editors added suggestive titles that were like magic wands endowing the confessor's simple words with romance. The blurbs or explanatory paragraphs under or over the title were also editorial contributions designed to sell the story to readers: "They are," Hershey noted, "the distilled essence of the wish fulfillment in the literature of escape."[12] Blurbs could alert readers to the cosmic significance of the stories.

The blurb for "Movie Mad" led the reader on:

"A reckless but innocent girl, lured irresistibly by the silver screen, daringly endeavors to crash her way to fame."

For "Not Made to be a Wife" the editor blurbed:

"She loved both men madly and they returned her passion. But she failed to find happiness in marriage with either. Why?" Why, indeed— who would not want to read on to discover what ailed this woman?

Scoffers had no place in the editorial office. Editors who conceived the blurbs appreciated the importance of their art and revelled in their ease of composition as they gained experience. It was not what the blurb said that mattered as much as how it was said. The plot must not be revealed; it must be hinted at to tease the readers's interest, to draw him in seeking an answer to a tempting question.

Among the qualities of the stories treating temptation, young love, marriage, motherhood, family, fame, and both good and bad fortune there was little humor. It was impossible to have a light touch when dealing with life-shaking matters. The intrusion of the comic would be in extremely bad taste. How all the confessors knew this is not obvious but Macfadden and his editors knew it and the publisher's own seriousness was reflected in the contributions. He was the leader of a great crusade, always threatened, often resisted, continually derided, and it was not in him to crack jokes like some easy-living traveling salesman.

Chapter 8
Nemesis

I am the symbol of truth and tolerance for the entire field of national health.

Bernarr Macfadden

Macfadden's place in the field of national health was a matter of unhealthy, apoplectic debate among the nation's doctors. They considered him a blatant quack and were concerned about the extent of his influence and the hazards created by his simplistic theories of diagnosis and treatment. And, while they could never admit it, they were also upset by the assaults on their pocketbooks by Macfadden and all other advocates of unorthodox medical practice.

The doctors, through the American Medical Association, kept a long watch on the activities and publications of Bernarr Macfadden. His rise to fame gave no pleasure to those who longed for the day when his pernicious villainies would be thoroughly exposed. Macfadden really caused great pain to the established healers. Often enough they asked, "How long, Oh Lord, must we endure this faker?"

Two AMA officials, Dr. Arthur J. Cramp and Dr. Morris Fishbein, led the extended counter-propaganda campaign against Macfadden. Cramp opened the initial file on Macfadden and wrote the earliest warnings against the physical culturist, giving way to Fishbein in later years. Cramp, a shy, introspective man with a fine flair for the cutting phrase, joined the American Medical Association's Chicago headquarter's staff in 1906. His purpose in life was as strong as Macfadden's. Earlier his daughter had died under the hands of a quack doctor, a tragedy that drove him to study medicine, and, after finding medical practice incongenial, into an editorial position on the *Journal of the American Medical Association (JAMA)*. Fortune smiled on this crusading knight soon after he joined the AMA. The organization decided to implement a long-term effort against quacks and patent medicine vendors and established a Propaganda Department, later renamed the Bureau of Investigation. Before this move by the AMA there had never been a concerted attempt to expose quackery by government agencies or anyone else. In fact it was the government's action in 1906 in legislating the first Federal Food and Drug Act that inspired the AMA to investigate quacks. For the first time the government would be empowered with the means of protecting the public from manufacturing and sales practices that were unsanitary or otherwise threatening to health.

Journalism played a large role in bringing about this federal health reform legislation. In October 1905 Samuel Hopkins Adams, a 34-year old magazine writer, shocked the nation with a series of articles in *Collier's* that exposed the health products upon which Americans were spending seventy-five million dollars annually. He showed how the cunning of advertising bunco men assisted the manufacturers of phoney remedies in a colossal fraud on the public. Initially he focused on the "bracers," tonics rich in alcohol. Peruna was the most popular of the proprietary tonics that were guaranteed to cure all ills except alcoholism. Oceans of the stuff were consumed. One doctor believed that more hard liquor was taken in tonics than was dispensed by the nation's licensed liquor dealers. Peruna made good money; it cost eighteen cents to make and sold for one dollar. Peruna's advertising for its mixture of alcohol, water, burnt sugar and flavoring emphasized its value in treating catarrh, which its maker considered the base of all disease. Adams interviewed Dr. S.B. Hartman, Peruna's maker, who willingly admitted that drugs did not cure disease but he insisted that Peruna had "produced good results."[1] Adams' investigation showed that Peruna-type medicines had probably been a great killer of tuberculosis patients whose powers of resistance were diminished by the alcohol. It appeared too that typhoid victims went undetected for a long time because the Peruna stimulant disguised the problem of disease. Evidence that Peruna had created great numbers of alcoholics was even stronger. Adams suggested that the government collect the liquor tax the tonic vendors had been able to avoid and require that the alcoholic content be noted on labels.

From bracers Adams turned to magnetic healers like Dr. L.C. Thacher of Chicago, who advertised widely that "I can cure any disease that afflicts the human race...I am as positive that I can cure them all with the famous Thacher Magnetic Shields as I am that the sun will rise in the morning."[2] When Adams called on Dr. Thacher he observed that the doc wore several magnetic shields and heard that the AMA had been unjustly alerting newspapers that usually carried Magnetic Shield advertisements to their vendor's fraud. Opposition made Dr. Thacher sad. He was not a quack. "My object," he said, "is to spread the light, to rescue humanity. I can cure them of anything. In time I will compel the authorities to notice my methods."[3] Thacher recited specific case histories—successes with insanity by restoring the harmonious vibrations of the brain; and paralysis: "Had five cases. Couldn't wink or speak or move finger or toe. Cured 'em right off. Winked. Spoke. Got up and walked. Paralysis? Pish!"

Magnetic healers did not have as easy a time with rivals as with disease. A man like Thacher had to stir himself and beat the bushes for custom because the giant house of Sears, Roebuck sold Electric Liniment, Magnetic Insoles, Electric Battery Plasters, and Electric Rings. Rings were popular catalogue purchases because people liked ordinary rings well enough and the Electric Ring gave them energy as well as decoration. Sears insisted that "these are the first genuine electric rings introduced in the United States. All others are imitations."[4]

Next Adams visited Mr. Isham, who, like other quacks sought to capitalize on all the publicity over the discovery of radium. Isham sold the California Waters of Life, a sure-fire cancer cure. Isham, a young, articulate fellow, affirmed that he bottled water that was identical to that Moses had released from a rock by striking it—exactly as his advertisements alleged. The vendor was not so clear on the location of the various testimonial writers whose glowing endorsements he used in his ads. One was a Professor Fogg, presumably a very learned man, who lived, Isham thought, somewhere on Long Island. Like Dr. Thacher Isham was not into selling his wonderful healing water for the money: his profits were designated for a scheme to abolish poverty and suffering by means suggested to him by God.

It was easy for Adams to buy large quantities of morphine from both the St. James Society of New York and the St. Paul Association of Chicago. In advertisements of a distinctly religious tone these secular establishments offered to cure the morphine addictions of their mail order patients with the same daily dosage of the drug buyers were accustomed to using.

In ten articles that were later published in book form Adams thoroughly documented what he termed "The Great American Fraud." It was a wonderful example of muckraking journalism at its best, attacking powerful, vested interests with no holds barred. Adams heaped scorn on the press as well, charging that it was at "the beck and call" of the patent medicine industry: "Not only do the newspapers modify the news affecting these interests, but they sometimes become their effective agents."[5] He exposed the practice of awarding advertising contracts that always included a clause providing for automatic cancellation should that state's legislature pass bills unfavorable to the patent medicine industry. The AMA made effective use of the series, which ran until September 1906, in encouraging congressional sponsors of reform legislation.

Another literary work stimulated the last stage of battle for federal legislation when Upton Sinclair's novel, *The Jungle,* exposed stockyard conditions. Sinclair did wield his crafty pen deliberately to evoke nausea among meat-eaters and foster vegetarianism, as had Dr. John Kellogg a year earlier with a book entitled *Shall We Slay To Eat?* Kellogg did not have as many readers as Sinclair did, but the public was not interested in the primary message expounded by either. People remained calm about the working conditions of stockyard laborers and the health-inducing qualities of vegetables but became passionately excited about eating decayed beef and other filth in their sausages. Thus *The Jungle* became a weapon for the AMA in overcoming congressional resistance to food and drug legislation and, for a time, Sinclair was a hero to the doctors. The doctors' gratitude was short-lived; it did not survive the close relationship Sinclair established with Macfadden a few years later and his enthusiastic espousal of various off-beat health treatments.

The AMA has never been one of the more popular professional organizations in America. While neither as powerful nor as monolithic as its foes imagined, it did lobby effectively at times to get the kinds of state and federal legislation doctors favored. Progress was anything but swift in encouraging the states to establish uniform standards of medical licensing and other measures considered by the AMA to be essential to effective health treatment. Since Cramp's concern was with quacks he fought causes that were neither ambiguous nor too controversial, leaving others to combat "socialist medicine," the great dread of the AMA. The doctors, like other groups, favored government intervention in some areas but abhorred it where it was likely to restrict their incomes or dominance. Quacks and other foes of the AMA like Macfadden labored persistently to convince the public that the AMA was suspect on all fronts—and were remarkably successful.

For many reasons, some of them rational, large segments of the public have been very hostile to doctors generally and the AMA in particular. The treatment of illness is a delicate, personal matter, one that for many is tied to deep religious convictions. To many rural folks and urban workers doctors represented a privileged class, one professing great scientific knowledge (in itself suspect to fundamentalists) while grasping for fees from poor sufferers. Of course, there were individual well-loved doctors in many communities, practitioners revered for their selflessness as much as for their skills, but the better established stereotype was quite different from the kindly, gentle "sawbones" depicted by illustrator Norman Rockwell and other sentimentalists.

Whether a doctor was selfless or grasping he was not likely to favor Bernarr Macfadden or anything he represented. The physical culturist possessed the means of broadcasting his "lunatic" ideas widely and seemed eager to promote a variety of quacks and nostrums. Macfadden, by his own admission, was utterly innocent of scientific training yet pontificated and advertised himself nationally as a health expert—even daring to diagnose and prescribe by letter.

Quackery is an ancient problem. It is said to have originated when the first fool met the first charlatan and it certainly flourished during Europe's medieval era and before. The practice of the first European quack in America in the 16th century is well documented because explorer Cabeza de Vaca, forced into quackery by his Indian captors, described his experiences. He had laughed when Indians initially demanded that he employ their remedies: "They cure by blowing upon the sick and with their breath and imposing of hands they cast out infirmity."[6] "Why don't they ask us for our diplomas?" joshed Cabeza with his comrades. But the pleasant raillery at superstitions and the Spaniard's resistance gave way when the Indians punished his refusal to cure by refusing him food. Suddenly Cabeza started performing in first class fashion, blowing, touching, and muttering prayers with gusto. The prayers were sincere calls for his patients' recovery, motivated by fear of reprisals if treatments failed.

In the course of time Cabeza's practice was taken up by untold numbers of charlatans, as well as by honest men who lacked educational requirements. Licensing standards were left to the individual states where resistance among doctors and legislators, who favored a *laissez faire* attitude to keep treatment costs low, reflected individualism and a distaste for regulation. Among the thousands of quacks who imposed upon the unwary there were many whose shocking ignorance and unshakable beliefs in their own ridiculous theories encouraged the premature filling of graveyards. A twentieth century quack and contemporary of Macfadden was Dr. John Brinkley. He was one of the greatest in terms of blatancy, employment of new advertising technology, and cunning resistance to regulatory forces, and one who stirred the frenzy of Cramp and the AMA. Doc Brinkley gained his license in Texas in 1919 but it was while practicing later in Kansas that he conceived his most infamous con. Like Macfadden the doc had observed that people were very interested in sexual rejuvenation even if they didn't talk about it very much. Macfadden could only offer a few special exercises, modest inventions, and some books, but Brinkley sold a surgical transplant of powerful goat glands to aging men who wished to regain their former sexual prowess and overall good health. The doc prospered because he pioneered in radio programming, emitting the strongest signal in the country to carry his message of hope all over middle America. When federal authorities stripped away his radio license and Kansas declared his medical credentials phoney Brinkley moved to Del Rio, Texas where he continued to prosper. He located his new radio station just across the Rio Grande in Mexico to evade the federal authorities and fought off Texans keen on taking away his license to practice.

Macfadden did not favor Brinkley's surgical panacea or any other transplants because he did not approve of surgery. He considered Brinkley to be a knife-happy quack not too far removed from the mainstream practice of surgeons. Macfadden was much more attracted to quacks who avoided the scalpel, even if it was in favor of mysterious electrical boxes or other contraptions. He was a tolerant man and even showed a fleeting interest in the wonderful electric machine invented by a pillar of the California medical establishment for the diagnosis of ailments. In the field of quack technology in the aid of diagnosis or treatment no instrument has ever surpassed Abrams' box. Doctor Albert Abrams, a University of Heidelberg Medical School graduate, returned to his native California to practice with distinction. In 1889 he was honored by election as vice-president of the California State Medical Society and he was a professor of pathology at the Cooper Medical College. Abrams diverged from his orthodox course in 1909 with the discovery that the reflex centers of the spine could be stimulated by hammering on a patient's back. Later Abrams began turning patients over to percuss or hammer the abdomen. These were not aimless thumpings because it had long been established that tone qualities from the body under percussion aided the diagnosis of pneumonia, tuberculosis, and other diseases. But Abrams' exploitation of his theories took a spectacular turn when he discovered the radio. Many other Americans were experiencing the joys of radio at the same time but Abrams saw other prospects in the marvelous new machine.

Abram's invention, a maze of wires, coils, and batteries, lent extraordinary powers of diagnosis to its users. By testing a drop of a patient's blood Abrams, and the many physicians eager to buy his box, could determine whether the subject was suffering from syphilis, sarcoma, carcinoma, cancer, typhoid fever, malaria, gonorrhea, tuberculosis, or other diseases. The patient himself did not have to be on hand because the doctor utilized some other healthy individual as a control whose vibrations upon thumping were carried to the box. This fascinating instrument also identified the exact place within the body where the disease of the absent patient was located.

As a character of lively imagination, Abrams found other uses for his box through further experimentation. By plugging in to the signature of a dead person he could find what malady had carried him off and what his religious persuasion had been. Although Abrams never explained the value of religious identification anyone could see that the box's possibilities were limitless. As Abrams began publishing his own journal, selling boxes, and increasing his expensive instructional courses plenty of scoffers derided his invention, but numbers of learned medical disciples gathered at his feet. Soon he realized that buyers of the box would benefit more by using it for repeated treatments than for a single diagnosis for each patient so he created the oscilloclast, which was designed for treatment. The original box sold for $200 but the oscilloclast could only be leased because its money-making potential was boundless, although it did not differ much from the original. Lessors paid $200 or $250 down and a five dollar monthly fee.[7]

Litigation in 1923 gave a physicist the opportunity to examine the box. He found that the tangle of wires had no apparent purpose and many lacked connections. It was as if the wires had been chosen and placed with an eye to their color and design appeal. He did concede that the box emitted an interesting hum. Abrams died in 1924 without joining in the general derision of his invention. For a time Upton Sinclair had been quite taken with the fraud's claims and had contributed an article on him to *Physical Culture*.

Abrams and Brinkley were great quacks but individual quacks did not occupy Cramp as much as manufacturers of patent medicines. Keeping track of the various offerings, investigating and exposing them, and encouraging government action kept Cramp very busy. The advertising and sales of countless dubious specifics had been a scandal since colonial times and the attempt at reform with the 1906 federal legislation was welcomed by the doctors and most of the public. But the exposures of Samuel Hopkins Adams and the new laws did not bring about immediate changes. The patent medicine manufacturers constituted a powerful force and they were very slow to reform. As time passed the major companies found it beneficial to conform to the law but others battled on with the power of their advertising purse. People continued to learn all about the wonderful pills, tonics, medicines, and appliances, which were available from their druggist, their doctor—quack or otherwise, or by direct mail. The Indian Medicine Shows faded away in the 1890s as vendors of Kickapoo Indian Sagwa and other marvelous cures but thousands of other remedies were advertised as certain cures for constipation, female weakness, liver complaint, restoration of lost manhood, dyspepsia, indigestion, loss of appetite, obesity, rheumatism, chills, fever, cancer, heart failure, or any other disease.

Many newspapers in the early decades of the century survived on regular patent medicine advertising. Full page and double spread ads were common but there remained room for many modest announcements of instant comforts to mankind. Hyperbole reigned. Charlatans trumpeted the cure of cancer without the knife, the elimination of sexual weakness with electric belts; the treatment of rheumatism with electric insoles; and relief from any and all diseases, pains, discomforts, insecurities, embarrassments, deficiencies, disabilities, and misfortunes. Some of the oils, lotions, and tonics were harmless compounds of water, sugar, and coloring. Others used drugs that could do serious damage and, of course, a great many featured an alcohol base to the great comfort of secret alcoholics and the thirsty folks whose religious beliefs denied them the comforts of an occasional snort. Quacks ventured into every field of health with their "secret" ingredients. Their secrets gave them a competitive edge and became the particular point of attack under the new federal legislation, although it took some years and several amendments before the law's teeth became sharp enough to do the job. Tell the consumer what he is using, cautioned the law, and, reluctantly, slowly with many sharp delaying tactics that prove the elasticity of language, the peddlers have had to comply. One secret anemia cure was made of sand; a useful pill for all ills was made of cottage cheese; a liquid tonic designed to fix up any sufferer was largely kerosene; and the promoter of a cancer cure with "radium-impregnated fluid," only impregnated his water base with a bit of alcohol and quinine sulfate.

Of the thousands of medicines and nostrums offered to suffering humanity by public benefactors out for the buck the case of the Microbe Killer is particularly instructive. Its creator's medical theories resembled Macfadden's in several respects although the latter did not believe microbes were important enough to warrant a drug campaign. William Radam, an Austin, Texas gardener until the public's response to his medicine forced him to abandon his fruits and vegetables for more lucrative manufacturing, boasted of the simplicity of his discovery, achieved in the late 1880s: "I had discovered a remedy that would cure disease, and...that there is but one disease and one cause of disease, no matter how varied the symptoms in different cases might be...I laid claim to being the only man that could prove these things."[8] Unlike Macfadden, the gardener was enthusiastic about the findings of Pasteur and Koch and believed what they said about germs causing disease. Radam thought about these things as he looked around his garden. Now, he reasoned, one just has to invent something that will kill the germs. Killing germs or microbes in people was a lot like killing bugs on plants. So he concocted a powerful microbe killer for all who had health woes: "I treated all my patients with the same medicine, just as in my garden I would treat all weeds alike. There are endless varieties of weeds, a very large number of which are familiar to me by name, but that would not cause me to pause about their extermination, or the method of effecting it. What matters is what the scientific name of a weed might be? So long as it is a weed, that suffices...So it is with disease in the human body. We are not to waste time and endanger the patient's health by trifling about special symptoms: let us remove that cause, and the person will be well."

Like other quacks Radam was criticized by orthodox physicians but he set a standard for defense with vigorous, all out attacks on the medical establishment. By his reckoning doctors had conspired against their patients' welfare and endowed their arts with "a halo of mystery" by indulging in the diagnosis of disease. "Diagnosing disease is simply blindfolding the public, but physicians dare not acknowledge it, for if they did, their glorious work would be undone, their services would not be needed, and they would have to fall back on other occupations."[9]

Before the passage of the Food and Drug Act gave examiners the opportunity to make a purposeful test of the Microbe Killer's ingredients Radam only had to worry about competitors and an enterprising New York doctor who publicized his own tests. Radam sued his imitators and his detractors and did not finally get his comeuppance until a federal investigation in 1912. The feds showed that the tonic was 99.38 percent water with a few other minerals and a dash of wine to give the mixture a healthy pink color. There is nothing wrong with water, as Radam himself observed: "I killed nobody and of course any man may cure another with water if he likes."[10] All this was true but sellers had to mind their labels and advertisements in 1912. Radam's label claimed the microbe killer a cure for cancer, syphilis, yellow fever, leprosy, small pox, constipation, asthma, headache, neuralgias, croup, mumps, measles, whooping cough, worms, diptheria, tonsillitis, consumption, dyspepsia, indigestion, gastritis, colds, and "every disease," and that the Killer could be applied externally or taken internally with equal effectiveness.

Cramp understood the need to educate doctors and the public to the menace of quackery. He published the reports of his investigations and of product testing in the AMA's journal. In the hope of reaching a larger public he made compilations of his journal notes for a "veritable Who's Who in Quackdom," a 500 page book entitled *Nostrums and Quackery,* published in 1911. Later two other volumes were published. Cramp's book proved to doctors and the public that skilled testing of medicines had been undertaken on their behalf. It called attention to the existence of something like a national complaint bureau, a center to which individuals could denounce spurious practitioners and phoney treatments.

With the necessity of exposing hundreds, or perhaps, thousands of fake doctors and blowing the whistle on the fanciful—and sometimes deadly—outpourings of the powerful proprietary medicine industry Cramp was a busy man. Thanks to federal legislation and the progress through the 1920s of regulatory agencies on commerce and radio the AMA's efforts gained increasing support, but policing was still slow-paced. While the post office's jurisdiction over mail fraud gave relief in some cases and the Federal Trade Commission began pouncing on frauds affecting interstate commerce in the 1930s more effective regulatory amendments of the Food and Drug Act of 1906 were long deferred. The original act did not require manufacturers to list the ingredients of their nostrums on the label except for alcohol and certain narcotic drugs.

Nonetheless it was a great step forward as it banned fraudulent claims on labels and advertising circulars distributed with the product.

Macfadden liked to remind doctors that he had published articles in 1906 exposing quacks, as he had, and that they should not bad-mouth him.[11] Considering his exemplary record in health reform he was deserving of the AMA's highest praise. So why did the AMA withhold praise and make it a point to castigate his works. Was it jealousy? Was it fear? Was it part of an economic war for patents? He concluded it was all these things. He told the truth about doctors so they were out to get him. And what was the truth about doctors? As simply and repeatedly stated by Macfadden it was that doctors were unnecessary but because they refused to admit this they constituted a dangerous as well as a parasitic class.

These were hard words for doctors to hear. Others had uttered such disparagements before Macfadden came along but his heresies were broadcast widely in many magazines, newspapers, and public appearances. As a sensitive man Macfadden understood that his dismissal of the entire medical establishment and the learned institutions supporting it were upsetting to the AMA. He did not wish to be unfair or unkind (he had met some honest doctors); he would stop hectoring the AMA if they abandoned their pretensions. Why should doctors persist, Macfadden asked, when all their diagnosis and treatment was based upon an utterly false comprehension of the body's functions and needs?

Cramp's interest in Macfadden accelerated after he read a *Physical Culture* editorial blast at the AMA in March 1911. "It is the intention of the AMA," Macfadden asserted, "to secure control of a National Health Department, to crush all publications that made a business of advising the public in regard to health."[12] *Physical Culture* was high on the AMA's crush list because "drug sales are down because of our fight against drugs" which has brought thousands of "powerful enemies" against us. Macfadden's reference to "our fight against drugs" was a fair enough description of his constant condemnation of drugs and doctors. Cramp's annotation of this clipping indicated his concern: "A typical illustration in the form of one of a vast number of this unscrupulous imposter's monstrous misrepresentations of the medical profession. Well worth reading and considering. This rascal deserves thousands of powerful enemies in the AMA and they ought to take advantage of the opportunity I am offering them to crush him." Despite his militant language Cramp's tactics were limited to a warning to the membership which was hardly likely to bring destruction to Macfadden.

A weapon of more potential against Macfadden's influence was suggested by an offer to Cramp from H.G. Hedden, a disgruntled former associate of the publisher. Hedden had a wide range of accusations against Macfadden but AMA officers doubted whether his evidence was adequate and were concerned about a possible entrapment by Macfadden through Hedden. "If we take this up," Cramp advised his superiors, "Macfadden will claim that doctors are trying to ruin him for revenge."[13] Hedden was advised to approach newspapers with his story. If he did so he did not convince them that his sensations were interesting or trustworthy because nothing was published.

Another reason for the AMA's growing alarm over Macfadden was his establishment of the Healthatorium, a sanitarium, and the Macfadden College of Physcultopathy in Chicago, Cramp assumed that the Healthatorium was probably violating some laws even if there were physicians on the staff. He could not imagine why any "respectable physician" would work for someone as "grossly, dangerously ignorant" as Macfadden. Cramp had been involved with quackery long enough to realize that the public was susceptible to persuasive characters regardless of their ignorance or eccentricities. And many of those Cramp had to worry about were even more dubious than Macfadden. It was because he encountered such individuals that Cramp kept a copy of *Alice in Wonderland* on his desk. Reading a few paragraphs daily reconciled him to the fantasy world of his professional endeavors.

Cramp gathered information about Macfadden from doctors and others. A physician who headed the University of Washington's physical training department told about a Seattle farmer who suffered from psoriasis and, as a reader of *Physical Culture,* consulted Macfadden, then journeyed to Macfadden's Healthatorium in Chicago for treatment. As a cure was guaranteed him the farmer paid over $248 in cash, then, after talking to other patients, learned that the place was "a fake concern."[14] The farmer went home but did not get his money back. Whatever the farmer's disappointment he may not have done better had he heeded Macfadden's first advice, which was to consult Dr. Linda Hazzard, Seattle's starvation specialist.

Occasionally Cramp could take positive measures to redress one of Macfadden's transgressions. Reading a Macfadden ad in 1921 he was amazed to come upon an endorsement of the physical culturist's health ideas by Admiral Cary T. Grayson, President Woodrow Wilson's personal physician. "No, no," cried the exasperated investigator, it can't be that an eminent medical man could fall for Macfadden's absurd notions. The endorsement in question was limited in reference to venereal disease and stated:

"SEE WHAT ADMIRAL GRAYSON SAYS. ADMIRAL GRAYSON, PRESIDENT WILSON'S PERSONAL PHYSICIAN SAYS 'I have just read your chapter dealing with venereal disease. I am in full agreement with all that Macfadden, the eminent physical culturist, wrote. He has a remarkable grasp of the situation. A copy of his clear-visioned discussion of an important subject should be placed with every mother and father and adolescent boy and girl in America.' "[15]

Grayson was a busy man what with treating the president through his fatal illness but not too busy to answer Cramp's query. Grayson had not endorsed Macfadden and complained to Orr J. Elder of the publication company who agreed to discontinue use of the endorsement. Neither Elder nor Macfadden explained nor apologized for the unauthorized use of the doctor's name.

Macfadden took a page from the book of Norman Baker, a contemporary cancer quack of singular aggressiveness who answered the AMA's efforts to shut down his hospitals with much vilification of the doctors and the formation of a defense league. Macfadden announced the establishment of the American Protective League, dedicated to saving people from "absolute autocracy," and inviting members to help him save the country from the doctors. "Are you going to submit to medical tyranny,"[16] Macfadden asked the public? Help against an "insidious movement designed to give the medical trust absolute power to determine the fitness of any and every practice of healing citizens." The AMA's lust for autocracy exceeded anything in the civilized world—"the Russian Czar and his dukes no longer being contestants for this honor."

Such ill feeling did not deter Macfadden from requesting editorial courtesies from the AMA. Publishers commonly exchange issues of their magazines and in 1923 Macfadden's manager offered any one of his eight magazines in exchange for the AMA's *Hygeia* but got no response. The *Hygeia*, a new AMA publication that year, was one that its editor, Dr. Morris Fishbein, hoped would be found in every doctor's waiting room and in the homes of many lay people concerned about better health. Among its articles some of the more infamous quacks and dubious patent medicines would be exposed. Fishbein understood that the *Journal of the American Medical Association* had few readers except among doctors and wished to reach the general public.[17]

Macfadden's American Protective League did not attract any support so he tried another ploy in 1927. He sent out a form letter to doctors around the country recommending they read *Hygeia* and soliciting their correspondence on health matters. He assured them that he was quite willing to recommend "sound" doctors to his readers. He admitted that "we may have differed occasionally in some of our beliefs,"[18] but professed to believe that doctors shared his interest in national health. The editor of the *Texas State Journal of Medicine* was one of many doctors to write to Cramp with alarm: "I have had several inquiries from doctors in Texas about the whole proposition, and some of them seem to be falling for the thing...please advise." Cramp prepared a form letter to doctors and warned the Texas editor to keep cool: Macfadden is "utterly discredited" with intelligent doctors; "it would merely be playing into the hands of the Macfadden fakers to give any space to the latest attempt to gather in the shekels." Cramp explained Macfadden's tactic: "After damning the medical profession from Dan to Beersheba, and thus playing for the support of all the cultists, faddists and quacks, he now turns around and attempts to get the doctors to say that they believe in his particular brand of physical culture. Those who are willing to admit this he will 'recommend' as physicians who are safe to go to. It should be quite obvious that any recommendation from Bernarr Macfadden is a heavy liability for a decent physician."[19]

Some doctors did not mind telling Macfadden directly what they thought of his proposition. Dr. E.O. Harrold of Marion, Indiana spoke frankly: "You seem to want to know what we think of you and your ambitions. I don't think I can tell you. Old 'Mother Wright' used to run a big, successful whore-house here but, Bernarr, she was a piker. She should have nationalized her 'institute' and published a few magazines and covered more ground. I believe you are a lot smarter than Old 'Mother Wright' even if you seem to have about the same ideas. You will go further, I believe."[20]

Dr. M.A. Moore commended Macfadden's campaigns for sunlight, exercise, and diet baths, but scorned his propaganda against vaccination and drugs: "It is so pernicious that it undoes a million times all the good your former publicity has done...the harm done by the warped and ignorant ideas you advocate is not against the physician it is against the public at large."[21]

The Bureau of Investigation's file on Macfadden grew thicker in the early twenties. Cramp clipped articles by alleged doctors like Dr. Edmund Gray who advised treatment to Macfadden's magazine subscribers. A victim of cirrhosis of the liver, for example, was advised to try fasts of three to six days every month and keep to a milk diet between the fasts. Colon flushing and twisting exercises that expanded and compressed the body area near the liver would be a help.

Cramp was cheered around this time because a scandal involving the Healthatorium made the Chicago newspapers "despite large advertising"[22] by Macfadden. It seems that a sanitarium inmate got smallpox and passed it along to eight others. Macfadden tried to keep things quiet but the word got out and city health authorities, over Macfadden's strident protests, removed all the diseased individuals from the place. Cramp also had the report of the deaths of an aged couple at the Healthatorium. He was not a ghoul but the accumulation of such reports suggesting Macfadden's treatment of individuals in unorthodox ways could eventually lead to his destruction.

Macfadden's direction of a syphilis test was also brought to Cramp's attention. Macfadden wanted to use his natural treatment methods on twenty men who had been infected with the disease earlier and had been treated by standard methods. Macfadden sent the test candidates to Dr. Eugene A. Fisk for examination. Two of them definitely needed medical treatment but, on Macfadden's instructions, they declined to be treated. Fisk remonstrated to Macfadden who denied that he had planned natural treatment of the men and admonished the doctor to appreciate that some individuals just did not care to be treated by doctors. Cramp was not surprised at Macfadden's falseness—"in fact, I should be more surprised to see him telling the truth."[23] Macfadden, of course, had to be wary of charges that he was practicing medicine without a license.

Fishbein and Cramp decided it was high time to expose Macfadden after he began publishing the *New York Graphic*. The newspaper was a powerful weapon in the publisher's war on the AMA and he was using the new vehicle with apparent glee. Editorial cartoons provided a provocative means of exposing the doctors. One such cartoon in 1924 showed an unpleasant looking ruffian called "Medical Trust" being supported by a top-hatted fellow called "Comstockery" in ordering a little citizen to obey laws on compulsory vaccination and others beneficial to the trust and censors. "I will regulate your morals," said the Comstock figure while the Medical Trust shaped up his health treatment.[24]

Compulsory vaccination was an anathema to Macfadden for years. It outraged him that children could not attend school unless their parents submitted to vaccination. This forced him to keep his own children out of the public schools and forced him also into some dubious stories about vaccination. The *Graphic* even dared to try to convince a mourning nation that movie star Rudolph Valentino had died because of a serum injection. Anti-vaccination articles were standard fare in the *Graphic* and in *Physical Culture*. The AMA did manage to expose some of these efforts as with an article by G.W. Desbrow, M.D., entitled, "Vaccination Killed my Two Sisters." After a furious exchange of letters Macfadden conceded that "there is no such person" as Dr. Desbrow.[25]

Fishbein's two-pronged assault on Macfadden in the *Hygeia* focused on Macfadden's advertisements in 1924 and the general failures and follies of the magazines in 1925. Fishbein hoped to convince the public that Macfadden was a greedy hypocrite of no fixed principles.

It seemed wrong to Fishbein that Macfadden "has lent himself to the promotion of dozens of now discredited notions," and was willing to employ dubious physicians in his attacks on the medical profession. "It should be obvious to any physician that the lending of his name and his M.D. degree to the periodicals of Mr. Macfadden constitutes a definite departure from his scientific training, and certainly from the ethical ideals which were conferred on him with his medical education." Among doctors who aided Macfadden's "pernicious propaganda" was Edmund C. Gray. Gray earned a degree from Bennett Medical College in 1914, "apparently without preliminary education in a college or university." The Bennett Medical College was not of the caliber Fishbein favored and probably did not give Gray much of an education. Fishbein wondered why Gray did not practice until 1918 and moved around quite a bit after that. Probably Gray had not been too successful, hence was ripe to offers of Macfadden's coin.

Macfadden also used an article by Lee A. Stone, said to be an army surgeon. Fishbein checked and found no record of Stone with the army. Another frequent magazine contributor was Dr. Frank Crane, presented as a medical man but who was in fact a graduate in theology. Crane was not even "a practicing reverend but a syndicated producer of trite aphorisms for daily prayers and Babbitt-hunting periodicals. He is the apotheosis of the Pollyanna school of thought." Like the case of Dr. Desbrow, a man who did not actually exist, Macfadden had published other medical articles by Dr. Edwin C. Bowers and Dr. Frederick Collins— who also did not exist.[26]

Fishbein asked why Macfadden resented the efforts of the AMA and state legislatures to protect the public by requiring a legitimate M.D. degree of practitioners? Why does he promote actively "the interests of the manipulative cults, including chiropractic and osteopathy; of the Abramites, with their fantastic electronic conception; of the naturopathic cult, with its emphasis on barefoot walking in the morning dew; of colonic flushing and vegetable diet; of the antivaccinationists and antivivisectionists; of the fanatical groups that feel that their personal beliefs are more important than the good of the community; and, indeed, of any of the extraordinary fads which have risen for a moment above the horizon of medical practice only to sink rapidly to oblivion."

Recent issues of *Physical Culture* exposed Macfadden's brand of science. In July Upton Sinclair defended Albert Abrams while Macfadden defended naturopathy and the notion that deformed eyes could be improved without glasses. Two issues held a symposium devoted to the triumphs of osteopathy and there was also an article arguing that the bobbing of womens' hair caused their baldness. Fishbein concluded that the articles and advertisements in *Physical Culture* did incalculable harm by destroying public confidence in the printed word and perverted public intelligence with editorials "on matters pertaining to scientific medicine."

Fishbein said Macfadden's magazines "reek of sex." Any reader could see that both the illustrations and the stories appeal to the sexual and the erotic. "It is the belief of at least many editors," Fishbein said, "that Macfadden periodicals, with their sex stimulation and appeal, promote unchastity." Fishbein was saddened by Macfadden's much publicized board of ministers who ruled on articles for the confession magazines. "Shall one criticize more Mr. Macfadden or the ministers who have lent themselves to his exploitation." And what of the article by Byrne

Macfadden, Bernarr's daughter that "she learned to shimmy from Gilda Gray!"

Fishbein claimed Macfadden was not really following the ideal of the Greeks he liked to praise. The ancients had discouraged immodesty and salaciousness. "The Macfadden gospel is essentially an appeal to a large minority of persons whose eyes are aroused by the flash of nakedness or whose weakened wills succumb to every new health fad. He has taken what should be a beautiful search for health, for vigor and for strength and made of it an ugly and discouraging thing to every right-minded individual."

If Macfadden was a dirty-minded panderer, a menace to public morals it was easier to understand his persistent opposition to doctors. Records of the Bureau of Investigation suggested the reason why an unscrupulous man like Macfadden would vilify a noble profession. In 1907, Fishbein asserted, doctors had received a letter from Macfadden's sanitarium, offering "a 50 percent kickback" of fees to doctors whose patients came to the sanitarium. "Possibly this proposal brought letters from physicians that embittered Macfadden against the entire medical profession. His present attitude lends color to such a supposition." While Fishbein's theory was interesting it is unlikely that he believed it. He must have known that by 1907 Macfadden had already been opposing doctors for a long time.

The heavens did not crash down upon Macfadden as a result of Fishbein's articles which were probably read primarily by those who shared the doctor's views. Macfadden did have his defenders, notably Annie Hale, an advocate of natural healing whose book, *These Cults*, examined several victims of AMA assaults. She called Macfadden, "a genial, courteous gentlemen with much less aroma of self-inflation about him than one senses in most self-made men of notable achievement."[27]

Hale knew all about Bernarr Macfadden's early life and his conversion to the cause of national health. She knew all about *Physical Culture* magazine too, but she was aware that the magazine's early drab illustrations had given way to "lurid pictorial sections which gave offense, not only to prudes and vestal-virgin minds in the medical profession, but to others less prejudiced, who felt nevertheless that it was possible to depict physical culture and vigorous health stunts without recourse to the extremes of contortion and daring poses affected by the Macfadden magazines."[28] Sales zoomed under the editorship of Carl Williams (1916-23) and some important authors like Havelock Ellis, Homer Croy, and Albert Edward Wiggam appeared in the magazine. There were also many contributions from inferior writers "and its pages have been marred by literary crudities not found in periodicals of equal popularity and power." Hale did not deny that the magazine provided both instructive health information and "some of questionable value."

Having established that she did not view Macfadden's world with blinkers Hale made a pertinent defense of charges that he "capitalized the erotic." "What of it," asked Hale, "is it not the universal practice of novelists, dramatists, poets, musicians, and dancers?"[29]

Hale struck at the falseness of Fishbein's concern for Macfadden's erotic emphasis. If the publisher was able to avoid trouble with postal authorities and others officially charged with protecting the public from obscenity, what were the doctors worried about? "Does their modest calling naturally make them more sensitive to such things than mere postal clerks accustomed to the seamy side of life?"[30] Sex appeal had been loosed on the world before "Macfadden emerged from the Missouri wilds with the nefarious purpose of utilizing it in health propaganda...Now all this scandalized mouthing in medical circles...is pure buncombe." Macfadden's real crime was in showing "the laity how to be independent of doctors...the war between Macfadden and the medical profession is an economic war, pure and simple, natural, logical, and inevitable."

Health preachments in *Physical Culture* certainly differed from what doctors taught but it was not necessarily false. To Hale it seemed wonderful that Macfadden taught everyone they must bear personal responsibility for their health. Obviously, doctors, authors of a system "which discourages laymen from taking any thought about their own bodies—as something risky, not to say impious,"[31] that urges all to see "a reputable physician" for fixing ills, do not like Macfadden. And why should the doctors cry out against the publisher's erotic appeals when they relied upon fear to lure patients?

The AMA's attack on Macfadden might have benefited by a concerted wave of publicity with newspapers and magazines around the nation rallying to the cause with heavy reliance on Fishbein's articles. It did not happen, although one magazine, *Detroit Saturday Night,* waded into Macfadden with a vengeance. Editor N.H. Bowen had prepared for a scheduled lecture by Macfadden in Detroit by asking the AMA for information on the publisher and then quoted Fishbein extensively. Bowen called Macfadden "the bare torso king" who turned out "shoddy sex magazines" that constituted a grave danger to his readers. Macfadden's readers were "undeveloped, semi-literate, half-baked mentalities that cannot truly think, seekers of thrills, near morons. There may be worse magazines in the world...but, if there are, intelligent people would rather be burned at the stake than be forced to read them."

Bowen had resented the preparations Macfadden made for his Detroit visit which included mailings of proof sheets of his article "Health Hints" to all the newspapers, giving permission to reprint in exchange for their agreement to print a free ad for his books. These 'Health Hints' scintillate with such soul-stirring questions as "Why not throb with superior vitality? Why not possess the physical energy of a young lion?" He also resented the insult that sponsors of Macfadden were offering the physical educators and the physicians of the city. Macfadden was not the founder of modern physical education, as he claimed to be, nor was he trained to give health advice. "Macfadden is unquestionably the King of the Bare Torso Brigade—those gentlemen of strange mentality who seem to be obsessed with the idea of continually flaunting before the public portraits of themselves in the nude. Their advertisements invariably contain these pictures with the subjects in melodramatic pose, wearing 'manly,' smug expressions that probably make quite an impression on very green youths and raw flappers."[32]

Throughout the rest of Macfadden's career the Bureau of Investigation maintained their watch on him. Other defectors tried to capitalize on the association's enmity to Macfadden but they were not judged too respectable themselves. Dr. Jesse Mercer Gehman, a doctor of naturopathy rather than of medicine, whose letterhead showed his well-muscled body, identifying him as "formerly personal trainer to Bernarr Macfadden, Father of Physical Culture," and former associate editor of *Physical Culture,* wanted to give the AMA information on Macfadden's neglect of a mental patient and exploitation of him in the *Graphic.* Gehman also offered the editor of *Hygeia* articles on exercise, bathing, dietetics, and natural living, "subjects of vital concern to the readers of your publication." The editor declined to answer the innocent author's letter but it was placed in Macfadden's file.[33]

Another defector about the same time was Arthur Leslie, Macfadden's publicity man. Cramp and Fishbein could not doubt that Leslie was in a strong position to know where Macfadden buried his bodies but they did not rise to Leslie's bait. When Leslie's wires and letters were not answered he made his proposals through a relative, including documentation of his effective work for Macfadden. It was Leslie who handled a rather clever ploy that gained a good deal of publicity for *Physical Culture.* The magazine published the report of a writer who went to eleven doctors with his health complaint and got eleven different diagnoses. This had been an effective promotion of Macfadden's ideas and one that was achieved at modest expense without any fakery. It was also Leslie who had developed techniques for the promotion of Macfadden's books through his lectures in various cities and the pre-appearance mailings of publicity material that had infuriated N.H. Bowen of *Detroit Saturday Night.* Leslie apparently offered the AMA the best kind of material he could gather, including a number of letters from clergy protesting against Macfadden's magazines and reports on scandalous conditions in the sanitarium. But the material was not really as devastating as he imagined it to be; not was it anything that could be utilized in any effective way. Leslie was probably sincere in wishing to do Macfadden in. He had been fired and wanted new employment. "I'll show you how to build a backfire"[34] against Macfadden's attacks on doctors, he promised. Leslie's persistence over many months showed his desperation and misplaced conviction that he had something sensational to trade, but the doctors remained suspicious of a Macfadden scheme to embarrass them.

Down the years Cramp followed Macfadden's trail, marveling when *Graphic* readers were offered free treatments of chlorine gas for their colds, and the persistence of Macfadden's odd mix of the common sense with the nonsensical in giving medical advice. In 1929 Cramp got curious about Macfadden's involvement with Castle Heights Military School and sent for a school catalogue over his wife's signature. The school material was not very revealing but it went into the file along with numerous issues of various Macfadden magazines that were sent in from time to time. Macfadden was still going strong when Cramp retired but Fishbein and others carried on. As late as 1946 Macfadden felt good enough to wire a debate challenge to Fishbein. They would speak on the AMA's current cancer campaign "which arouses unnecessary fear." New York's Carnegie Hall should be the scene of the debate on the issue, "Resolved, that cancer is made possible by lowered vitality brought about by defective diet, lack of muscular activity, and other devitalizing habits, and cases termed curable by modern diagnosis can be cured by eliminating causes."[35] Macfadden wanted to take the affirmative side and donate $10,000 to the winner. Doctor Fishbein, an outgoing fellow who rather liked the limelight did not succumb to the invitation. In fact, he did not even reply.

Bernarr and Mary Macfadden and their children

Anthony Comstock

"Your Honor, this woman gave birth to a naked child!"

Cartoon of Anthony Comstock

Cartoon of Anthony Comstock

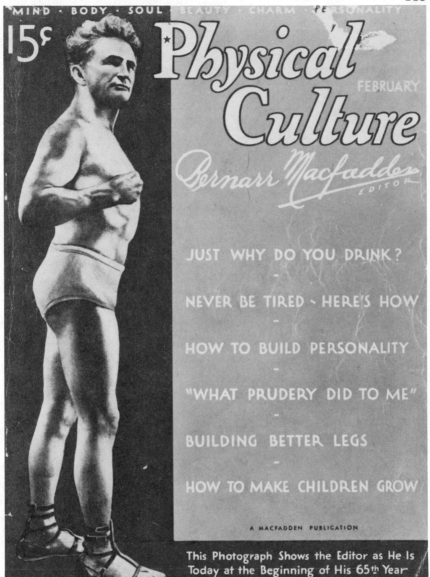

Macfadden at 65 on cover of *Physical Culture*

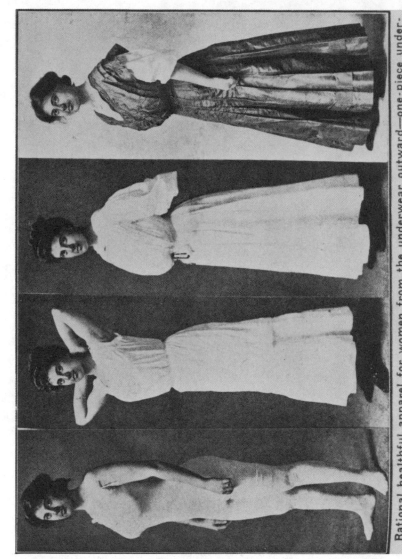

Rational healthful apparel for women from the underwear outward—one-piece underwear, one-piece corset-cover and underskirt, shirtwaist, yoke and skirt.

Illustration from Macfadden's *Encyclopedia* showing healthy clothes

A typical *True Story* cover girl

Arthur Cramp, nemesis of quacks at the AMA

Macfadden posing as a gardener for the *Encyclopedia*

Fulton Oursler, Macfadden's right hand man as editor.

Penny Restaurant, Inc.
16 West Lake Street
BERNARR MACFADDEN, *Founder*

Vital Health Foods
served at popular prices *in pleasant surroundings*

A Few Of Our Daily Specials

BREAKFAST		READY AT ALL HOURS	
Cracked Wheat	.01	All Soups	.02
Scotch Oatmeal	.01	All Cream Soups	.05
Hominy Grits	.01	Two Meatcakes	.05
Steamed Cornmeal	.01	Yankee Pot Roast	.12
One Fresh Egg, any style	.04	Corned Beef and Cabbage	.12
One Fresh Egg and Bacon	.07	Grilled Pork Chop	.07
Stewed Prunes	.01	Club Steak	.15
Stewed Raisins	.01	Sirloin Steak	.18
Stewed Apricots	.02	Beef Tenderloin Steak	.15
Stewed Mission Figs	.02	Beans in Tomato Sauce	.03
Pineapple Juice	.05	Wholewheat Macaroni and Cheese	.10
Tomato Juice	.05	Waldorf Salad	.05
Grapefruit Juice	.05	String Bean Salad	.05
One Half Grapefruit	.04	Cream Cheese Salad	.05
Sliced Pineapple	.03	Hot Biscuits	.01
Wholewheat Griddle Cakes, with syrup	.05	Puddings	.02 and .03
		Pure Jello	.03

Honey Tea, Raisin Coffee, Tea, Milk,

Buttermilk and Coffee

We Serve Chase & Sanborn Coffee

All Baking Done on Premises

We are serving 15,000 satisfied patrons daily

ONE CENT RESTAURANTS:
107 W. 44th St., New York 77 Bleecker St., New York
511 Third Av., New York 356 Pearl St., Brooklyn
125 W. 26th St., New York 1924 Pennsylvania Avenue Washington, D. C.

Menu from Macfadden's Penny Restaurant

ILLINOIS BRANCH

FOR PRESIDENT CLUB

Headquarters: 153 N. MICHIGAN AVE. CHICAGO, ILL.
Telephone: Randolph 1934
Bank: Mercantile Trust and Savings Bank of Chicago,
Jackson Blvd. and Clinton St., Chicago, Ill.

BERNARR MACFADDEN
... Native Missourian ...
New York Publisher, output 15 million magazines monthly. Health and anti-Communistic Crusader. Aviation enthusiast. Organizer of Penny Restaurants, National Youth Movement and non-profit Health Resorts. Willed entire fortune of several millions to beneficial trust. LIBERAL.

Dear Friend:

A new and dominant figure—born and raised to manhood in Missouri—a man whose rise in life has been as vivid and absorbing as that of Abraham Lincoln or James A. Garfield—has appeared on our troubled political horizon.

He was born in poverty on a farm near Mills Springs in Wayne County. As a boy he split rails and followed a plow on a farm, spending some of his early years working in a coal mine.

A man who early in life dared to lift his voice in behalf of his own class, the poor and the down trodden. A man who slowly step-by-step worked his way from a lowly printer's apprentice to the command of vast business enterprises.

This man is Bernarr Macfadden. His recent address before the St. Louis Republican Club so stirred the nation that great popular demand forced him into the political spotlight. Here indeed is a man capable of administering the world's greatest business—our government.

As emphatic endorsers of all his fundamental ideas voiced in that memorable St. Louis speech, and as admirers of his great political editorials, convinced of his sincerity and unequalled business ability—we are glad and proud of the privilege of advancing the name of this great American and native Missourian for the highest gift of the American people.

We feel sure that you will want to share our pride and pleasure in seeing Bernarr Macfadden in the White House, and will want to join in this great voluntary movement to put him there.

May we therefore ask that you detach the coupon on the 4th page of this letter and mail it to these headquarters together with your contribution. For we are confident that you will want to be identified with this laudatory and unfettered effort to safeguard constitutional government.

Sincerely yours,

C. S. Peterson

Illinois Branch
BERNARR MACFADDEN for PRESIDENT CLUB

The club officials would like to show Mr. Macfadden the names of every one of his readers and friends on the list of contributors even though they cannot afford to donate more than 10¢.

In a recent presidential preference poll conducted in 41 cities and totaling over 7500 individual ballots, Mr. Macfadden stood first among all Republican choices. Sample of ballot used in this poll is enclosed. We can send you 100 of these ballots to test out our candidate's strength among your friends if desired (6¢ postage).

Presidential campaign letter (1936)

Upton Sinclair, always a health fan of Macfadden's

Dr. Linda Burfield Hazzard, "the starvation specialist"

Advertisement for the Physical Culture Hotel, Dansville, NY

Typical ads in *Physical Culture* (p. 93)

Ad in *Physical Culture*

"What? Learn Music by Mail?" *they laughed*

"Yes," I cried, "and I'll bet money I can do it!"

ONE day after lunch the office crowd was in the recreation-room, smoking and talking, while I thumbed through a magazine.

"Why so quiet, Joe?" some one called out.

"Just reading an ad," I replied, "about a new way to learn music by mail. Says here any one can learn to play in a few months at home, without a teacher. Sounds easy."

"Do you suppose they would say it was *ard?*" laughed Fred Lawrence.

"Perhaps not," I came back a bit peeved, but it sounds so reasonable I thought I'd rite them for their booklet."

Well maybe I didn't get a razzing then! red Lawrence sneered: "The poor fellow ally believes he can learn music by mail!"

"Yes, and I'll bet money I can do it!" I ried. But the crowd only laughed harder han ever.

During the few months that followed, Fred awrence never missed a chance to give me a ly dig about my bet. And the boys always got good laugh, too. But I never said a word. was waiting patiently for a chance to get the *1st* laugh myself.

My Chance Arrives

Then came the office outing at Pine Grove. After lunch it rained, and we had to sit around nside. Suddenly some one spied a piano in the corner. Fred Lawrence saw a fine chance to have ome fun at my expense.

Pick Your Instrument

Piano	Violin
Organ	Clarinet
Ukulele	Flute
Cornet	Saxophone
Trombone	Harp
Piccolo	Mandolin
Guitar	'Cello
Hawaiian Steel Guitar	
Sight Singing	
Piano Accordion	
Voice & Speech Culture	
Italian & German	
Accordion	
Harmony & Composition	
Drums & Traps	
Automatic Finger	
Control	
Banjo (Plectrum, 5-	
String or Tenor)	
Junior's Piano Course	

"Ladies and gentlemen," he cried, "our friend Joe, the music master, has consented to give us a recital."

That gave the boys a good laugh. "Play the 'Varsity Drag'!" shouted Fred, thinking to embarrass me further. I heard a girl say, "Oh, let the poor fellow alone; can't you see he's mortified to death?"

I smiled to myself. This was certainly a wonderful setting for my little surprise party. Assuming a

scared look, I began fingering the keys, and then . . . with a wonderful feeling of cool confidence . . . I broke right into the very selection Fred asked for. There was a sudden hush in the room. But in a few minutes tables and chairs were pushed aside, and the whole crowd was dancing. I played one peppy selection after another until I finished with "Crazy Rhythm" and the crowd stopped to applaud me. As I turned around to thank them, there was Fred holding a ten-spot right under my nose.

"Folks," he said, "I want to apologize to Joe. I bet him he couldn't learn to play by mail without a teacher, and believe me, he sure deserves to win the money!"

"Learn to play *by mail,*" exclaimed a dozen people. "That sounds impossible! Tell us how you did it!"

I told them how I had read the U. S. School of Music ad, and how it was the biggest surprise of my life when I got the first lesson—everything was as simple as A-B-C. No scales or tiresome exercises.

"And," I continued, "all it required was part of my spare time. In a short time I was playing jazz, classical pieces, and in fact, anything I wanted. Believe me, that certainly was a profitable bet I made with Fred."

Play Any Instrument

You, too, can *teach yourself* to be an accomplished musician—at home—in half the usual time—through this simple new method which has already taught over 600,000 people. No matter which instrument you choose the cost averages just a few cents a day.

Free Booklet and Demonstration Lesson

If you are in earnest about wanting to play your favorite instrument—if you want to gain happiness and increase your popularity—send at once for the Free Booklet and Free Demonstration Lesson which explain this remarkable method. The booklet will also tell you all about the amazing new *Automatic Finger Control.* No cost—no obligation. Sign coupon below. Instruments supplied when needed, cash or credit. U. S. School of Music, 182 Brunswick Bldg., New York.

Ad in *Physical Culture*

"I have reduced the prices on my more important health books. Prices are cut to the bone, now you can save as much as 50% — and get a book FREE, besides"

Bernarr Macfadden

Not only have the prices of many Macfadden health books been drastically cut, but you are also offered the great book "Good Health" Free with every order amounting to $4.00 or more. Here is a book that should be in every home—vitally essential and useful every day of your life. And remember it costs you absolutely nothing for if you order $4.00 worth of the books listed below—

You Get This Great Book FREE

Physical Culture Cook Book—A real guide to health. Written by Bernarr Macfadden. Tasty menus—appetizing recipes. Novelex binding—372 pages. Price $1.00.

Keeping Fit—A veritable encyclopedia of health information. With special exercise chart included. Red leatherette binding—215 pages. Price $1.00.

Tuberculosis—At last a substantial hope is held out to all sufferers of this dread disease—if the patient is sufficiently confident and persistent. Cloth bound—288 pages. Price $2.00.

Preparing for Motherhood—Prepare yourself along the simple lines recommended in this great book and enter upon the ordeal with a mind free from worry. Cloth binding—264 pages. Price $2.00.

Fasting for Health—Is unquestionably the most masterful work on fasting that has ever been written. Blue cloth binding—211 pages. Price $2.00.

Eating for Health and Strength—This book shows you what and how to eat in order to maintain your vitality at high water mark. Cloth binding—176 pages. Price $2.00.

Strengthening the Eyes—Enables you to train the muscles of the eyes so you can make them work properly without effort or strain—210 pages cloth bound. Price $3.00.

Strengthening the Nerves—Bernarr Macfadden in this book shows you how to recharge your undernourished nerves and acquire glowing health and vitality. Cloth binding—256 pages. Price $2.00.

Strengthening the Spine—Shows you how to develop a strong healthy spine—211 pages—illustrated. Cloth binding Price $2.00.

Asthma and Hay Fever—Simple, easy treatment for asthma and hay fever that gives relief. Cloth binding—180 pages. Price $2.00.

Foot Troubles—This book tells you in simple terms how to banish foot troubles forever. Cloth binding—210 pages. Price $1.00.

Tooth Troubles—Tells you how to eliminate tooth troubles which cause disease. Cloth binding—210 pages. Price $1.00.

Vitality Supreme—Build vitality, energy, virility and health the Physical Culture way. Own this book. Durable binding—185 pages. Price $1.00.

Diabetes—Bernarr Macfadden's own treatment for diabetes. Cloth binding—235 pages. Price $2.00.

Predetermine Your Baby's Sex—A most thorough treatment of sex determination. Cloth binding—168 pages. Price $2.00.

Rheumatism—Let nature treat your rheumatism. Bernarr Macfadden explains the commonsense way in this great book. Cloth binding—198 pages. Price $2.00.

Skin Troubles—Tells how you can have a really beautiful complexion. No more pimples or blotches. Cloth binding—283 pages. Price $2.00.

Digestive Troubles—Are you troubled with stomach and bowel disorders—then this great book is meant for you. Cloth binding—270 pages. Price $2.00.

Constipation—To be constipated is to be poisoned. Bernarr Macfadden tells you in this book how to avoid and treat it. Cloth binding—277 pages. Price $2.00.

Colds, Coughs and Catarrh—Eliminate these bothersome ills—and do it nature's way—as explained in this book. Cloth binding—214 pages. Price $2.00.

Headaches—Are the danger signals of health. This book tells you how to eliminate them. Cloth binding—211 pages. Price $2.00.

The Miracle of Milk—Milk is the great curative agent. It has given health to thousands. This book tells you how to use it for health. Cloth binding—204 pages. Price $1.00.

Hair Culture—You can have the beautiful head of hair you desire. This great book tells you how. Cloth bound—190 pages. Price $2.00.

Physical Culture Food Directory........$1.00
How to Raise the Baby.................. 2.00
Manhood and Marriage................. 3.00

Gaining Weight........................$ .50
Reducing Weight........................ .50
Womanhood and Marriage............... 3.00

Macfadden Book Company, Inc., Dept. P. C. 2, 1926 Broadway, New York. N. Y

I am interested in..

Please send me a copy by return mail. I will pay the postman $....... plus postage upon receipt of the book. It is understood that if for any reason I am dissatisfied with the book, I can return it at any time within 5 days after receipt of the book, for a refund of my money. (If your order amounts to $4 we will send the book "Good Health" Free.)
We prepay postage on all cash orders.

Name..

Street...

City..State................

Canadian and Foreign orders—cash in advance.

Ad for Macfadden's books

Ideal feminine physical development calls for elasticity, grace and lightness of movement. All these are conveyed by dainty Dora Duby, an American dancer who now has Paris at her feet

(Krydove)

Healthy cheesecake photo in *Physical Culture*

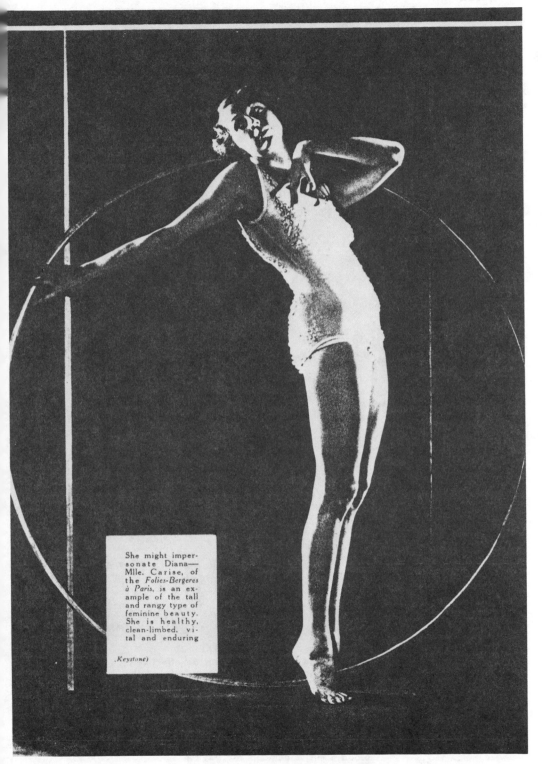

She might impersonate Diana—Mlle. Carise, of the *Folies-Bergeres à Paris*, is an example of the tall and rangy type of feminine beauty. She is healthy, clean-limbed, vital and enduring

(Keystone)

Cheesecake photo in *Physical Culture*

One form of resisting exercise that can be effectively
used with the full breathing—inhaling a full breath,
holding it, flexing the arms, one behind the back and
the other behind the head, endeavoring to pull the
head forward with the right arm, at the same time
bringing the head far backward. Relax and repeat the
exercise, reversing the position. Remember that this
combination of muscular movements makes your breathing exercise far more valuable by creating in the
blood itself a demand for oxygen

Macfadden exercising

A Charles Atlas ad

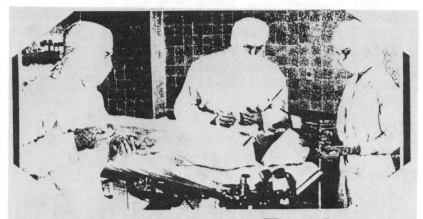

How She Had Dreaded This Operation
Her Third Trip *to the* Hospital in Two Years

FOR weeks the very thoughts of another trip to the hospital had been a hideous nightmare to young Marjorie Brewster. Doctors and nurses were but ghastly creatures of torture to her. On her two previous trips she had barely "pulled through." Now she must go through it all again. Certainly other women didn't have all this trouble.

Yet for all this torture—dreadful as it was—Marjorie could blame no one but herself. It wasn't as she explained—that hard luck and trouble had been her lot ever since she was married three years ago. It was indeed much more than just bad luck.

Married life for Marjorie Brewster had brought problems which she couldn't solve. She was as unequipped for marriage itself as she was for the birth of her child later on.

She didn't know her own body—its needs —its demands. Though considered well educated by everyone—she lacked the most fundamental of all knowledge—that of understanding her physical self.

Perhaps that was because there was no one to whom she could turn for

this information. It wasn't something she could talk over with her friends—something she could casually inquire about from her physician. Yet she could have found out— so easily.

Why Gamble
With Your Own Life

Really there is no excuse for anyone taking a chance with his own life today. No longer should there be whole lives pounded and broken upon the shoals of health ignorance. Essential health knowledge is available to everybody. Every man and woman may now have an expert health counsellor instantly at their command.

And after all the demands of health are cut from a simple pattern. Once you know your own body. Once you recognize your own physical needs. Once you recognize nature's warnings of sickness and disease. Then you can rule your health just as surely as you can rule your actions. This most essential of all human knowledge is to be found in but one place—The Encyclopedia of Health. Not just an ordinary

set of books to be sure. Rather a necessity for every individual—for every family in all matters of health and disease.

Not only does this great encyclopedia guide you in the certain ways of health but it also charts for you the course to follow in fighting every kind of disease. Tells you the symptoms of each ailment and outlines methods of treatment. Tells you what to do in cases of sudden illness, accidents— and emergencies. And the cost of it all is but a few cents a day.

You Owe it to Yourself and Your Family to Have this great Health Insurance

Send for this Free Book, "A Simple Guide to Health," and learn how you, too, may enjoy the security of good health—and abandon the fear of sickness and disease.

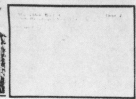

"How She Dreaded This Operation" another *Physical Culture* ad

Chapter 9
"The New York Graphic"

It educated readers up to a point where they were able to understand the other tabloids.

Alexander Woollcott

Without doubt September 15, 1924 marked a momentous day in the annals of American journalism—the birth of the *New York Graphic*. "We want this newspaper to throb with those life forces that fill life with joyous delight," announced Macfadden in the lead editorial. From its boisterous, exuberant start the paper drew more ridicule and outraged moral castigation than cries of joyous delight. Yet the "Pornographic," as some called it, throbbed all right, and its publisher fulfilled other promises: "We intend to dramatize and sensationalize the news and some stories that are not new...We want this paper to be human, first, last, and all the time."[1]

Being a citizen of New York City in the 1920s must have been stimulating for those who enjoyed newspapers and a great city's social ferment. Even the professional moralists like John Sumner, Comstock's successor with the Society for the Suppression of Vice, and others who answered the call to battle for righteousness must have been dizzy with the prospects: there was so much to be done! Pity the folks who rustled the pages of more staid daily journals, hearing dimly the clash of warfare among the steamy, charged-up tabloids, disapproving of them, and so missing the last great hurrahs of personal, scarcely responsible, and highly diverting journalism. Newspapers of the 1920s and through the '30s, full-sized and tabloids alike, were livelier and far better written than most of the poor, dull things available now. Our wretched daily fare, so cautious, and written with all the flair of a corporate news release, would provoke wonderment if seen by the reader of the 1920s, who would probably turn in despair to TV news were that hapless alternative available.

New York's first tabloid, the *Daily News*, modeled after London's *Daily Mirror*, hit the streets in June 1919 to open a new, sensation-seeking age in journalism. The *News* took readers away from conventional papers because of its vulgarity, unpretentious triviality, and breezy style— and, of course, because of its emphasis on photographs. Rival editors denounced the new paper's emphasis on pictures, large headlines, crimes and scandal, huffing at the "servant girl's Bible."[2] Quickly the city's servant girls and many other fascinated readers showed their preference for the lively tabloid. Circulation rose steadily from its initial run of 26,000 to one million by December 1925. The Sunday edition, started in May 1921, even surpassed the daily's success: by 1926 it lead the nation in circulation with 1,234,189 readers.

One of the *News's* outstanding attractions was its photographs, selected carefully and used copiously with concern for dramatic impact. Attention was given to clear printing of the photographs and the over-all layout of the pages. These innovations alone gave the *News* a fetching appearance that distinguished it from all other papers on the newsstand. And the paper's news coverage was somewhat innovative as well, featuring banner headlines and devotion to murder stories and juicy scandals. When short of colorful stories editors had to make do with misleading headlines and trumped-up, rumor-based stories for front page leads. If editors occasionally violated the canons of professional rectitude, it was not a transgression unknown to larger papers. And these short-comings were balanced by aggressive investigation of good story possibilities regardless of costs in staff time and support expenses, as well as by full attention to sports and features. Crime coverage was brilliant if sometimes a little biased. Without question the *News* was good reading. It was, as one admirer put it, "by turns sobby, dirty, bloody, and glamorous,"[3] covering news in a way that appealed to "elementary emotions of a truck-driver, and to the truck-driver in everyone."

William Randolph Hearst, long a front-runner among publishers of the so-called "Yellow Press"—an opprobrious term coined in the late nineteenth century to describe papers displaying more than a conventional interest in the scandals of the day—challenged the *News* in 1923. Hearst's *Mirror* resembled the *News* in all respects but its editors never managed to catch up with the News in circulation despite very determined efforts.

Macfadden's entry into the tabloid war had not been timely with the *News* and *Mirror* hogging the market. But he was accustomed to success and passionately committed to the unbounded possibilities for the propagation of his ideas that a newspaper afforded. If all or most New Yorkers started reading his paper he could convert them to physical culture. And once he had captured New Yorkers for his cause he would go after other cities with similar newspapers. The prospects made him shiver with excitement. Now he was the king of the magazine publishing field, but magazine readers represented an elite minority.

Leslie Cohen, a 23-year old with rather limited newspaper experience, was the new tabloid's contest editor. Cohen did not know too much about the world of journalism but he was aware that his paper was intended to be singular. The publisher made a speech on the first day of publication that astonished the young editor. Macfadden had appeared in the newsroom with Fulton Oursler and stood on a desk to address his staff. "He looked like an Indian," Cohen thought, "his gestures and bearing having some quality of the Noble Redman."[4] It was not so much the content of Macfadden's speech as the manner of presentation that struck Cohen: "It struck me as a combination of Old Scotch and Chotaw...I do not know Chotaw, but it seemed only Chotaw could sound that way." Cohen probably did not know Old Scotch either but he listened intently, as did the entire staff. Employees might make jokes privately about the boss but he was a legend and they respected him for his attainments in publishing. But they were a little uneasy because they were not sure what their paper would be and they did not want to be ridiculed by colleagues on other newspapers.

Macfadden told his staff that they would have a crusading newspaper. He rose on tiptoe and slammed his fist into his palm for emphasis. "We are going to...crusade for health!" he said. "For physical fitness!" And against medical ignorance!"[5] The newspaper would fight along side the publisher's magazines against drugs and "Prurient Prudery." Staffers may not have been aware until that day that these were the burning needs of the time, but they learned. Before long they would be smiling at the definition of the paper's editorial policy as expressed by some wit: "The newspaper was for fornication and against vaccination."[6]

Macfadden announced his aims in "Our Platform" in his first issue:[7]

1. Elimination of all intolerance, religious or otherwise.

2. Abolishment of all forms of government censorship.

3. Elimination of graft and favoritism in business and politics.

4. Direct primaries for all elective officials.

5. Amendment of all prohibitory laws that infringe constitutional rights as originally interpreted by the framers of the American Constitution.

6. A seat for every person in our subway and elevated trains.

These and other expressed principles showed a no-nonsense approach to lofty and local matters and the front page motto, "NOTHING BUT THE TRUTH,"[8] was also inspiring and elevating. Yet, incongruously, as some felt, the banner headlines to stories failed to catch the same purposeful mood. "SHE GAVE UP ART FOR A BARONET" was one. "I KNOW WHO KILLED MY BROTHER" was another. And then there was "MY FRIENDS DRAGGED ME INTO THE GUTTER." Both of the last two stories and others like them were written in first person form by non-professionals, in keeping with the democratic formula that had proved so successful with *True Story*. The "Gutter" story by Ann Luther was introduced in compelling terms:

"Sunk into the depths of loneliness, Ann Luther, motion picture actress, is today in hiding in Hollywood. Since she lost her $1,000,000 suit against Jack White, wealthy motion picture producer, she has been, she says, 'sick at heart.'[9]

"Once trustful of her fellow beings...she has turned against the world in bitterness. Yet, in her breast burns the desire to have the truth set right before the world, and it is her story of tragedy and battle that she reveals today for the first time to GRAPHICS readers."

Among novel features of the first issue was the "Daily Photo-Drama from Life," an attractive page three spread telling how "Radio Song Opens Gates of Prison to Convict."[10] Also on page three was the first of many contests for readers, a feature designed to increase circulation that was to become the despair of Leslie Cohen, the feature editor, and others who worried about its costs and the endless struggle to come up with fresh gimmicks. The "Miss Courtesy" contest promoted chivalry. Men willing to give up their seats on the subway to the unidentified Miss Courtesy, who would roam the underground world for the purpose, would win a cash prize. But Miss Courtesy would definitely not be wearing the nice bathing suit she wore in the photograph accompanying the contest feature story when she rode the subway.

Cohen gave Macfadden credit for suggesting the Apollo-Diana contest. The publisher had not tossed the idea out merely as a crass popularity scheme. He wished to encourage marriages among young couples resembling Apollo and Diana, "perfect mates for the human race."[11] As readers of *Physical Culture* knew, Macfadden was fascinated by eugenics and devoted to the hope of improving the human race through sensible breeding. But he did not want to worry young, attractive, single New Yorkers with heavy theoretical considerations. All they had to do was come forward, identifying themselves to the *Graphic* and the rest would follow. The newspaper solicited photographs from "marriageable men in full possession of unusual strength and general excellence" and from women who met equally high standards and were ready to provide their measurements and signify interest in "an ideal marriage." Editors would choose the most worthy candidates who would then be introduced to one another at a special banquet. What happened next was up to the winners, but if a romantic spark inspired a couple to marry they would receive a prize of $1,000—and much, much publicity.

After the marriage the couple would have time for serious planning. They would know, if they had read any of Macfadden's works on the subject, that marriage was not an end in itself. Apollo and Diana would not be likely to couple without giving a thought to race betterment. And the *Graphic*, appreciating their needs as well as those of the nation, would award $100 for each child born in the first five years of marriage. To would-be scoffers or prudes who might say unpleasant things about exploiting sex Macfadden had the perfect answer. He had consulted the three ministers who checked the morality of stories submitted to *True*

Story. The reverends had agreed unanimously that the contest did not violate the religious conscience. The Apollo and Diana contest was not Editor Cohen's favorite, nor was one heralded by the headline: "WHO IS THE MOST BEAUTIFUL ITALIAN GIRL IN NEW YORK?" or "WHO IS THE CITY'S BEST CHARLESTON DANCER?" But Cohen did think well of certain contests and believed strongly that the contests, the composite photographs, and Walter Winchell's column were the leading elements in the paper's circulation gains. His heart was in the crossword puzzle contests which attracted thousands of new readers anxious to win the prizes that totaled $1,000. Macfadden was jubilant over the results of the contest as 35,000 individuals sent in their puzzle sets. Against Cohen's advice he insisted that a $25,000 puzzle contest be announced. He was annoyed when only 36,000 sets came in as he expected the same 25 to 1 return achieved on the initial contest. Fleetingly, Cohen headed the biggest department on the paper with a staff of eleven helping him grade puzzle sets.

As drama critic and entertainment editor Walter Winchell presided over a generous allotment of two middle pages. Eventually the *Graphic* lost Winchell to the larger world where his status as America's prime gossip gained him great eminence in journalism and on the radio. Who could recall his truly irritating rasp calling out to radio listeners, including "all the ships at sea," to hear his banalities without reflecting that, in some respects, the world has improved?

Other features included a serial, "The Romance of an Artist's Model." It resembled those in *True Story* and had the kind of romantic photo support and caption that *True Story* readers loved: "He pressed me tightly against him so that I could feel the trembling of his heartbeats."

There were other news columns and features and, of course classified ads and sports. For several years Ed Sullivan served up sports until going on to greater fame as a Hollywood gossiper and, later still, as one of the stiffest, least personable and most inarticulate of early Television show hosts.

Features also included a health page where Macfadden's theories were presented daily. Young Cohen did not like the publisher's attacks on doctors because he revered the memory of his doctor father. Cohen did agree with some of Macfadden's opinions but "his recurrent use of the term Pus Peddlers for doctors who vaccinated and his everlasting spiel about the Body Beautiful rose in my craw."[12]

Cohen also objected to Macfadden's insistence that women bear children by "natural methods," without the assistance of a doctor. At the time he was worried about his pregnant wife and hoped doctors could ease her pains and perils. As a prospective new father he did not dare quit his job so he decided to kill the boss by encouraging him to run barefoot on the snowy fields of Central Park. The notion started as a prank over which he and a friend laughed uproariously. Cohen told his friend that Macfadden would turn out for a dawn run if assured that photographers would be present. "He'll get pneumonia; it'll kill him,"[13] Cohen said. But the attempt on Macfadden's life failed. "Mr. Macfadden ran like crazy in his bare feet. He didn't get pneumonia, he didn't die, he was the picture of his supreme idea: An Athlete's Triumph."

The *Graphic's* staff included two exceedingly talented editors. Feature editor Joseph Applegate's artistry in designing eye-catching layouts was even admired by his rivals. Layout was of prime importance in tabloids where the editors turned away with a vengeance from the dull side-by-side column fixation of most newspapers and magazines. On Saturdays Applegate's genius bloomed even more fully because much of the news gave way to features and, particularly, a magazine and rotogravure section. Managing editor Emil Gauvreau was also highly respected by other newsmen, or, at least, had been before taking over the *Graphic* after being fired by the *Hartford Courant* for crusading that annoyed his publisher. Finding a new job in New York under a publisher who valued modern approaches in a tradition-bound field and one whose zeal for crusades exceeded that of Richard the Lion-Hearted pleased Gauvreau mightily.

Gauvreau was an interesting man. In his youth his family moved from Quebec to Connecticut where young Emil was taunted by schoolmates because of his French accent. By the time he had to leave school for work, after only two years of high school, the lad knew English better than most pupils because he was an omnivorous reader. Music was his other passion and he only reluctantly abandoned his dream of becoming a professional flute player to take his first job as a cub reporter in 1909. Hard-working and perceptive he performed brilliantly and, at the age of 26, was elevated to managing editor of the *Courant*. As managing editor the young man wished to stir up the rather staid newspaper and was successful until one of his rousing investigations upset his masters in Hartford.

When Gauvreau called at Macfadden's office he was interviewed by Fulton Oursler, the publisher's right-hand man. Oursler liked the applicant's background and took him to the boss. Macfadden knew all about Gauvreau's work in Hartford because it had involved the exposure of medical diploma mills, revelations that had amused Macfadden tremendously. The publisher hired Gauvreau on the spot and put him to work immediately. Time was short and all three men and others labored for five months in planning the new paper, originally to be called *The Truth,* and hiring a staff.

Gauvreau complained that Macfadden's "sudden crusades for health led me into extraordinary bypaths,"[14] but he knew better than to resist any of the publisher's plans. The man hired to answer the health letters from readers "who felt badly, perhaps after having read our paper," told them to drink orange juice or paint it with iodine. Yet readers did tell Gauvreau that they improved after following advice given in the paper and he came to believe that an orange juice regime would have helped him more than the whiskey he poured down during those hectic years.

Gauvreau laughed at the articles the paper published on "brain breathing," involving a series of exercises of the neck to induce more active cerebration. The neck movements had to be coordinated with inhaling through one nostril only. Newsroom staffers, who tried the exercises out at their desks, reported wonderful recoveries from their hangovers. When Macfadden brought in a man who had cured himself of the drug habit through physical culture methods and had the paper announce free consultations to all addicts, Gauvreau was less amused. "That evening our editorial rooms were turned into a raving asylum by all manner of terrifying, shaking creatures who crawled with pawing hands over shuddering copyreaders, climbed on chairs and finally had complete possession of the place."[15] Staff had to call the police to get their visitors ejected.

Macfadden's adherence to his health principles did not, in Gauvreau's opinion, help the paper make money. People did not particularly want to hear "that right was on the scaffold and wrong was on the throne in medical affairs,"[16] but the editorial line was never abandoned. Sometimes the editorial line on doctors carried over into dubious news stories as with one in May 1925 insisting that the AMA Convention had broken up early: "Many of the 3,000 doctors are leaving to go home because of a fight in the ranks."[17] Most refused "to listen to discussions of the much advertised medical ethics, the values of certain much advertised medicines, and the reports of slip-shod work by physicians which resulted in the death of patients."

Gauvreau, while personally a man of refined, literate tastes, appreciated that most newspaper readers did not read Shakespeare. His intellectual friends, dismayed when the *Graphic* appeared, could not make the same distinction: "They were petrified with astonishment and shunned me as a pariah in a cafeteria where we had been gathering for breakfast for intellectual discourses."[18]

Gauvreau, a small, pleasant looking fellow who limped from a boyhood accident, was a favorite of Cohen. Another of his favorites was John W. Vandercook, the feature editor, who affected English "bags," as the then fashionable, extra-wide tweed trousers were called, and spoke in complete, grammatically precise sentences. Vandercook crossed swords with Oursler over some matter of editorial policy and resigned. Later he wrote *Black Majesty,* a best selling novel.

Neither Cohen nor Gauvreau could stand Oursler. Cohen described him as tall, lean, and secretive looking. Staffers appreciated his shrewdness but they did not trust him. Gauvreau respected but did not love his rival for Macfadden's ear, "a tall, dark, intensive man with penetrating eyes and a long nose, an executive of staggering energies who drained quarts of milk in his office and smoked cigarettes until he was shrouded in smoke."[19]

John L. Spivak was the *Graphic's* star investigative reporter, a skilled writer who would later include some reminiscences of his work with the paper in his memoirs. Another talented reporter was Alma Sioux Scarberry, tall, attractive, capable, part-Indian; she had transferred to the newspaper from one of Macfadden's magazines to become an effective reporter of murder cases and other sensational events. She made mild fun of the publisher's foibles but had harder words for Oursler. When, much later on, Oursler published his immensely popular retelling of the Biblical story, *The Greatest Story Ever Told,* Alma sneered at a man "who would take the Holy Bible and try to serialize it!"[20]

Macfadden had purchased the equipment and building of the defunct *Evening Mail* located on what was then City Hall Place. From the start there was a desperation to do better than the *Mirror* and the *Journal,* especially the *Journal,* another Hearst newspaper that was Macfadden's chief rival in the afternoon field. Gauvreau bragged of the angry reaction of Hearst in firing three of his editors in one afternoon for allowing the *Graphic* to catch up to the *Journal* in circulation, but for most of its existence Macfadden's tabloid did not threaten either the two leading tabloids or conventional newspapers. With his many other enterprises the publisher could not devote full time to the newspaper but his attention, day and night, was enough to keep Gauvreau moving in a frenzy: "My days became kaleidoscopic, my nights uncertain. Macfadden often awakened me at three o'clock in the morning with a circulation idea."[21] One of the ideas was good enough to boom circulation 30,000 a day, as when the publisher ordered him to run a front page photo of a convict executed at Sing Sing the night before. The photo must fill the entire page except for the two-word caption in two inch letters: "ROASTED ALIVE!" Macfadden hated capital punishment and never missed a chance to shock people into sharing his view.

Needless to say the paper had a contest on capital punishment, a best letter competition announced by the headline: "PEOPLE DENOUNCE LEGAL MURDER." Editor Cohen was pleased to work hard on this project because he supported the publisher's position. To lend respectability to the cause he was able to secure the cooperation of two famed lawyers, Judge Ben Lindsay of Denver, the juvenile court reformer, and the celebrated attorney, Clarence Darrow, whose eloquence on the subject had often swayed jurors to acquit his clients.

Gauvreau did not deny that the drive for circulation forced him to exceed journalistic niceties at times. He had to "make" the news on slow days: "We could no longer wait for calamities to happen. Characters were built up and paraded. Hot news became the wild, blazing, delirious symptom of the time."[22] One of the editor's most imaginative helpers was Terry Turner, a theatrical press agent Gauvreau valued because his audacity seemed limitless. Both men, however, were relieved when the American Medical Association stepped in to prevent one of Turner's schemes involving the separation of two female Siamese twins by surgery. Since the sisters were keen to marry they had gone along with Turner's suggestion that the newspaper sponsor an operation and keep a close look on subsequent events. Doctors refused to perform the operation and a great story—or perhaps a great disaster—was averted.

The *Graphic* dashed along its particular road as the twenties rolled on. A sampling of feature story headlines shows the consistent editorial policy:

I AM NOW THE MOTHER OF MY SISTER'S SON.[23]
I STARTED AS A NEWSBOY SAYS HEAD OF BANK.
HE BEAT ME—I LOVE HIM.
RUDY ASKS $1,433,000 FOR KISSES.
MY BACK WAS BROKEN BUT I KEPT ON LAUGHING.
LOVER'S LURE LEADS LAD TO GATES OF DEATH.
THOUSANDS APPLAUD WHILE WOMAN IS TORTURED FOR AMUSEMENT.
FOR 36 HOURS I LIVED ANOTHER WOMAN'S LIFE.
DANCER'S HEART BROKEN.

The lead of the dancer's story got right to the core of the matter: "Oh, if only my mother had told me the great truths of sex and if there had been a baby, it might have been different." Some might criticize a story like this with its wretched lead but the tale illustrated one of the publisher's favorite themes: the need for sex education.

One diligent student of journalism made a careful survey of the March 2, 1925 *Graphic's* 1,568 inches of space. Advertisements, to the publisher's regret, only took up 200 inches; news took 175. This left the remaining 75 percent of the paper for headlines, pictures, features, and fiction. Three front page headlines declared what seemed significant that day:

MILLIONAIRE TRIED AS SLAYER.[24]
SMOTHERS DANCE HALL LOVE.
FUROR OVER ANTI-PRUDE SCHOOL.

The last story was a scoop. No other New York newspaper reported on the small school in Suffolk, England, where students were allowed to play in the nude. The very brief story about the incident on page 3 did not make clear what the furor had been over the pre-adolescent students. It was as if the devotion of one third of the front page to the headline had drained all that might have been newsy about the topic.

The paper was refreshing. Where else could one read a new play's review by some private individual, an amateur or "man-in-the-street," who sat next to Winchell on opening night, then wrote his opinions which received equal billing with that of the illustrious Winchell? What other readers received free singing classes or ukulele lessons and could hope to meet the love of their life through the lonely hearts feature? Where else could you find free medical advice, including the opportunity to come into the newspaper office for a consultation? Who else dispatched a woman to do comparative shopping around town (a novelty then) and published the prices of various items she purchased? And where else were reporters directed to ignore the pretense of aloof neutrality in news reporting and comment on the moral implications of the event?

Walter Winchell's popularity was one of the *Graphic's* conspicuous successes. Gauvreau had hired him on Fulton Oursler's recommendation and the editor took some credit in his memoir for giving Winchell the freedom to gossip along lines that no other newspaper would have ever allowed. Yet no love was lost between Gauvreau and Winchell. The editor was astonished at the columnist's gall and arrogance, mocking his "hunched figure with a white lean face of deceptive humility...No stranger phenomenon has yet appeared in the newspaper business. Gossip acquired such a tangibility, such a grip on his life, chiefly from the bare nucleus of a slim fact that, many times, he was more often cleverly wrong than monotonously correct."[25]

Gauvreau expected the young man, who had had more time as a vaudeville "hoofer" than as a writer, to accept guidance. But Winchell had his own notions about writing: "his refreshing *insouciance* about the difference between a subject and a predicate became an ironical asset which preserved his personality and may have had the virtue of saving him years of learning to be like everybody else. In his pate rattled more than a grain of genius which was to produce a 'slanguage' often too puzzling for the venerable gentlemen of the courts who were not permitted to go to old man Webster."[26]

According to Winchell's biographer, Walter started off tamely enough with reports on show castings and some of his bad verse and jokes.[27] In time he developed his penchant for "verbal fornication," mating words like "cinemagic," "playbore," and others. Soon he turned to risque gossipy items linking stars and other celebrities in liaisons, sometimes regardless of reality. Gauvreau encouraged him initially when he began pulling more fan mail than anyone else on the paper. Walter grew ever bolder with his tidbits exposing the romantic affairs of celebrated folks and Gauvreau tried to restrain him. Restraining anyone on the paper was not a comfortable position for Gauvreau, the unblushing perpetrator of daily vulgarities that sometimes scandalized the most hardened newsmen in New York. A wag remarked that Gauvreau's sudden "morality" resembled that of a prostitute who objected to profanity.

As Winchell and Gauvreau, two power hungry characters, fought daily battles, the writer received the welcome support of Oursler. Why Oursler, who was always anxious about Gauvreau's excesses, would defend Winchell's reckless course is not clear. Probably it was out of perversity and hatred of Gauvreau, or because he hoped a disaster to Winchell would bring the editor down too. But, obviously, by the standards of the *Graphic*, which Gauvreau had done much to shape, Winchell was on the right path. Winchell revolutionized entertainment world reporting, paving the way for a multitude of imitators, including such popular modern expansions of gossip columns as the *National Enquirer*.

Among the wonders of Winchell's career was the forbearance granted his tortured but readable (it was always claimed) style and unsurpassed audacity by journalists who really knew how to write. Heywood Broun argued that Winchell was the only thing worth reading in the *Graphic*, which was probably not overwhelming praise. But Alexander Woollcott praised him in a magazine piece and other Algonquin Round Table luminaries felt good about discovering a new star on the vulgar scene. Only Damon Runyon dissented.

Gauvreau continued to take what pleasures he could from Winchell's presence by pointing out that he had inaccurately identified writer Emile Zola as a woman and had described an ocean liner docking at the port of Paris. But Winchell freed himself from his contract dependence upon the *Graphic* by showing Hearst editors a faked offer of employment from the *New York World*. Thus stimulated, and keen to take a popular writer away from Macfadden, Hearst matched the fake *World* offer. Macfadden refused to let Winchell break his contract despite the writer's harassing phone calls late at night. Finally, as Winchell's own story relates, he was inspired to threaten Macfadden: he would make it known that he had seen the publisher eating lamb chops and other meats in defiance of vegetarian principles. Macfadden released the gossiper who joined the *Mirror* with great glee. His joy faded some time later when Gauvreau showed up at the *Mirror* as his new editor.

In his published works Fulton Oursler made heroic efforts to defend the *Graphic*, arguing that the "bitterness and denunciations" derived in large part from critics who never read the paper. He liked to stress that the paper had many loyal fans. Gauvreau, too, had been surprised at the numbers and zeal of the paper's steadfast patrons, "a mysterious army of followers of the physical culturist's principles. In New York there were thousands of them, all loyal subscribers to *Physical Culture*. They bought Macfadden's daily paper religiously and soon came down in droves to help me run it."[29]

Both Oursler and Gauvreau believed that the loyalty of readers derived from the publisher's adherence to his principles. Macfadden had promised that the *Graphic* would be the first tabloid with a "serious purpose" behind it and never backed away to gain popularity. Historians of "Jazz journalism" have insisted that the *Graphic's* only aim—and one it remained true to—was circulation building. Of course, the aim of circulation building does not really need to be defended and perhaps would not be attacked were it not for Macfadden's insistence that his motivation was elevated and the aping of this shaky assertion by his loyalists.

Oursler's true feelings on the *Graphic* differed considerably from those he expressed publicly. He blamed Gauvreau for creating "the Frankenstein monster"[30] of the newspaper world: "It was a riotous, red-hot, rampaging scandal sheet." The editor's trade-mark was "manufacturing scandals for the paper to expose," and the low point was the Daddy Browning and Peaches affair, an escapade conducted by the participants under contract to the *Graphic*.

Edward W. Browning, an eccentric, middle-aged, millionaire rake, married Peaches Heenan, a ripe 15-year old, in a mismatch that upset society and intrigued newspaper readers. When the couple's bliss ended in a divorce suit even the conservative newspapers like the *World* and the *Times* covered their screaming, defamatory courtroom appearances. But the *Graphic* made the couple's shattered romance a story of transcendent import. Gauvreau, according to Oursler, left nothing to chance after agreeing with Peaches that her true story would appear in a series of articles explaining her desperate need to escape from Browning. On the night the editor and Peaches selected for her flight from the Browning mansion Gauvreau provided the ladder.

Oursler complained often to Macfadden, begging him to restrain Gauvreau's mad-cap schemes, only to hear the publisher brag about increases in circulation. Macfadden went even further to show his appreciation of Gauvreau by thanking Oursler heartily for introducing him to such an inventive editor. Oursler's attempts to ignore Gauvreau's excesses were no more successful than efforts to slow him down. Macfadden required Oursler to spend his mornings at the *Graphic* before taking up his afternoon duties supervising all the magazines. The hours at the *Graphic* were not productive because Gauvreau ignored him and because the newsroom was conducted like a madhouse. It would be easier,

Oursler believed, for a minister, while delivering a sermon, to ignore a naked lunatic dancing up and down the church aisle than for an editor to concentrate in the newsroom. Besides, Oursler's duties included that of cleaning up after Gauvreau's work as libel suit followed libel suit, asking in all a total of $7,000,000. Oursler conferred with the *Graphic's* lawyers on strategy and the team did very well standing off injured parties—only $5,290 was paid in damages and settlements, which indicates the solicitude of the courts for freedom of the press.

Poor Oursler could not even laugh at incidents that sent waves of merriment through every newsroom in the city. The best of these stories concerned the misfiring of the *Graphic's* justly popular Lonely Hearts Contest that had evolved into a kind of a dating bureau. One day a furious woman burst into the *Graphic's* newsroom, deposited a bundle on Gauvreau's desk, and shouted: "That's one of your god-damned lonely hearts."[31] After she stomped out the staff warily examined the bundle to find a cooing baby.

John Spivak, a *Graphic* reporter, credited Oursler with directing an effort to bring more "romance" to the paper. Spivak followed up a *News* story of the previous day recounting the suicide of an unidentified young man in a Newark rooming house. While trying to figure out how this sad event could become newsworthy Spivak bumped into Norman Carroll, brother and business manager for Earl Carroll, the famed showman whose "Vanities" was the rage of the New York stage for years. Carroll and Spivak put their heads together over a drink and came up with a chorus girl and a front page story in the following day's *Graphic:*

"Possessed by a mad and hopeless love for a young and beautiful Broadway dancer who extended him many kindnesses but rejected his frenzied wooing, an unidentified young poet ended his life yesterday by inhaling gas...In a farewell letter he disclosed his infatuation for the charming 23-year old member of Earl Carroll's 'Vanities.' Because of her coldness...he had decided to 'cash in his chips on this merry little game of life and love.' "[32]

Another *Graphic* involvement with Earl Carroll was anything but the result of a collaboration. Macfadden may have been a little jealous that Carroll's much bally-hooed bathing beauty contests at Coney Island had become popular events in a field that he had pioneered. But, whatever his motivation, the *Graphic* charged that the contests at Coney Island and Atlantic City were fixed. The exposure made a great story because bathing beauty contests were stimulating, popular events—and the *Graphic* gained circulation. Whether Macfadden actually had more than a rumor to go on is not clear and was not determined by legal proceedings after Carroll and the city managers of Atlantic City sued the publisher for $4,000,000. After dragging on for some time the suit was dropped. Macfadden continued to bad-mouth Carroll through unfavorable reviews of the promoter's various shows.[33] Other papers joined in the fun on occasion. A writer in the *Morning Telegraph* wondered why nudes were "art" in Macfadden's publications but "orgy women" in Carroll's shows.[34] Macfadden sneered at those who could not distinguish his service to strength and health from the lascivious sex scenes Carroll featured.

The *Graphic* had a hand in Carroll's criminal prosecution over another matter. As the popular Irishman and *bon vivant* gave as much care to entertaining guests in his home as on the stage he once gave friends the spectacle of one of his lovely showgirls bathing naked in a tub of champagne. After inquiries were made in connection with a lawsuit Carroll lied about it: "it was ginger ale,"[35] he said under oath, and then was tried and convicted of perjury.

The most shameful exploitation of a murder case that occurred in the twenties can not be added to the long list of tasteless treatment of sensational events for which the *Graphic* was responsible. The murder in 1922 of a New Jersey minister, Edward Hall, and his choir-singer lover, Eleanor Mills, remained an unsolved case for a long time. But the ingredients for a true newspaper sensation compelled the *Mirror* to campaign relentlessly for the indictment of the minister's widow. By the time of trial the affair had become so celebrated that there were 200 reporters covering it, many representing distant newspapers. Mrs. Hall was acquitted and it became apparent that the prosecution's case had little more substance than that provided by editor Philip Payne of the *Mirror,* whose use of the case for circulation-building was exposed.

But the barrage of post-trial criticism of newspapers also included the *Graphic* and Macfadden saw a chance to show his essential high purposes. In an editorial he challenged the New York press to limit their coverage of the trial of Ruth Snyder and Judd Gray which threatened to be as sensational and as well covered as the Hall-Mills fiasco. According to police, Snyder and Gray were adulterous lovers who killed Ruth's husband for their own convenience. The press saw it as the great story of 1927 because a woman was involved and stood a good chance of being executed. Newspapers ignored Macfadden's offer to limit his coverage if they would limit theirs and made the sordid, banal killing a tremendously publicized event. Macfadden tried to shame the other editors by limiting his coverage to an extremely modest 500 words daily.

Macfadden hired the famous Los Angeles evangelist, Aimee Semple McPherson, to write about the proceedings. He did not usually believe in using big names as writers but figured that Aimee would have particular insight because of her clerical connection.

Aimee accepted the assignment to earn a few dollars and distract public attention from one of the great sex scandals involving preachers in the early twentieth century. Her disappearance late in 1926— presumably an accidental drowning—and reappearance with a far-fetched story of a kidnapping had been heralded by the *Graphic* and other newspapers. It was generally believed that she had been living in sinful bliss with a married man on the beach at Carmel. Aimee's popularity fell off somewhat but her career demonstrated that California held lots of gold for a beautiful young woman whose sexy voice exploited the Scriptures on the radio. Novelist Sinclair Lewis probably used Aimee as the model for a leading character in his *Elmer Gantry* although he denied her inspiration.

Aimee's reports on the Snyder-Gray affair were as effective as her preaching. She knew what the *Graphic* wanted and provided stirring accounts of "sin caves," the gaudy nightspots that attracted Judd Gray and weakened his spine to the point of planning a murder to keep his illicit lover. What shall it be, Aimee asked, "the sunshine of the cross or the shadow of the chair? As ye sow, so shall ye reap."[36] As for Ruth Snyder, well, any writer might describe her problem, but hearing it from Aimee shortly after her own exciting escapades was particularly tantalizing: "Lust is the poison that drives women mad."

Snyder and Gray were convicted and sentenced to death. Now the *Graphic*, perhaps regretting its handling of the trial, grasped for a chunk of the action. Following its long-established ploy the *Graphic* sought to thrill readers and frustrate rivals with a major coup:

"Don't fail to read tomorrow's *Graphic*. An installment that thrills and stuns! A story that fairly pierces the heart and reveals Ruth Snyder's last thoughts on earth; that pulses the blood as it discloses her final letters. Think of it! A woman's final thoughts just before she is clutched in the deadly snare that sears and burns and FRIES AND KILLS! Her very last words! Exclusively in tomorrow's *Graphic*."[37]

As the management of the *Graphic* waited for the execution they had reason to feel that they had a scoop of unheard of proportions. And, in an orderly world, they might have been right and reaped just rewards. But the world of the twenties' tabloid journalism was not orderly and the *News* schemed to scoop its rivals as they had never been scooped before. The *News* dispatched photographer Tom Howard to the death house at Sing Sing. Taking pictures of an execution was banned, of course, although it is hard to imagine what use could be made of such pictures were they allowed. Who would publish such gruesome pictures? What readers would wish to see a woman writhing on the electric chair in her death agony? *News* editors knew the answer to both questions. Howard raised his ankle just before the juice went on, snapping the scene with a miniature camera strapped to his lower leg. The precious photograph was then rushed to the *News's* art department for some touching up that reflect the most electrifying moment of the scene and, next day, the infamous picture filled the front page. An extra edition sold 250,000 copies and a second extra of 750,000 copies went too.

One of the Gauvreau innovations that was much criticized was the use of composite photography, which was the polite and technical term for a faked photograph using models to support a news story. Gauvreau always insisted that he had no intent to deceive because such photographs were always identified as "composographs," although a reader required very good eye-sight and much curiosity before he might notice any identification. It was the thrilling society divorce case of Kip Rhinelander that inspired the first use of composographs. The wealthy playboy demanded his freedom from his wife, claiming that she had not mentioned before marriage that she was part black. She argued that Kip or anyone else should have been able to see her obvious racial characteristics and offered to unveil herself in court to make her point. For this occasion the judge cleared the courtroom of non-essential watchers so Gauvreau turned to his art department for help. The result was a great circulation-building front page photo of a courtroom scene, a group of lawyers, and a woman stripped to the waist—a fine studio production.

With such a success at the start the composograph became a standard feature. It certainly did help liven news stories, particularly crime stories, but it was used whenever Gauvreau thought that it would be effective, as in illustrating the visitation of the Holy Ghost in the form of tongues of fire to the congregation of a popular preacher and, most notably, in promoting the serial biography of film idol Rudolph Valentino after his death. "I produced an illustration, by our new method," Gauvreau recalled, "showing the moving-picture actor entering the spirit world and meeting a number of celebrities who had passed on before him."[38] Readers responded: circulation increased immediately by 100,000.

But Gauvreau admitted his mistake with the Browning story, which represents one of the most tasteless uses of photography, real or faked, in the annals of journalism. Daddy and Peaches had happier moments early in their marriage and Peaches told about how much fun they had playing "doggie." And there they were, posed by models but with their own faces attached, pictured on the floor of their bedroom under the headline "WOOF, WOOF, I'M A GOOF." Daddy Browning was a great help to Gauvreau in keeping the scandal alive. He agreed to accept a gander as a pet and led it around the streets of the city, presumably so that a photograph captioned, "HONK, HONK, IT'S THE BONK," could be published.

The composograph had not originated with the *Graphic*. It had been used sparingly by other papers from time to time. In 1925 the *News* used such a photo to illustrate an earthquake and perhaps inspired Gauvreau to take up the art. But only the *Graphic* used it frequently and, happily, the art form did not pass into general use after the *Graphic* folded.

John S. Sumner, Comstock's successor at the New York Society for the Suppression of Vice struck at the *Graphic* for its treatment of the Browning story in February 1927. He had frightened Macfadden into the abrupt suspension of his first newspaper, *Midnight*, a weekly which appeared briefly in 1922. The thrust of *Midnight* was that New York was coming apart at the seams. Usually a clergyman wrote an editorial denouncing the city's moral depravity, then the news pages illustrated social frivolity and crime with relish. But, with the *Graphic*, Macfadden refused to buckle under. Macfadden wanted New York's best criminal attorney and tried to retain William Travers Jerome, famed as the prosecutor of Harry Thaw, the crazed millionaire slayer of architect Stanford White, and for many other celebrated court battles. Jerome, an old man past his prime was not up to dealing with the tawdry world of tabloid sensationalism, but his response to the newspaper created the best among a legion of stories on the paper. After listening to Gauvreau and Macfadden explain Sumner's charges Jerome asked to see a copy of the tabloid as he had not previously heard of it or of Daddy Browning. Jerome looked the paper over, adjusted his glasses to make sure they were right, then hurriedly returned the paper: "Plead guilty,"[39] he urged and showed his callers out.

Max Steur, equally famed as an attorney but younger and more active as a criminal lawyer, knew all about the *Graphic* and Daddy Browning. Nonetheless he took the case with enthusiasm and won an acquittal. The great days of Comstockery were past.

Time magazine waded into Macfadden over the Browning affair, castigating him for his "orgy of pornography"[40] and for trying to get more mileage out of the long-running Harry Thaw scandal. Thaw had escaped from an asylum so the *Graphic* refreshed readers' memories of an earlier scandal with a composite photograph showing Thaw trying to strangle a young girl. The magazine derided the newspaper's claim that its intent was only to warn young girls to be careful. "What maid, wife, or widow," asked the magazine, "needs further warning against Harry Thaw?" In a review of Macfadden's brushes with the law and attempts to improve New York's health from 1901 the magazine concluded: "He was as militant as any Irishman with an undigested dose of religion; he was out to make the world safe for healthy bodies," but, eventually, this "apostle of the corporeal" learned that big money could be made in exploiting the human form.

Macfadden's own defense of his paper was probably best expressed by Clement Wood, one of his biographers, an effusive writer who earned every cent the publisher paid him. Although Wood smoked and avoided fasting like the plague he admired Macfadden and all his works with all of his being. He believed that the editorials in other newspapers were mere "applesauce" compared with those his boss penned for the *Graphic*, and his tone commands our respect: "Look at it, in its startling entirety: editorials on raw turnips, on eliminating breakfast, on curves of the bust, on eliminating hats, on wet feet, fat wives, white flour, sleeping sickness, Henry Ford's eating, and so on and so on. The collective force of these new-visioned editorials is worthy of measurement by Einstein."[41]

Charges that the *Graphic* was a "pandering sheet," that it exploited sensational stories for the purpose of depraving public taste, were, Wood insisted, clearly refuted by a review of the paper's contents. "There is no pandering, no incitement to depravity, no cheap hothousing of sex...There are, instead, swiftly moving, brilliantly written stories, which present the gist of the news at a tempo attuned to the hectic rush of modern city life...and, of course, the flood of pictures interpreting the stories, so that the eye may fully understand what is to be said."[42] Wood believed that the *Graphic's* editorials made the paper a positive force so great "that any faults elsewhere in the paper shrink to nothingness." Macfadden was a great and wise man: "He is an Elijah, a Paul, a Savonarola, preaching the gospel of health," increasing the health, beauty, happiness, and success of thousands of people.

Gauvreau believed that the *Graphic* followed the standard ploy set by Macfadden-Oursler for all publications: "First, you denounced and deplored, in a blazing editorial, what you were going to print: then you went ahead and printed it with astounding illustrations."[43]

In discussing the newspaper in his autobiography Oursler did not insist that he was "holier" than Macfadden and Gauvreau during his early years with them: "In those days I could accept anything that could be made to pay with the public." He wanted money, fame, and influence just as they did—but he does confess that he was "cannier" in understanding what was going on: "Whether from cunning or experience, I knew that they were wrong. Not all the things we did were wrong, but they were done in the wrong way."[44]

With the economic crash of 1929 the *Graphic's* circulation was 350,000, far short of the publisher's expectations. The *News* and even the *Mirror* became more serious about social issues as the depression deepened while the *Graphic* continued along its familiar way. Since Macfadden had always been serious about the purpose of his newspaper he saw no reason to change anything just because the world was falling down. Critics thought that his resistance to more somber times was a perpetuation of the gay abandonment that had been the spirit of the twenties, and advertisers, always a little leery about using the *Graphic*, liked the tabloid even less. Circulation dropped in 1930 and Macfadden's stockholders who objected to the lack of profits, forced him to close down the newspaper in 1932.

Chapter 10
Age of Macfadden

Money, beyond the power it gives, has but little value to me.

Bernarr Macfadden

Did success spoil Macfadden and draw him to rich foods and soft living? Indeed not. The Spartan warrior used all of his increasing wealth and influence in the twenties in persistent rides—more like cavalry charges—on his familiar hobby horses. Among the folds and seams on his aging body he found new muscles to flex and nurture, and for his number one patient, the American public, he devised new blessings. As he had never taken a vacation during the first half century of his life he saw no reason to hold back from his mission during his second half century. He would not live forever—only 125 years, by his careful calculation. When one has learned how to milk the heart of a nation to the magnificent purpose of creating the Kingdom of Health it is not time to relax. Awareness of one's power and influence for good made his heart light and his step brisk. The trumpets of stern duty sounded louder and louder, making the most beautiful music a dedicated man could hear.

He seemed always to know what to do next and how best to ration his day. As he fostered new magazines and the *Graphic* he did not neglect *Physical Culture*, his flagship and favorite, nor his health research and new inventions. But first and last he was a crusader for the best causes. Look to the *Physical Culture* editorials to see what these were: the promotion of the harem skirt ("loose fitting, thus healthy");[1] grass eating ("nutritious for humans too;" this was not really his idea but a photograph of the author grazing in a field in top hat and opera cloak was); having babies without doctors ("nature's way"); boxing with feet ("devastating"); headstanding to cure baldness ("a matter of currents"); wearing fewer clothes ("sensible"); discarding hats ("they cause baldness"); and teaching folks how to live on five cents a day ("nothing to it").

Macfadden could see the success of his teachings in the 1920s. Girls started playing tennis in shorts and sweat shirts, discarding hampering skirts. Other had joined his anti-white bread campaign and hat manufacturers were extremely angry over his attacks on hats. More people were exercising and concern about diet was widespread. He noted that

153

much of the diet faddism had more to do with the evolving terror of obesity than a sensible selection of the healthiest foods, but people were eating less if not for the correct reasons. No one had to worry about getting fat if they exercised, lived a healthy life, and fasted periodically to keep the system running sweetly.

He had threatened the livelihood of corset makers who now advertised new "healthy" models but he made no headway with cigarette and cigar smokers. He attacked colleges as "cesspools" of alcohol filled with cigarette suckers. Self-made men did not usually champion education and students, in their turn, found much humor in lampooning his muscle emphasis.

No one ever accused him of having a thin skin. He loved to court publicity by demonstrating to news photographers the benefits of standing on his head for some time every day. If people laughed, so what. He did not mind risking ridicule but it was not because of his fun-loving ways. Fun and humor were not too important to one who was devoted to a heavy, earnest mission. He knew himself to be a great teacher and proved it by various ways, as by showing newsmen how he scrambled around on all fours gorilla fashion for a time each day. At the moment he had been very keen on the discovery that the gorilla movements made the spine stronger and, if family members would all adopt it, they would make expensive furniture obsolete.

So people laughed and mocked but continued to read his magazines (*Physical Culture* readers, it should be said, did not laugh). Mary Macfadden did not like to see him becoming a figure of ridicule but he dismissed her concern: Let them laugh. "The fools are giving me a million dollars' worth of publicity. Ford is being laughed at the same way."[2] Occasionally he won a major disciple and gained favorable publicity. The public really admired Henry Ford in the twenties even if they did not quite love him. When all the newspapers showed photographs of Ford and Macfadden chatting together in amiable agreement on many facets of life, Macfadden's stock rose with the public. Ford liked the notion of a cracked wheat diet for working men and opposed their drinking of alcohol. Both men agreed that "history is bunk" without reading any; they agreed too that labor unions were bunk. As captains of large industries catering to public taste each man could see how the other fit into the world. Macfadden could not help thinking that his obsession was more beneficial to mankind than making automobiles likely to make lazy folks lazier, but he did not say this to Ford.

Macfadden believed that he had influenced the changing sex mores of the early 1920s. It was not that he approved of illegal drinking or the place of the automobile in creating opportunities for lovers, but he liked shorter skirts for women and the public's receptivity to serious discussions of sex. He was enchanted when the muckraking author George Creel, who had been the nation's chief of public information during World War I, introduced him to Judge Ben Lindsey. Lindsey had first attracted national attention for his reforms of the Juvenile and Family Court of Denver, his battles with public utilities companies of Colorado, and his provocative criticisms of laws on prostitution and other sex crimes. Lindsey wanted to write a series of articles for *Physical Culture* on the youthful generation, emphasizing its sexual conduct and attitudes, and Macfadden was delighted with the idea. Lindsey collaborated with a professional writer, Wainwright Evans, and the articles appeared in the magazine in 1924 and as a book, *The Revolt of Modern Youth,* in 1925. Lindsey's articles evoked a great stir and much public controversy. He had used case histories of young women in their teens and early twenties as the basis for his observations on the inadequacy of parents and the society in responding to sexual matters. This was one of Macfadden's familiar editorial themes and it was heartening to him that a recognized authority had evidence to confirm his theories.

Lindsey's work was timely and of lasting value. He indicted clergymen, educators, and all others who wished to "terrorize people into being good."[3] He believed that they acted out of cruelty, ignorance, and smugness and were responsible for ruining many young lives. Two years later Lindsey produced another book that created a storm of controversy, *The Companionate Marriage.* Macfadden did not get the chance to publish the original articles this time but the themes included some he heartily supported. Lindsey called for compulsory sex education, legal contraception, and liberalization of divorce laws.[4]

Bernarr and Mary changed residences several times before finding a suitable home at Nyack, New Jersey, then, more permanently, at Englewood Cliffs, NJ. Getting Bernarr to settle on a residence caused Mary some difficulty as he liked the idea of making his home in a building that could also earn money as a sanitarium. Mary continued to argue the needs of the growing family—her fourth daughter was born in 1918 and Helen, offspring of Macfadden's second marriage, was also part of the family. And more "perfect" Macfadden specimens were to come. Bernarr, who had changed his own name to make it more impressive named his children Byrne, Byrnece, Beulah, Braunda, Beverly, Berwyn, and Bruce.

The Macfaddens were reasonably social despite the demands of business and family. Week-end visitors were common although they tended to be magazine editors and writers. Sanford Bennett was one favorite of Mary's because he was an elderly countryman with whom she could exchange reminiscences of England. He helped edit *Physical Culture* and his manner of dieting intrigued Bernarr, who figured that Bennett would probably live to be 100 years old. Mary always called

Bennett "the Old Roman Regurgitator."[5] As an accomplished *raconteur* Bennett would probably have been welcomed widely as a dinner guest save for his diet methods. After a hearty meal and stimulating talk he excused himself to vomit into the brass bowl he always brought along. Mary believed that the nerves of many hostesses, who could have found no reference to the situation in Emily Post, were spared when Bennett choked to death on a chicken bone.

At Nyack neighbors thought Macfadden a little eccentric in ordering the construction of Missouri-style porches around the perimeter of the large family home. They were also amused by what they knew of his carrot eating propensities and the signs of intense physical training noticeable around the place, particularly as the girls grew older. But Macfadden ranked a distant second among characters when compared with Oom the Omnipotent, who also lived in Nyack.

Oom was a physical culturist who discovered the means of restoring youth to wealthy women of the post-menopause age. The slender, pasty-faced man of high forehead, long nose, dimpled chin, whose eyes could look deeply into the hearts of women had taken a twisted path to Nyack and fame. As Pierre Bernard, born about 1875, he had followed the trade of his father, a barber of Iowa, in Chicago and California. New York police arrested him in 1905 when he called himself Homer Stansbury Leeds, for an indecent assault on a minor. He moved to Seattle to found the Tantrik Order of America and marry a dancer named Blanche. He claimed to have learned his Tantra system from a Syrian who had picked it up in India. Tantra was a Sanskrit cult of magic and mysticism derived from the dialogues between the Hindu god Siva and his wife, Parvutti— chats that included some richly salacious exchanges. Tantriks sought the beautiful and the sublime through communion with nubile young girls in a sex worship service.

When Tantrik failed to grip Seattle Bernard moved to New York as Oom in 1910, taking cheap premises on the West Side. On the complaints of two teenage girls police broke in to discover signs that Oom's physical culture training was a cover for an erotic cult. A nice scandal and successful prosecution was ruined when the young women, very late teenagers, confessed that Oom's delay in marrying them as promised had induced their charges of abduction.

Oom moved to upper Broadway where neighbors were upset by the late-night arrival of fancy cars bearing fashionably dressed women and, later yet, an unpleasant mingling of screams with Oriental music. Oom protested the persecution by police of his "Sanskrit school," then moved to Nyack in 1919 to found the Braeburn Country Club. His kind of physical culture attracted up to 100 women who wore bloomers and sandals while exercising. By 1924 Oom was rich enough to pay $200,000 for a 265 acre Nyack estate.

Oom and Macfadden were friendly neighbors. Oom consulted Macfadden on the diet he prepared for his special guests and always greeted him by bowing low and extending his arms, palms down. Macfadden was interested in Oom's work just as he had been fascinated by John Alexander Dowie and Thomas Lake Harris, other great pitchmen of the erotic and exotic.

Although his turban, robes, and mystic mumbo-jumbo had contributed to his fortune Oom came in time to prefer conservative English tweeds and mainstream participation in life. He became a bank president, a chamber of commerce treasurer, the director of a trust company, and a partner in two factories. When interviewed in 1931 he boasted of having 400 members in his country club—"just a lot of nice wealthy people interested in beauty and books."[6] Members included such great names as Vanderbilt, Alexander, Mills, and Turnbull. Old Oom had come a long way from his disreputable storefronts of Seattle, the West Side, and Broadway. His summation of an amazing career revealed something of the giddy horizons imaginative physical culturists might aspire to: "I'm a curious combination of the businessman and the religious scholar," he told Joseph Mitchell. "I'm just a man of common sense in love with beauty and that sort of thing. There ain't no nudist cult here. No sir, nothing like that. Acrobatic exercises for men and women, lectures on art and philosophy, nice little things like that. We take sufferers from melancholia, old boys threatening to commit suicide, and build them up."[7]

Oom became richer and richer and achieved a formidable respectability down the years. He built the Nyack Stadium and helped train some heavyweight boxers. Perhaps it was because he was not nearly as earnest and sincere as Macfadden that he died far richer during the same year and at about the same age as his former neighbor.

Macfadden was inclined to be tolerant of other physical culturists even if he did not accept all their views. He doubted Oom's claim that the cultivation of a sixth sense could be achieved through refining, rather than enlarging, muscles. Oom told his students that if they studied hard enough they would be able to send their astral bodies through space. At such a specious—and spacey—promise, all that was based in the sound earth of the Ozarks in Macfadden rebelled: "That I don't go for," he told Mary. "We've got to keep both feet on the ground."[8]

Macfadden transformed his large, sixty-five year old home in Nyack to meet his peculiar needs. Besides the porches designed to encourage more outside sitting and playing he added a swimming pool, tennis courts, miniature golf course, and all the physical training paraphernalia—swings, trapeze, chinning bars, punching bags, he could find room for.

To a great innovator, teacher, and entertainer whose capital resources were expanding by leaps and bounds as fast as confessionists' woes could be set to type, Macfadden was a natural sucker for the movie makers. Americans were going crazy about films in the 1920s and Macfadden was easily encouraged to believe that he could carry his magazine successes into pictures. His first film, called "Zongar," showed his common-man's infatuation with exotic names. He wrote and produced the story of superman Zongar's adventures, fully confident that people would go batty about Zongar, who represented the perfection attainable through physical culture.

The Macfadden kids loved the film but Mary and other adults could make little of it: "People gasped at Zongar," she said, "rubbed their eyes, and blinked as it opened with a conglomeration of Men of Muscle dashing by, followed by a long series of acrobatic leaps in the air, pointless gaps in which Amazons exercised with dumbbells, daredevil stunts from a high-flying plane, and what not. Occasionally a girl, who must have been the feminine lead, hurried headlong in obvious distress, pursued by a villainous character."[9]

Poor reviews for "Zongar" did not discourage Macfadden: "Idiots can't be expected to appreciate the first physical culture movie." He kept at it with "Wrongdoers" starring Lionel Barrymore and managed to work in a scene of Lionel dancing with young Helen Macfadden; "False Pride," with Owen Moore and Fair Binney—a story more complicated than "Zongar" in that it treated realistic characters who expressed emotions; the sad story, "Broken Homes" which Macfadden directed, featuring Alice Lake as heroine and a wonderful climatic scene showing her recovering poise and health by chewing carrots at a time of deep distress; and "Wives at Auction," a morality tale exposing the woes of married folks who scorned the doctrines of physical culture. Rumor said that the director of this film, Hugh Dierker, quit in fury and disgust, throwing carrots to the cast as he exited.[10]

There were many other films including a whole line that adapted stories taken from *True Story* and others more properly belonging to the self-promotional genre that feature Bernarr exhibiting his physical prowess. He did love to see his body on film and did not see why a film showing him visiting a fat suburban couple in their mid-thirties with exhortations to change their lazy ways should not foster his ideas. Such films were actually for training and featured the proper ways of exercising at home. It did no harm to add a story line and scenes showing the once-paunchy couple looking fit some months after giving in to Macfadden's blandishments. As one might expect they had become proper models for Apollo and Diana. Macfadden pioneered the physical training genre that has since become part of the standard video and TV program fare.

Lots of good magazine income went down the movie drain just as lots more was lost on newspapers. It was very hard for Macfadden to accept restrictions on his genius. He believed that he understood films and film audiences and newspapers and newspaper readers every bit as well as the magazine world. But he was dead wrong. And, as he was from Missouri, where men bragged of their stubbornness, it took the passage of a decade to convince him.

Macfadden's plunging on films made Mary nervous but not so nervous as did his plans for family expansion, training, and exploitation to advertise his theories. It was difficult to live with a man "whose interest in the human body was like that of an explorer hoping constantly to traverse a country hitherto unknown."[11] Like other explorers, Macfadden yearned for the fame that came with making a unique discovery, and he always felt that he was on the verge of making astounding discoveries about the body. He expressed his infatuation in lectures: "Why go traveling," he asked audiences, "in order to behold the wonders of the earth...when you can find nothing in the world so wonderful as your own body!" It was such declarations and his posing that induced *Time* magazine to take up calling him "Body-love Macfadden," but Mary did not think anyone could guess at the travails of being married "to one of the most mercurial and unpredictable personalities yet produced by the upper vertebrates."

From the time as a young man when he had tinkered with an exerciser to make it more effective, Macfadden expended great amounts of energy on inventions. He conceived the idea of "Washed Air" and even formed a company to install what amounted to a primitive air conditioning system in buildings. The Majestic Hotel in New York and a brewery benefited from this cooling device before the enterprise faltered. Another favorite scheme was an echo of London's double-deck buses, the double-deck subway car. He pushed the idea hard on New Yorkers, despite the fact that the cars he planned would not fit the subway tunnels. He had his own version of double decking constructed in one of his publication office buildings to create more space for editorial staff. Those editors housed on the upper office decks were forced to keep a low posture for want of head room.

Macfadden liked Abraham Lincoln, "the first natural physical culturist in the White House," and believed that Lincoln had been an inventor too. Somehow his scheme for department stores was inspired by an alleged Lincoln device for raising sunken ships. Macfadden's plan was an in-store railway that carried customers around to the various departments. "This time, I think I've hit it," Macfadden announced, "women won't have to come home tired" and the insane scrimmages at sales will be halted; "we'll make our first cool million, and go on from there!"[12]

While pondering over an article describing a silencer someone had invented for a Maxim gun Macfadden decided that private phone conversations should be protected. He invented a contraption but, as it did not work well, he improved upon one that was marketed and used it all the time. It worked fine although it looked like an iron mask. Employees and visitors to his office gossiped that the publisher was a very secretive fellow—as he was.

As one who thought a lot about sexual vitality Macfadden naturally came up with a number of inventions that would remove the embarrassment of men inflicted with temporary impotence. His favorite device was called the Wimpus but in several tests made by other men it failed to accomplish what it was designed to do.

Mary made fun of the Wimpus but she was impressed with the numbers of Macfadden inventions that were improved upon by others and successfully marketed. He was sure that the basic shoe design was all wrong. Toes needed room to spread out and they needed air. High heels were destructive to foot health. Eventually a shoe manufacturer designed shoes that incorporated the features Macfadden considered vital and even marketed it as the Physical Culture shoe. Macfadden's gratification was limited because his lawyers could not force the manufacturer to share his proceeds. All Macfadden could do was shake his fist at every Physical Culture shoe advertising billboard he saw and tell his companions, "I don't like to be skinned out of a money-making idea."[13]

Some of Macfadden's faddish notions inspired others to make practical use of the essence of his ideas. His practice of sleeping on the floor to gain the benefit of the earth's magnetic influences and a healthy hard surface led to specially made boards to insert between the spring and mattress of a bed. Even doctors began recommending that patients with spinal problems use a bed board—but they did not give Macfadden credit for the concept.

It was not in the field of mechanical invention where Macfadden left his clearest mark on the world, but rather his ideas on diet and exercise. His urging of whole wheat bread helped popularize it and many of his diets and suggestions for heart disease victims came into general use. Even his doctor enemies conceded that his advocacy of healthy living was useful. Doctors could not help pointing out that much of the physical culturist's advice was based on common sense, but this deprecation should not stand. Educating the public to observe "common sense" in healthy living habits was no easy task. To the extent that Macfadden contributed his editorial genius to this effort for fifty years he should be commended, even if some of his advice showed a silly or dangerous side.

None of these Macfadden diversions with inventions and other ideas interfered with his appreciation of the value of his magazines and he supervised a steady expansion of his empire in the twenties. His chief aide in magazine editing was the singular and talented Fulton Oursler, who answered an ad in 1922 promising a "glowing opportunity"[14] for an imaginative, resourceful editor of "America's fastest growing magazine enterprise." At the time Oursler was editing a music trade magazine for $50 a week while trying to free-lance his short stories and other writings. Oursler believed that he would become a great writer in time and his wife believed in him too. The couple had just moved to New York from Baltimore for the magazine job after several years in newspaper work.

Fulton Oursler was born in Baltimore in 1893. He left school after the eighth grade, worked at construction, then ran a butter and egg route before clerking in a law office for three dollars a week. While still in his teens he got a reporter's job with the *Baltimore American*. At leisure he expressed his deep love for literature by wide reading of classical and modern works and teaching himself to read French and German. And always he was writing—stories, plays, novels, and even confessional pieces for the *True Story*.

Oursler, a tall, dark, lean, melancholy looking man was something of an enigma to his colleagues. He was a good amateur magician, capable enough to become a pupil of Harry Houdini and make several professional appearances, and also a ventriloquist and hypnotist. It may have been his showman's style of dress and portentous air that attracted Macfadden to him because the simple man from Missouri liked mysterious folks. But, after a bit, first impressions did not matter too much because Oursler proved to be the perfect assistant, hard-working, imaginative, daring, and absolutely loyal. Other Macfadden lieutenants came to hate Oursler, as did Mary, who believed him to be the evil Richelieu whose encouragement of Macfadden's political and other ambitions resulted in the destruction of the magazine empire.

As a very clever, articulate, and informed man Oursler could have talked rings around Macfadden but learned not to do so. Mary believed that Oursler learned to control Macfadden through flattery, but her view was biased. Macfadden did respond to Oursler's suggestion made at their first meeting that he buy the *Metropolitan* magazine, a monthly literary magazine that had seen better days and more subscribers than it then entertained. The magazine's well known editor-publisher, John Brisben Walker, wanted to sell and Oursler argued that the magazine's prestige would counter-balance more spectacular new magazines like *Midnight*, another scheme in the planning stages. Let's take a chance even though we might "get a bloody nose,"[15] roared Macfadden, delighted to have found an assistant with some audacity.

As supervising editor for Macfadden Publication Company Oursler was busy enough, yet always managed to find time for writing, and eventually achieved his goals of becoming a playwright and a best-selling author. Oursler found more resentment than friendship within the editorial offices, which is understandable given his powerful position, but he was helped by John Coryell, the most prolific "hack" writer of his day.

Coryell's death in 1924 saddened Oursler very much because Coryell had warned him of the "many unsuspected pitfalls"[16] in his new duties and "was the first to tell me I could write real stuff." Coryell had long been Macfadden's favorite writer because he hated fine writing—"simplicity was his literary god." Yet Coryell's reading taste embraced the whole of classical literature. Coryell had espoused many of the theories of Horace Fletcher as well as socialism and anarchism. In his last years he made tolerance his cause—it seemed the ultimate goal and the only means of salvation for mankind.

John Russell Coryell, born in 1851 in New York, was an established writer when he first met Macfadden. His most popular books, written under pen names like Nick Carter, were detective novels, including the *American Marquis* (1889); *Old Detective's Pupil* (1889); *Wall Street Haul* (1889); *Among the Nihilists* (1898); and others. For Macfadden Coryell took on more serious topics like *A Child of Life: A Startling Story of the Struggle of a Girl Born Out of Wedlock Against the Sins and Perversions of Today*. Coryell wrote this moving work under the name of Margaret Grant and wrote many similar books under the name of Bertha Clay.

Coryell's ancestors played some historic roles. His grandfather, Lewis, was President James Monroe's secret emissary to Texas in securing the annexation of the republic. His father, Miers, was a marine architect who installed the engine in the ironclad *Monitor* during the Civil War. John studied in New York's public schools and City College before traveling at age seventeen to China where his father was building ships. At Canton, Shanghai, and in Japan, John held posts with the U.S. Consular service. In 1875 he left the orient for California where he tried his hand as a ship broker before working as a newspaper reporter in San Francisco, Sacramento, and Santa Barbara. With such an adventurous literary apprenticeship he was well-armed to return to New York in 1878 to write juvenile stories and even published his own boy's magazine. His first great success was under the pen name Nick Carter in the 1880s. *The Old Detective's Pupil* was translated into twelve languages.

From crime detection Coryell turned to romances and wrote hundreds of novels under the name of Bertha Clay and others. Readers, mostly women, had developed an insatiable appetite for romances and Coryell showed an amazing profligacy. At one point he held a contract with a publisher that called for one million words of fiction each year and in magazines like *Family Story Paper* it was not unknown for six of his serials to be running at one time—under various pen names. Early in this century Coryell began writing for *Physical Culture* and was Macfadden's mainstay for many years. In 1920 Coryell joined Macfadden's editorial staff where he fostered *True Story* to success. Mary Macfadden shared her husband's appreciation for the fatherly Coryell, who had discreetly treated her to a fabulous meal in Paris during a time when Bernarr had restricted her diet. "He could write anything by the yard,"[17] she said, "from sports, and the water cure for pneumonia, to the art of love in the world of physical culture." Coryell wrote persuasive articles about fasting and the like under the name of H. Mitchell Watchet but at the table he was his own man—a splendid gourmand. Despite Macfadden's rigidity in regard to diet and exercise he did not attempt to impose his Spartan ways on his gifted staff members. Coryell, Oursler, Gauvreau, and other editors smoked, drank, and avoided exercise diligently without offending Macfadden's sensibilities, although he did feel sorry for them. Macfadden did not hold it against Coryell that he had written *Wild Oats,* the book that came close to landing its publisher in prison for two years, because the subject was one he had urged on the writer.

Among writers with Macfadden that Oursler did not like was Clement Wood, "the foul-mouthed poet and scribbler,"[18] who shared the dubious literary distinction with Oursler of writing a fawning biography of the boss in 1929. Wood raised the art of gushing over biographical subjects who retained him to an almost sickening level. His eloquent enthusiasm for Macfadden was only equalled by the amazing puffery he performed in the commissioned biography he did of the infamous, goat gland quack, Doc John Brinkley, and in the ghosted autobiography of Norman Baker, the blatant cancer quack.

Macfadden also had a writer named Grace Perkins with whom Oursler fell in love. Fulton and Grace married in 1925 before Arthur Garfield Hayes, the famous attorney and one of the founders of the American Civil Liberties Union, secured Oursler's divorce. The impatient couple married anyway, then stayed in Mexico and Europe until the divorce was finally completed. During these difficult months Oursler could not oversee the Macfadden publications but the publisher accepted everything the couple wrote for him, a total of one quarter of a million words, "mostly pot-boiler" stuff for the magazines and the *Graphic.*

Without question Oursler's influence on Macfadden's publications was extensive. It is difficult to compare its relative importance to the contributions made by the publisher himself. Like many other employees Oursler saw himself as the guiding genius of the enterprise, the man who took *True Story* from a circulation of 200,000 to over 2,000,000.

When he was writing biographical profiles of the boss Oursler gave him all the credit for the publishing empire's successes, but, at home, he spoke of his own "complete editorial command."[19] Except for the publisher's "rare intervention," Oursler literally put his stamp of approval on all copy for all magazines. No article, title, or illustration was printed until it bore the stamp "OK FO" on it.

When Oursler spoke of writing being the passion of his life he may be believed. In 1926-27 he enjoyed the success of his Broadway play, *The Spiders*, which ran for 500 performances. Thus he moved to a lofty place as a creative writer.

Some of Oursler's work for Macfadden did give him special satisfaction. He was proud of suggesting *True Detective* to the publisher and defending the concept of a true crime magazine against the objections of the company attorney who feared libel suits. Macfadden compromised initially by directing that stories be fictionalized and names be changed. After a few issues appeared without any clamor Macfadden accepted the "true" concept. It was at this time that Macfadden hired John Shuttleworth as editor, a man who proved to be very able. For years Shuttleworth resented Oursler's heavy hand on editorial policies but the magazine did well regardless of the conflict among editors. The detective magazine, like the confession magazine, was a true innovation in magazine publication that spawned a number of imitators. Confessions always sold much better than the detectives but both types of magazine have shown the wisdom of their originators: *True Detective* and its imitators are still to be found on newsstands after well over a half century of publication.

Uninformed readers often lump the detective magazines with confession and/or pulp magazines in general condemnation, yet a distinction should be observed. The true detective magazines are a very rich historical source on national and international crime. The standard of writing is higher than that of daily newspapers and the coverage is at once more cohesive and more complete than that provided by newspapers.

The overall understanding reached between Oursler and Macfadden at their first meeting resulted in an audacious expansion. Macfadden relied upon *True Story*, a true gold mine, to support a string of new magazines. Each new magazine would have its own editorial staff and would survive only if it gained respectable circulation figures.

Macfadden formed the Macfadden Publishing Co. and invited investors in 1924. With stock sales he was able to bring out new magazines. Aside from his several entries in the confessional and detective field he published *Dream World, The Dance, Fiction Lovers, Modern Marriage, Muscle Builder, Ghost Stories, Own Your Own Home*, and others.

Some publications did not last. *Brain Power* was one magazine that failed, perhaps only because the name was wrong. The content, featuring self-improvement themes that were then in the vogue, was attractive enough, but somehow it did not do to suggest that one could get brainy by buying a magazine. The magazine was launched in 1922, then dropped after several issues.

While the *New York Graphic* was the star of Macfadden's newspaper empire he had another New York tabloid that was more successful. The *Daily Investment News* sold for ten cents and answered a genuine need. It gave simple, clear advice on the market to ordinary people who were not sophisticated enough to benefit from market letters or the long, complex articles in other newspapers. Allene Talmey, a magazine journalist of the day cited the investment tabloid as illustrative of the publisher's ability to find a public. He has "an uncanny divining rod which tells him where lie rich formations of those submerged millions to whom the usual form of reading matter does not exist. They are virgin property to him. He takes his readers away from no other publisher. He creates a reading public."[20] It was this ability that helped Macfadden become the most successful publisher of magazines in American history. Estimates of numbers of his readers vary widely. None of his other publications sold anything like the two to three millions of *True Story* sold each month, but during his peak years he reached tens of millions of readers.

And, of course, he also wrote books which were heavily advertised in his magazines. His books appeared from the *Physical Culture* press with great regularity. In 1901 he published *The Power and Beauty of Superb Womanhood; How They are Lost and How They May Be Regained and Developed for the Right Degree of Attainable Perfection.* Other titles were shorter like *Constipation, Its Causes, Effects, and Treatment; Health-Beauty-Sexuality, from Girlhood to Womanhood;* and *Strengthening the Eyes.* There were other books on the treatment of baldness, on fasting, cookbooks, books on tobacco, and on *Marriage, A Lifelong Honeymoon; Life's Greatest Pleasures Secured by Observing the Highest Human Instincts.*

The 1920s have been given many tags like "the jazz age," "the flapper age," and others, but Macfadden would not have complained if it had been labeled "The Age of Macfadden." Certainly the publisher revealed a definite regard for his place in history by commissioning the publication of three separate biographies in 1929. While it is likely that Macfadden's political ambitions suggested the biographical treatment the oddity of tripling the dose probably derived from his serious considerations on his value to the world. H. L. Mencken expressed his astonishment in a review of all three books in the *American Mercury:* "I can recall no more passionate anointing of a living man even in the literature of campaign biography."[21] The published tributes came from the pens of Fulton Oursler, Clement Wood, and Grace Perkins, writers who worked for their subject. "The authors," wrote Mencken, "of these brochures do not spare the goose grease...poor Macfadden chokes and gurgles in it on every one of their 825 pages...a hero without a wart, spiritual or temporal, sworn only to save us all from the Medical Trust and make us strong enough to lift a piano with our bare hands, with maybe a couple of gals and a bartender sitting on top of it."

Clement Wood's book compared Macfadden to Abe Lincoln and the abolitionists who freed the slaves; Macfadden would free men from "the shackles of weakness and disease, superstition and prudery."[22] He was a man wonderful to look at with his fine thicket of dark brown hair, dominating eyes—although kindly—and muscular body. "He stretches out a hand to grasp yours: he is as democratic as sunlight or shower. Unless you are prepared for it, you will be amazed at the pulsing vigor, the iron strength, of his clasp. For good health is as radiant as the sun; and somehow you feel like shading your eyes a trifle, when he comes close to you." At age sixty Macfadden was a marvel of physical strength and beauty: "There is utter symmetry, utter grace, in the powerful lines of the figure. His physique today is smoother, more powerful, more Atlas-like than at any previous stage in his development. Powerful corded muscles in the legs, a torso like a sculptured Hellinic god, a magnificent chest expansion...When he walks with you, you have the general sensation that you have somehow become juvenile, a novice, close behind the steps of a matured adult."

Fulton Oursler's book cannot compare with Wood's in gushy effusions but he did his best. He said Macfadden "is one of the last few survivors of the old race of medicine men, which flourished from the fire circles of savage tribes down to the dawning of our own century."[23] Macfadden had always been despised by doctors who feared the truth of his teachings but had himself, lately, become more tolerant of doctors despite their false practices. The biographer's grip on social history was not strong so he accepted Macfadden's assertion that he had been the first health expert to warn the public about the unhealthiness of liquor. Macfadden's energy was probably not exaggerated by any of his biographers. He did rise early and take walks of up to twenty miles along the way to his office, and sometimes keep at his work there until 10 P.M. He was never idle because of his sense of responsibility towards the public and his stockholders and because he loved the strenuous, hard-working pace of life he had become accustomed to leading.

In one way the book by Grace Perkins, Oursler's wife, was the most interesting of the lot because it paid more attention to the Macfadden family. She painted an idyllic picture of the family's life at Nyack and discussed Bernarr's theories on education at great length. Great respect was accorded all of Macfadden's views on health, including his bitter denunciations of vaccination. Perkins treated all of her employer's pronouncements on sex with touching reverence. The Macfadden children were not allowed to linger in bed in the morning because they might be tempted into bad habits. But the greatest bulwark erected in the family against unseemly sexual passion was in providing a proper diet: "The conventional diet acts as an irritant spur to the imagination as well as to the physical expression of sex activity...the regime he gives his children is helpful in aiding them to gain and keep in control their sex natures."[24] It may have surprised any readers who thought of Macfadden as the nation's leading purveyor of licentious literature to learn that "he disapproves heartily of licentious, underworld material which is put in some sex novels. These novels and stories written without an outstanding moral purpose excite the passions and debase the mind." Perkins had a nice image to explain why his treatment of sex, contrary to what the small-minded prudes claimed, was good: "Evil must be brought into the open and destroyed. A covered, unventilated cess-pool will always give off bad odors. Sunshine and clear, purifying air will eliminate the stench together with the cause of it. And so it is with moral turpitude." Perkins also commended Macfadden's courageous stand in denouncing laws that banned the dissemination of birth control literature.

Whatever good Macfadden anticipated from his sponsorship of these three curious books did not seem to flow to him in the 1930s. Looking back he may have marveled at his discernment in choosing the year 1929 to add the three book monuments to the full-sized bronze statue that stood by his living-room fireplace, because the depression thirties gave him, as countless other Americans, a very rough time.

Chapter 11
Presidential Timber

Macfadden has made his fads pay. Perhaps no other man has had such lucrative foibles.

Alva Johnston

When Californians rewarded Macfadden for establishing a sanitarium in the state by naming a mountain after him it seemed an auspicious start to the 1930s. The *Journal* of the AMA scoffed at the tribute of naming Macfadden Peak in the Castle Crags near Castella but the physical culturist was very pleased.[1] But in the summer of 1930 he had even more important things on his mind, after deciding impulsively to travel with Mary to Europe to meet Premier Benito Mussolini of Italy. The urge had come upon him so suddenly that he had to wire Fulton Oursler, then vacationing in Europe, from the steamer *Berengaria,* to secure passports so that they could land and also to arrange for the interview in Rome. Oursler came through on both assignments, thanks to the American Consul and some Italian friends.

Macfadden was too thoroughly egotistical to admire many men, living or dead, especially if they were not physical culturists, but Italy's "Iron Man" intrigued him. Since he believed that he would eventually hold the office of president or some other high position it made sense to learn some statecraft from the no-nonsense dictator who was forcing the pleasure-loving Italians to become more serious and responsible. Like other Americans Macfadden, who rode trains often, had been captivated by reports that Mussolini had even managed to get his nation's railroad running on time. Macfadden felt that he would hit it off with the premier and that the resultant newspaper publicity would establish his credentials as an international statesman. He realized that the pressure of other affairs had left him outside the main stream of foreign affairs. Not that he minded because he did not much like foreigners anyway. But, political considerations aside, Mussolini, "the strong man of Europe," was bound to be a physical culturist and could open the way for the continental triumphs of Macfadden's doctrines.

Macfadden also hoped that the voyage would bring about a reconciliation with Mary, who had been down in the dumps for a long time. She had gotten fat and he had to impose a firm training program for her betterment. She blamed the constant child-bearing for her weight gain but such excuses did not justify her weakness in Bernarr's eyes. Other things also annoyed him. Nothing he did seemed to meet Mary's approval. She opposed his presidential ambitions, abused Oursler and other key associates, decried his efforts to sell the *Graphic* to Hearst, opposed his negotiations to purchase *Liberty* magazine, and worried about his heavy investments in New Jersey real estate—a housing development projected near the George Washington Bridge. Now, on shipboard, having earned her trip by losing 35-pounds, she was cold to his ardent suggestions that they conceive another male child at sea. He thought that two more boys in the family would balance the sexes effectively in "the physical culture family." While Macfadden had laid down the rule in the *Encyclopedia* that a wife "should be the supreme dictator"[2] in the matter of procreation, he liked to dictate all matters in his home. Yet Mary's stinging words and her shudder at his touch put him off.

In Paris matters worsened. They stayed at the luxurious Hotel King George near the Place Vendome where, Mary said, Bernarr spent a good deal of time looking up at the statute of Bonaparte ("a great physical culturist"). Apparently Macfadden saw a lot of himself in the famed general-statesman and after spending some hours in contemplation at the hero's tomb at the Invalides he reached a decision. According to the super-charged scene Mary described much later, Macfadden drew himself up in a Napoleonic pose to announce: "Woman, you are no longer necessary to my success."[3]

Even if Mary's retrospective account of events and past moods cannot be fully trusted, Bernarr's conduct after the death of their infant son in 1922 could well have determined the eventual end of their marriage. Nothing could be more tragic than the death of an infant, and what could mend a relationship if each parent blamed the other for the fatality? Byron, whom the parents called Billy, was eleven months old when he suffered a sudden, violent convulsion. His father, whose invariable cure of colds was a plunge into hot and cold tubs, plunged the child into a hot bath to stop his muscular spasms. "For the love of Christ," Mary screamed, "call a doctor!"[4] Whether Bernarr would have done so is a moot point: Billy's light apparently flickered out before anything more could be done.

After the child's burial Bernarr took Mary and their four daughters to Atlantic City: "Nature has a cure for this, as it has for everything else," he said. "The cure is exercise. We will walk it off."[5] And walk they did every day for a week, but still Mary could neither eat nor control her tears. Naturally he berated her for obstinacy—and his harshness did not heal her wounds. The family returned to New York for a short time, then Bernarr took them to a farm school in Athol, Mass. where the girls were left while the parents took off on a 14-day walking tour.

Billy was rather a famous boy in physical culture circles because his birth established Macfadden's discovery of sex determination. While there is no reason to doubt that Macfadden cherished all of his children the unbroken succession of female births had aggravated him. Perhaps he wondered if folks were saying that a truly virile man should not be incapable of making male offspring. As the girls appeared, pretty and healthy as they were, he redoubled his researches on the mysteries of sex-determination. Finally, he found the answer. Nature decreed that conception on particular days of the month determined the child's sex. Readers of *Physical Culture* learned all about this startling scientific break-through and saw lots of pictures of Billy and his doting father.

Personally Macfadden was deeply shocked and aggrieved by the loss of his first-born son, but he had professional considerations as well. Does the "father of physical culture" lose a son to some mysterious ailment? What could explain this sudden death? He had to think about this while Mary was preoccupied with her grief. What should he tell the world? What would his disciples and his foes say if he kept silent, as he had thus far, making sure that newsmen did not learn of the burial? On the walking tour he made his decision, wrote an editorial for *Physical Culture*, and mailed it off without saying anything about it to Mary.

Later she read "The Story of Little Billy," and wept bitterly. How could he do it? They were back in New York and she knew herself to be pregnant again. In part she could understand his need for a public confession to his disciples. She was used to his confessional habit, a passion, as a writer once noted, for taking the public into his bosom. But she could not understand or forgive Bernarr for his outrageous lies.

Bernarr told readers that the child had suffered a serious fall a few days before his death—which was not true. He charged that the child's loving mother, in her usual response to the charming child's domineering ways, had over-fed him. "Mother love is perhaps the most beautiful of all things human, though there is but little intelligence associated with it. It is simply a mad devotion of the mother for the object of her affection,"[6] he wrote.

The father did affect a sharing of the blame for the tragedy: he had been negligent too in not supervising his wife and not resuming the exercises he had been giving the boy when he was two and three months old. He had discontinued the exercises because the boy's response to the training was so enthusiastic: "He reciprocated so vehemently that I saw signs of his becoming bow-legged. . . . Consequently I discontinued his special exercises,"[7] and did not get around to starting another program that might have strengthened the lad against the effects of his accident. The tragic death should not have occurred, Bernarr told his readers:

"It is time for parents everywhere to realize their own responsibilities and to stop blaming God for their own neglect and indifference to the needs of parenthood." When Billy fell ill "the exact same methods that were used so effectively with all our children, and in vast numbers of homes where drugless methods are favored, were depended on for results. That the same favorable reaction did not take place will always be a puzzling problem to me. The medical and non-medical practitioners who were called on the case rendered conscientious service, but without avail."

Perhaps it is understandable that Macfadden told readers that he had called in a doctor, which he did not. Just a few months before Billy's crisis Mary had suffered a miscarriage and only the furious insistence of a friend overwhelmed Bernarr's refusal to have a doctor in the house. The doctor was allowed to come for only a single visit, then a midwife supervised Mary's recovery. "Don't call the doctor," was ever Macfadden's message to others. When, a year after Billy's death, Mary gave birth to a near "blue baby" being strangled by the umbilical cord at birth, the midwife demanded a doctor. Macfadden refused but, fortunately, the midwife was up to the emergency and no harm was done.

Fulton Oursler's part in this scalding family drama is telling. He and Mary did not hold each other in tender regard, yet Oursler urgently objected to his employer's publication of the Billy story when he saw the draft. It was one of the few differences the men ever had and a rather personal one for the intrusion of a recently hired employee, but Oursler felt bound to speak out. It was obvious to Oursler that Macfadden was lying about the boy's death, but he did not dare tell the boss his suspicion that a refusal to call a doctor sealed Billy's doom. Always the tactician, Oursler tried to convince Macfadden that any public discussion of the child's death was in "bad taste," particularly when it involved blaming the mother for the death. Later Oursler learned to appreciate that appeals to "taste" rarely penetrated the publisher's consciousness.[8]

Thus it was that Mary and Bernarr were still at odds years later in Europe. Things were patched up after the Napoleonic scene at the Hotel King George, but there was little joy in their relationship.

All the incidents of the European visit in 1930 were not so unpleasant as these domestic matters. Macfadden did meet Mussolini and the two strong men got on very well. There are two irreconcilable versions of Macfadden's role in undertaking the conditioning in New York of some Italian soldiers. Mary claimed that it had been Macfadden's scheme to gain fame and help the Italian leader by training the "muscular nucleus"[9] of the dictator's army at his own expense. Fulton Oursler, reporting on the arrangement years later when it did not do to discuss Macfadden's infatuation with fascism, recalled its accidental origin. Macfadden had chided Mussolini: "Your soldiers eat too much. If I had a few of your men for three weeks, I guarantee they'd be better soldiers!"[10] It was just a joke but some months later thirty Italian soldiers arrived at Ellis Island addressed to Macfadden. Macfadden did wonders with the young men at one of his resorts, then shipped them back to Italy. Mussolini sent Macfadden the Order of the Crown of Italy in March 1932. Ten years later, when American forces battled the Italians and Germans, Macfadden did not brag about helping Mussolini, but he must have been relieved that his "muscular nucleus" scheme did not entirely rejuvenate the Italian forces.

Macfadden's longing for political office emerged sharply in the late 1920s. His motivation was simple. He had been endeavoring to save the country from weakness since 1900. The national weakness that concerned him was not measured by the size of armies or quantities of armaments but rather in the failure of its citizens to adhere to principles of physical culture. A strong people did not have to go to war, which was the recourse of weaklings and cowards. Because the medical trust condemned him he had not been able to prevent World War I by making people stronger.

Macfadden showed an increasing interest in sanitariums and health resorts around this time. Perhaps political hopes influenced the widening of his geographic range with the purchase of the large Arrowhead Springs Hotel in the mountains near San Bernadino, California in 1930 and the acquisition of a Miami Beach hotel, called the Macfadden Deauville, around the same time. He told newsmen that he was planning a chain of hotels that would rival that of Conrad Hilton but did not pursue the notion.

When New York's Tammany Hall got wind of Macfadden's longing to be a political force its leaders found ways to tap the wealthy publisher for money. Macfadden was somewhat of a political innocent but he did know the power of the purse and he was willing to pay other politicians for help in gaining high office. Payment did not have to be entirely in cash as campaign contributions, the publisher reckoned, because he could open the pages of the *Graphic* to politicians who wished instant influence or literary immortality. Macfadden courted Mayor Jimmy Walker who responded with a civic celebration awarding Macfadden the key to the city but the mayor proved the wrong horse to back. Governor Al Smith, Fiorello La Guardia, and others fed up with the city's corruption encouraged an investigation by a legislative committee headed by Judge Samuel Seabury which exposed Walker's wrong-doing. The crusading of Editor Howard Swain of the *Graphic* helped kick off the investigation with Macfadden's blessing.

By 1932 America faced another crisis of weakness and desperately needed a strong leader: Macfadden was available, but stepped aside when Franklin Roosevelt seemed able to fill the bill. But it is likely that Macfadden, being Macfadden, did not believe his own professions of faith in Roosevelt. How could a cripple be strong enough to lead a great nation? Macfadden editorialized for Roosevelt in 1932. It may be that he was motivated more by the hope that the new president would establish a Department of Health with him as chief rather than by any feelings of compatibility with the Democratic platform. In 1929 he identified himself as a Southerner who respected states rights and feared the encroachments of federal power. He thought that there was far too much law making already. One of his editorials compared the simplicity of the ten enactments of the Mosaic code to the 51,482 laws passed by congress. As always he made his point directly:

"The federal government was originally designed to deal with foreign and interstate problems.

Affairs within the states were to be dealt with by the states themselves.

But we are witnessing a rapid and unresisted encroachment of the central government upon the sovereignty of the state—just as there is a rapid and unresisted encroachment of the state upon the autonomy of the individual...

There is too much law.

There is too little liberty."[11]

Aside from these traditional views Macfadden expressed a rather intense contempt for reformers at this time. A reformer considered himself "the paragon of all virtues, and resents all criticism,"[12] and was a menace to the nation. He knew all about reform. It could only be done through public education: "You have to develop their will power, strengthen their characters. You have to give them knowledge which is essential to make better men and women of them." The reformers Macfadden hated were those whom he usually identified as "prudes," those "loud-mouthed reformers that voice their personal hatred of every human soul who fails to agree with them...people that would make us go to church by law. That would bind one wife and one husband to each other, even if they were fighting like cats and dogs...Reformers of this type are unbalanced mentally."

Macfadden also expressed strong views on democratic participation. Everyone should vote so a poll tax of five to fifty dollars should be imposed upon all who were eligible. If they voted they would have the tax refunded.

He called for a square deal for farmers, old age security, "an aggressive merchant marine," and a World Court. But the outstanding need of the nation was for a Secretary of Health in the cabinet "and he should be non-medical."[13] This officer would "renovate and reform the health activities of this government" and would investigate the healing art, "free from the prejudice that is always found in one particular school of healing."

Writing about Macfadden's call for a Secretary of Health in 1929 Clement Wood, his biographer, noted his subject's admirable qualifications for such a post. Yet, despite all Macfadden's editorial urging, "both of the great parties rejected his demand. They will not forever persist in this incredible stupidity."[14]

The Secretary of Health idea had been proposed some years earlier by Irving Fisher, a distinguished professor of political economy at Yale. Fisher, who had been profoundly influenced by Horace Fletcher, became a health crusader and considered his work for health more significant than his economic studies. In 1908 he was among those chosen by President Theodore Roosevelt to report on the nation's natural resources and the waste of them because of bad health practices. Fisher was an effective advocate. He related health to national efficiency: "The prevention of disease...increases economic productivity...The nation loses much through undue fatigue" that could be easily remedied.[15] Fisher credited Fletcher's work for showing what could be achieved when an individual assumes personal responsibility for his health. In 1908 Fischer and Fletcher founded the Health and Efficiency League of America to build a better understanding of health. Understandably, the first lesson taught by the league was learning how to chew and properly taste food.

One of the ironies of the national health department proposal was that some congressmen opposed the idea out of fear of a too powerful medical trust. As a candidate for secretary Macfadden conspicuously stood against the medical trust.

Sometimes Macfadden grew impatient with democracy, particularly when labors' demands got on his nerves. It was then that other systems attracted him: "There are times when I believe that America needs a Mussolini, as never before."[16]

Little wonder that Macfadden became frustrated. As a longtime Republican he had given his party a chance to do the right thing. The GOP failed. He turned to Roosevelt and the Democrats in 1932. They failed. In 1936 he called for a fresh candidate: Bernarr Macfadden. He now shifted away from the Democrats back to the Republicans and told newsmen that the GOP would miss a good bet, "if they nominate an old-line Republican, they'll be beaten worse than last time as sure as shooting. They've just got to nominate a man who'll draw some Democratic votes, someone outside the political field. That's my chance, my duty."[17]

On a visit to St. Louis in September 1935 for a speech to the local Republicans, Macfadden agreed to accept the presidential nomination if offered. When the Convention neglected to offer it, Macfadden put himself forward as an independent. Campaigning was expensive. He had to borrow $250,000 from his publishing company, but later used his authority to cancel the debt which was a violation of law.

Macfadden's campaign did not excite the nation. Aside from a certain constituency among the health enthusiasts, he was generally viewed as a crank. Even allowing for the fact that 1936 was not the best year to challenge the popularity of Franklin Roosevelt, Macfadden's campaign was viewed with unusual indifference. The only occasions on which the public showed any warmth were those when audiences hooted Macfadden down for attacking Roosevelt too severely. He had to quit trying to address the Advertising Club of Baltimore when their heckling and hooting made continuing impossible. Since he had made considerable personal sacrifices to become a candidate in the hope of "saving the Constitution" he expected a more positive reception. His talk was provocative, warning of "enemies within the secret chambers of our government"[18] who advised Roosevelt, including Felix Frankfurter, the Supreme Court justice, who was "listed in the Red Network." When this exposure did not go over any better than his cries against government spending, Macfadden warned about "the Yellow Peril—the possibility of war with Japan." This was the last straw and the crowd's disorder could not be silenced.

Needless to say Macfadden did not quit accusing Roosevelt of selling out the country just because people heckled him. He continued his attack in other speeches, detailing the president's submission to Frankfurter and Rexford Tugwell, a presidential advisor, "supporters of communist doctrines."

In the course of his messages to the American electorate Macfadden had stressed that he planned to run the country according to "sound business principles." This conceit like his other much repeated suggestion for keeping the peace—let the businessmen get together to prevent war— was a projection of his changing assessment of himself in the 1920s- '30s. He saw himself as a great businessman as well as the father of physical culture. He was entirely accurate in depicting himself as a business leader yet the public did not see him as the millionaire tycoon of publishing. His public image remained fixed as a health nut and muscle man, an eccentric who liked to walk barefoot and stand on his head. Newspapers derided his statement that he was willing to disregard his personal interests unselfishly because the nomination was "an honor no American can afford to refuse." To one harsh editor "he sounded like W.C. Fields might sound if he had been put in the sun to dry. Like a man who could sell hair oil in Apelousa, Louisiana, if he wanted to."[19]

In the tedium of any political campaign the press yearns for the color a fringe candidate sometimes offers so Macfadden did get some attention. Newsmen treated his few press conferences as a carnival of fun. "It was something like interviewing the manager of the 'House of Glee' at Coney Island," Mary Macfadden complained. "They were all to have a corking (or rather uncorkable) good time out of it and wind up with columns of hilarious stories about the muscle man who was not adverse to doing his setting-up exercises as President each morning after jumping out of Abe Lincoln's White House bed."[20] When the candidate sponsored a rally at Carnegie Hall a newspaper lead to its story began: "Set 'em up again, Joe, so I'll forget a Bernarr Macfadden political rally."

The Macfadden campaign for president in 1936 was a waste of time and money but he did a little better four years later running for U.S. Senator in Florida. Political defeats did not discourage Macfadden. He was not the kind of weakling who indulged in self-doubts: he knew in his pure heart that his lust for power was not personal. Political power, like money, was only useful if it could be utilized to reform the nation. The candidate survived the ridicule as easily as he withstood the voters' apathy. As a showman he appreciated the publicity and his heavy crust of self-esteem armed him against verbal abuse. He had known for a long time that the great prophets in history had always been ridiculed because they were so far ahead of their time. A crusader needed courage— and he had never run from a fight.

Macfadden's interests were not limited to politics. He embraced aviation with great enthusiasm, getting his pilot's license in 1931. As a flier he was maligned by those who observed his absent-mindedness and indifference to the instrument panel. He depended more upon his instinct than anything else and suffered a few minor crashes, in part because he did not concern himself with either the weather or the state of a landing field when he was ready to go. He was also casual about ownership after he sold his plane and started renting. Some companies refused to risk their planes to him. Their caution did not slow him down. Once at the airport he was likely to jump off in any plane handy without consulting the owner. There was some question about his eyesight although he was able to pass the tests even in his eighties. Critics noticed that he had to hold a newspaper at arm's length to read it but would have died before putting on a pair of glasses.

It was perhaps the depression that stimulated Macfadden to establish the Bernarr Macfadden Foundation in 1931. He claimed to have given it $5,000,000 to carry on his health reforms but perhaps he exaggerated. His contribution was largely in properties that the foundation was to manage, including the Castle Heights Military Academy at Lebanon, Tenn., the Dansville, New York health hotel, a sanitarium at Liberty, New York, some summer camps, and other holdings. By this arrangement he gave up some income and assets but assured that a tax-free organization would exist despite whatever vagaries of the depression affected his magazines.[21]

The depression also encouraged Macfadden to revive the penny restaurants he had started many years earlier. People were hungry and he could feed them in cafeterias like the two he established in New York at a penny a dish for wholesome food. In 1932 he summoned newsmen to a dinner party in the restaurant on 43rd Street where he was treating Eleanor Roosevelt and her daughter to lunch. All ate heartily and each full meal only cost a dime. As the depression worsened Macfadden offered to send a staff member from the foundation to any city in the nation willing to establish a penny restaurant. The foundation representative would plan and start up the whole operation without any fee. Let's feed the hungry, cried Macfadden, it does not take much. He could show people how to feed one million hungry folks for a mere penny each daily.

The penny restaurant did not spread across the nation to relieve the hunger of the depression but his scheme was praised. Considering his eccentricities and status as a somewhat bizarre celebrity, attacks on him in the press were relatively rare. *Time* magazine was an exception. Its editors delighted in knocking the publisher. They considered him a phoney who had learned that more folks would read his lectures on whole-wheat bread, muscle building and deep breathing if he offered them "a nicely rounded female without too many clothes."[22] Later Macfadden discovered that "a sermon on ethics would gain the ears of millions if the text is a parable of the stenographer who lusted for her employer." Relying on these truisms, "aided by a complete lack of good taste," Macfadden's magazines reaped fortunes.

On this occasion *Time* was reporting on the bankruptcy of the *Graphic*, "a daily magazine of sexationalism...that shrieked, screamed, leered, turned its collar around and preached." All decent journalists held the paper in contempt, seeing the publisher's fake pretense of selling sex and scandal to "help tear down false prudery" and "demonstrate the benefits of physical culture."

The *Graphic's* failure in 1932 put 400 men and women out of work. Macfadden had tried hard to save the paper by toning down content to a level of comparative respectability but it was too late. From a peak circulation of 350,000 the paper fell to 237,000 and, as with other Macfadden publications, advertising revenues were low. He also had to sell the *New Haven Times* for a paltry $10,000 to its rival which swiftly shut it down. He also sold several small dailies in Michigan. Eventually he got rid of the *New York Daily Investment News,* the *Philadelphia Daily News,* and the *Automotive Daily News.*

With all his business woes Macfadden's domestic travails also worsened. A.C. Adams sued him for $100,000 for alienating the affection of his wife but a jury acquitted the publisher.

Mary Macfadden commenced her battle for a divorce and property settlement that was to go on for a decade. They separated in 1933 under a court-administrated agreement providing for family maintenance. Mary got the Englewood estate, custody of the children, and $15,000 a year. Later that year the couple was back in court because Bernarr was in arrears of his payments. He argued that financial reverses had prevented him from keeping up with his payments and sued for divorce, naming Baron Rosencrantz and Charles Wynne as parties to Mary's adulteries. Mary cross-filed for divorce, charging Bernarr's adultery with Betty Bennett at the hotel in Dansville, NY. In June 1934 Bernarr withdrew his petition for divorce and agreed to continue the terms of the separation agreement.

Two years later the Macfaddens were in court again. Mary was demanding $2.5 million, half of the reported $5 million that Bernarr had given the Bernarr Macfadden Foundation. She argued that they had made a life-time agreement in October 1914 that they would expound to the public through books and magazines "their personal precept of the science of physical culture." Bernarr had breached their contract by giving their joint gains to the foundation. It was in the course of this suit that Mary tried unsuccessfully to convince the court that she had originated the idea behind the *Physical Culture* magazine. She also failed to establish that an actual contract had been made. Apparently the court felt that the couple's separation settlement had provided her with adequate compensation for her contribution to the marriage partnership.

The next court skirmish was comparatively minor. In June 1937 Mary refused to allow Bernarr custody of the two youngest children, Berwyn, 13, and Brewster, 12. During the school year the children attended a military school but Bernarr had the right to designate a particular summer camp for their holiday time and wished to bring them to his office on occasion "because someday they'll inherit shares in the business."[23] Mary was ordered to observe the previous court order.

Divorces were hard to come by in states like New York. The couple's effort to gain one in 1945 was rejected for inadequate grounds but succeeded in 1946 when they made their differences clearer. Among other things he complained that she called him a "crackpot" while she insisted that he had always imposed his physical training program on the children against their will and contrary to her assessments of proper health measures. She also said that he had been unreasonably critical of her gains in weight.

One newspaper, the *Bridgeport* (Conn.) *Herald,* was rather like *Time* in gleeful recounting of the publisher's woes, perhaps because of his entry into the New Haven newspaper field. It amused the Bridgeport editor to note that Macfadden, cross-complaining to Mary's suit, accused her of neglecting the physical culture teaching of her children while being wooed by Baron Rosencrantz. Mary and this fellow, a Danish noble, smoked, drank cocktails, and visited speakeasies instead of attending to their health and the children's education.

Other gossip that charmed the editor concerned Yale University and Macfadden's yearning for an honorary degree. It was in the hope of achieving a degree, the *Herald* claimed, that Macfadden started publishing in New Haven and gave a lavish "blow out" to the chamber of commerce. "The employee who could have secured him a degree would have received a cool million,"[24] but authorities would not give in to the ambitions of a "gross vulgarian." No other evidence of Macfadden's longing for academic standing exists and it is probably the product of editorial imagination. Certainly Macfadden would know how to exploit the title "doctor" if he had it, but he had spent most of his life deriding those who bore the title and had not otherwise shown much regard for scholarly institutions save for those he founded. Arranging an honorary degree from an institution of higher learning would not be too tough had he wished to do so.

Fulton Oursler and Macfadden had another magazine brainstorm in 1932 that involved Eleanor Roosevelt. Oursler convinced her that her editorship of a magazine to be called *Babies, Just Babies* would be a grand thing. She would receive $500 for each issue from April 1932 and, if the magazine survived for a second year, $1,000 per issue, but only "if you are living in the White House or the magazine is profitable."[25] Eleanor's daughter would receive $200 monthly for secretarial help and Eleanor could veto any "objectionable" story material. The magazine was a dismal and almost immediate failure through no fault of Eleanor's. Apparently it was just a poor idea. The association with the Roosevelts continued despite the magazine's failure. Eleanor contributed to *Liberty* and Oursler enjoyed several invitations to the White House.

Macfadden gained a prestigious magazine in 1931 by exchanging his *Detroit Daily* newspaper to publishers Joseph Patterson and Robert McCormick for *Liberty*. *Liberty* had been founded in 1924 to challenge the well-established *Collier's* and *Saturday Evening Post* in the field of large, quality magazines featuring fiction, factual articles, and features. In its first years the new magazine featured the stories of popular writers like Ring Lardner, Fanny Hurst, Ben Hecht, and Westbrook Pegler, and the better-known illustrators as well. Leslie Thrasher did the cover illustrations that featured the same family of characters involved in some amusing incident in what amounted to a long-running cartoon serial. Other innovations included the one-page, short-short story; a notice of the reading time needed for every story and article; and a number of lively features, including contests.

Macfadden wanted Oursler to take over as editor but Oursler feared that a weekly magazine would take more of his time than his general overseeing of all the other magazines—and he needed time for his own writing. On the other hand Oursler was tempted because the new duties on a better class journal would allow him to move in more elevated literary circles. Eventually, Oursler relented to take up the reins he was to hold for the eleven years that *Liberty* lasted as a Macfadden publication.

The new management did not make radical changes in the content of the magazine. They did give up the Thrasher covers, however, and used more pieces by celebrities like Albert Einstein, Winston Churchill, Benito Mussolini, Mahatma Gandhi, and others. The Gandhi article represented Oursler's fondness for startling couplings of author and subject: it was entitled, "My Sex Life."

Oursler had a very hard time getting Macfadden to pay the prices demanded by top authors, particularly for fictional serials. His rivals at *Collier's* and *Saturday Evening Post* could offer up to $15,000 for a serial but Oursler was only able to work his fee up from less than $3,000 to $10,000 after many, long whining sessions with the publisher. Macfadden was tightfisted: "If we use a new author continuously," the publisher warned, "we will not only have to increase our price, but we will in a way be 'making' him, which will not only be costly, but at any time we are liable to lose him to the SEP and *Collier's*."[26]

One of Oursler's solutions was to commission his wife, Grace, frequently. She was almost as prolific a writer as he was. The editor also enjoyed the opportunity to commission true crime stories. Early in his tenure he got Edmund Pearson to do stories on some fascinating old crimes and he found other writers to look into some sensational current crimes. The magazine featured an essay contest which gave the winner a $1,000 prize. As the national debate over capital punishment raged in the thirties because of the Leopold-Loeb case the issue was a natural choice for an essay topic. Macfadden had long been a zealous foe of capital punishment but neither he nor the editors could resist awarding the prize to an advocate of execution: the author was a woman whose father was on trial for murdering her mother.

Liberty reached a high point in 1935 when it made a profit for the first time. As the nation was showing signs of recovery from the depression much of the popular press had turned against Roosevelt and his New Deal policies. Until late in that year, however, Macfadden continued to shout for Roosevelt in his editorials and the public and advertisers responded to praise of the president. The excitement over gangsterism in the thirties helped too because the magazine featured stories on the criminals and their nemesis, the G-Man. *Liberty* warmly aided J. Edgar Hoover's campaign to enhance his own and the FBI's reputation and Hoover reciprocated by doing favors for Oursler. But the political defection of Macfadden from Roosevelt towards Republicans and himself was obvious in 1936 and earnings that year reverted to the familiar red. Oursler managed to keep on good terms with the Roosevelts and Eleanor continued to write for *Liberty*. Readers also responded to good magazine coverage of the abdication of Edward VII and the birth and raising of the Dionne quintuplets.

Liberty recorded the coming of World War II in an interesting way. Macfadden, a consistent opponent of war, who had denounced World War I as insanity, and insisted that businessmen would band together to prevent another such disaster, wrote editorial after editorial denouncing war. He also showed his toleration and Oursler's persuasiveness in allowing the editor to call for England's resistance to Hitler after the breach of the Munich agreement. He did not give up, but let Oursler place his editorial beside his own charges that European statesmen were trying to draw America into a war. Oursler's piece was entitled, "This is No Time To Talk of Peace, Mr. Macfadden," and Macfadden's view was "Must We Be Prepared For Hell?"[27]

In *Liberty* readers rarely found anything directly expounding the publisher's health theories. The few exceptions to the rule were lively accounts of certain activities as with Edward Doherty's "Found—The Fountain of Youth," a story on one of the many cross-country hikes Macfadden sponsored. Even the *New York Times* and other newspapers gave pretty good coverage to these events involving several hundred pedestrians and hundred miles of walking, usually to Macfadden's sanitarium at Dansville, New York. Doherty interviewed the marchers of "Bernarr Macfadden's Cracked Wheat Derby,"—as one participant called the hike—near the end of a 260 mile trek from Cleveland. The marchers were singing when Doherty met them:

> Cracked wheat Monday,
> Cracked wheat Tuesday,
> Cracked wheat Wednesday,
> Cracked wheat Thursday,
> Cracked wheat Friday,
> Cracked wheat Saturday too![28]

Macfadden was with the walkers and he glowed when Doherty praised the youthful appearance of even the older members of the brigade. "They've found the Fountain of Youth," the leader said. "It flows out of their feet. I wish every man and woman could learn that. Nobody needs any gland transplantation, any operation, to become young again. He needs only to walk. These people are proof of that statement. Talk to some of them and you'll be convinced."[29]

And sure enough, when Doherty talked to the folks he heard all kinds of stories about doctors who had warned individuals that they might drop dead any minute and wonderful accounts of transformations from obesity. All the marchers praised Macfadden for encouraging their concern with diet and exercise and for providing the "cracked wheat wagon" which provided their meals along the way.

Liberty's greatest embarrassment came through the contributions of writer George Sylvester Viereck. Oursler alleged that he tried to discourage Macfadden from using Viereck's work when he first started work as an editor in 1924, after pointing out that Viereck had been jailed as a German propagandist during World War I. Macfadden did not believe the German-American's earlier patriotism made any difference and Oursler talked to other important men who felt the same way. Thus in the 1930s Viereck was contributing interesting articles to *Liberty*, including an interview with Adolph Hitler that revealed the staunch anti-communist posture of the leader.

Mary Macfadden blamed Oursler for employing Viereck just as she blamed him for every other bad decision her husband made. She argued that Bernarr was "basically ignorant" of foreign affairs. "He had never, during our married life, shown any interest in news dispatches concerning political diplomacy."[30] Oursler recognized that Viereck revered Hitler but continued to use his material because it was also evident that he rejected Hitler's anti-Semitism. As the war pressures grew Oursler had to start rejecting the stories he received and later the Justice Department prosecuted Viereck successfully as an alien propagandist. It does not appear that the propagandist had much luck in keeping Americans friendly to Hitler with his magazine work and the exposure did not harm the reputations of Macfadden and Oursler. Before Pearl Harbor Macfadden was ousted from his place as publisher by stockholders and Oursler took up war work. Under new management the magazine carried on until 1950.

It appears that *Liberty* was much more Oursler's magazine than it was Macfadden's. Its content was dictated more by its own history and the needs of competing with the *Saturday Evening Post* and *Collier's* and did not usually represent the passions of the publisher. Yet it was not Macfadden's way to leave any of his ventures solely at the direction of their staff: he wished to be involved in everything. He was comfortable enough with Oursler to allow him to spend several months in Hollywood when one of his films was in production with the understanding that he would not falter in his editorial duties, but the publisher was never long away from the office. The two men met often on weekends too. After Macfadden took up flying he often flew up to Oursler's place on Cape Cod. Macfadden liked to perform daredevil loops and spins near the Oursler residence before landing at an airport fifteen miles away.

Oursler always sent his car to pick up the boss but he preferred to run and walk alternately to the house. It was the gossip at Falmouth, according to Oursler's joke, that the Ourslers did not treat the old, white-haired man who visited them very well. They did not let him ride in their car, despite that he had no shoes, did not let him sleep in a bed, and, when they took him to a restaurant, they only let him have some juice.

The decade of the thirties brought out fresh aspects of Macfadden's potential for diversification, particularly with his political activity. He had always made something of a specialty of diffusing himself but he spread his attention dangerously thin with his whirlwind activities. The depression was unkind enough on men whose full focus remained fixed on continuing their commercial successes. People continued to read Macfadden's magazines during the depression but advertising income fell off. Traditionally, magazines depend upon advertising for the major share of their income and the Macfadden Publishing Co. was no exception. As major company advertisers tended to look down on Macfadden's magazines, he depended on smaller companies who were hard hit by the depression.

But the publisher's free spending was a sharper threat than the hard times. The president of a public corporation was not licensed to spend on whim: the day of reckoning was coming.

Chapter 12
The Ardent Lover

Give them love and more love and more love; any divorce is more news than any war.

Bernarr Macfadden

Leon S. Brach, a stockholder of the Macfadden Publishing Company, wondered why the publisher was running around Florida wooing voters when his magazines needed attention. Now Macfadden wanted to be the U.S. Senator from Florida and stockholders figured that they had been paying for his political campaigning since his presidential bid in 1936. In April 1940 Brach sued Macfadden for $1,400,000 in federal court, citing his cancellation of a $250,000 campaign loan from the company in 1936 and his wrongful drawing of a large salary while only devoting a little time to business.

At this ungrateful attack Macfadden was astonished. It seemed so unfair that some johnny-come-lately, a fellow who purchased his first stock in 1936, could dare question the wisdom and efforts of one who had given his all to the company for forty years. The publisher doubted that the suit really had anything to do with business. Like everyone in politics he experienced more than his usual paranoia in the heat of a campaign. "This is a trumped up charge," he told the press, "nothing else but political animosity could cause such a suit to be brought after four years of silence."[1] Back in 1936 Brach and other stockholders knew full well that the publisher's campaigning benefited the business. In fact, Macfadden argued with deep sincerity, his every act, every breath he drew, every handstand, and every public appearance was for the business.

But his forceful disclaimers did not help a bit. After thrashing matters out over a ten month period the lawyers reached an agreement on one thorny issue: Macfadden resigned as company president in February 1941. "Having reached the age of 73 years," he said graciously, "and finding that my foundation enterprises are demanding more and more of my time and attention, I have decided to relinquish control of Macfadden Publications."[2] The wording of this press release was extraordinary— not in the mention of his age, as he emphasized his age more with each birthday—but in hinting that the years in any way affected his energy.

His resignation created wide interest. *Newsweek* reported that the retirement of "the bushy-haired health faddist"[3] from the ten magazines worth $12,000,000 had been forced by officers and creditors who hoped "to lure advertisers frightened by Macfadden-inspired sensationalism." Macfadden was the majority stockholder but the printers and paper companies whose bills were unpaid had swung their support to the minority stockholders. The transition was smooth because most of the officers and editors kept their jobs. O.J. Elder, who had been Macfadden's business manager and advertising chief from the early days of *Physical Culture*, became the company president.

Newsweek was kinder to Macfadden than its rival, *Time*, was accustomed to be: "Now Macfadden may be out as a publisher but not as a health crusader. A walking example of his health theories, he will continue to fast, diet, exercise, and sunbathe to keep himself in shape."[4] Macfadden also had work to do with the foundation's "three schools, sanitarium, and three health resorts."

A few months later the court ruled on the minority stockholder suit. Macfadden must pay back $300,000 to the company, including the $250,000 campaign debt, return $200,000 in preferred stock, and cancel a contract requiring the company to spend $25,000 yearly at the Macfadden Deauville Hotel in Miami Beach. The bite could have been larger, as stockholders had even tried to get compensation for the $7,000,000 in losses accumulated by the *New York Graphic*, but it certainly reduced Macfadden's income. The reorganized company bought Macfadden's stock and he agreed not to compete with any of the magazines for five years.

Macfadden did not stay out of publishing for very long. After less than two years the company ran *Physical Culture* into the ground after trying to turn it into a beauty magazine. The company sold the magazine cheaply to its creator who quickly returned it to its familiar format. Some of the old magic still existed: Macfadden did manage to get the circulation up to 100,000—but that was far short of the 300,000 plus the magazine had attracted in better days. When the five year prohibition period ended Macfadden announced the debut of *Bernarr Macfadden's Detective Magazine*. Since paper stocks, depleted by the diversion of industry during the war, were not yet bountiful the publisher had to wait a little longer before launching a confession magazine and an auto magazine. As it turned out, for lack of financing or other reasons, no new magazines appeared. The original health magazine, now called *National Hygiene*, was the sole magazine venture he indulged in.

Even while fighting to retain control of his publishing empire Macfadden did not neglect to abuse his old enemy, the American Medical Association. In *Liberty* he demanded that the established school of medicine, known as allopathic, not be allowed to fill all the medical posts in the rapidly expanding military forces. He wanted equal consideration of homeopaths, osteopaths, naturopaths, and chiropractors, and cited statistics proving that his favorites did better than regular physicians. During the 1918 flu epidemic osteopaths only lost one fourth of one percent of their patients while regular doctors lost five to six percent. On pneumonia cases osteopaths only lost ten percent compared to the thirty-three percent loss rate of regular doctors. Chiropractors, by Macfadden's figures, did even better in saving lives.

The AMA's Bureau of Investigation always felt compelled to reply to published assaults on doctors' professional competence. Direct confrontation was difficult because the sources of Macfadden's statistics were mysterious and his use of them was more partisan than rational. On other arguments made by Macfadden the AMA stood on surer ground, as when refuting his charge that American soldiers overate. "He did not have the slightest knowledge of just how much soldiers eat...Officers will not permit themselves to be swayed by the extravagant claims of irresponsible cultists or by the distorted diatribes of Bernarr Macfadden."[5]

Pearl Harbor did not bring about a truce between Macfadden and the AMA. In late December 1941 the Bureau of Investigation was pleased to report that the Federal Trade Commission, after examining Macfadden's book, *Hair Culture,* had ordered him to stop stating in advertising that baldness could be cured by following his methods of treatment. Since Macfadden's long-established method, worked out when his hair suddenly started to vanish, called for tugging at the roots vigorously and "right living," his claim did seem a little exaggerated. Then as now the field of hair quackery was a very rich one. Over the centuries men poured oceans of odd mixtures on their scalps and some of them probably caused brain damage. One thing to be said in favor of Macfadden's treatment was that it did no harm unless a fellow was so determined that he pulled out roots and all.[6]

Around the same time the Federal Trade Commission pained the aging champion of vigorous life further by interfering with his advertisements for another book, *Strengthening the Eyes.* To be ordered to quit saying that "eye exercises are new, revolutionary and will correct defects"[7] made Macfadden think that the nation was going to the dogs. Had not he once overcome his own blindness, caused by overwork trying to meet a deadline for writing a book, through exercises? Over the years thousands of grateful men and women had written him with thanks for teaching them how to save their vision. Now this! Well, the doctors were certainly in the driver's seat.

Macfadden's commercial interest in eye exercises went back to 1917 when he teamed up with Dr. William H. Bates on a correspondence course that was offered by the Physical Culture Publishing Company and much advertised in *Physical Culture.* Bates had a curious history after graduating from a reputable medical school and practicing in New York where he also taught ophthalmology. In 1902 he vanished, then was discovered by his wife working at a hospital in London. Before that he had been admitted to the hospital, suffering from exhaustion. He told two stories to account for his movements: (1) he was performing surgery on a ship in New York harbor when it sailed off to Europe; (2) when he left New York he had been suffering from a complete loss of memory. Soon he vanished again and Mrs. Bates was still looking when she died. Bates surfaced in North Dakota where he practiced for several years before returning to New York to establish himself there.

At some point Bates reached the conclusion that anyone suffering from errors of refraction could train his eyes to perfect vision by exercises and exposure to intense light. One of his treatments, called "palming" required the patient to put the palms of his hands over his eyes and think of "perfect black." When a patient was able to see a perfect blackness he was on the road to improvement. Bates discovered, through a woman patient who was depressed by the color black that other colors worked as well. This particular patient experienced a correction of her sight by thinking hard about her favorite flower, a yellow buttercup. Exercises involved the shift and the swing. Shifting, moving the eyes back and forth until one gained an illusion of any object swinging, could be practiced visually or just mentally.

Macfadden sold the correspondence course for over twenty years. His advertisements made no bones about the wonders of the method: "THROW YOUR GLASSES AWAY. Eye glasses are not necessary to the average man or woman now wearing them. They can be discarded with joy and comfort, if you will strengthen your eyes." Later Macfadden dropped Bates' name from the course. Bates published a book, *Cure of Imperfect Eyesight* in 1920 and started a monthly magazine called *Better Eyesight*. Bates died in 1931 but Macfadden and others carried on. His theories made no sense except for the disorders involving the exterior muscles—walled eyes or partially crossed eyes, but their appeal still survives because many people hate wearing glasses. Bates' leading convert was the British novelist, Aldous Huxley, who wrote a book about his own "cure."

Macfadden's exercises varied from those developed by Bates. His book rejected the shift and swing as too complicated and went for moving the eyes up and down, from side to side, in nice rolling movements. Macfadden also recommended that the patient focus alternately on the tip of a pencil held before his eyes and a distant object. He liked frequent bathing of the eyes and opening them while the face was submerged in a bowl of water, and worked out a number of finger massages of the eyes as well. As perhaps the earliest disciple of Bates, Macfadden may have been annoyed when Gayelord Hauser breathed new life into the old bit of quackery with a book, *Keener Vision Without Glasses,* published in 1932. The book made lots of money over several reprintings with a text that leaned heavily on Bates and Macfadden with some of the author's own diet wisdom appended. Hauser believed that autointoxication contributed heavily to the cause of glaucoma and he sold healthy products to benefit victims.[8]

Despite these setbacks from government agencies Macfadden was still able to bark back at his old foes. He warned readers of *True Story* in a 1941 editorial that the AMA had a "death grip"[9] on health care and urged them to protest to the government. "Health advice has been commercialized to a scandalous degree," cried the man who had always argued that each individual should assume sole responsibility for his own health.

Macfadden also published an "Open Letter to President Roosevelt" in pamphlet form (not that he had any faith in Roosevelt on matters of health or anything else) that did not mince words: "Allopathic medical health authorities are to blame for all our physical deficiencies. They have made a ghastly failure of their efforts to protect the health of the American people." Roosevelt should reflect upon what could have been accomplished in American health if someone had taken charge of matters on a national level, Macfadden advised. He did not admire the "war-mad Germans" now fighting the world but they certainly showed the effects of their perverse education: "From the time its citizens are tiny tots they are trained to be ruthless murderers."[10]

As one of the nation's more celebrated men Macfadden was the subject of a two-part biography in the *Saturday Evening Post* in June 1941. Alva Johnston, a writer who delighted in colorful characters, caught his subject in mid-leap with bemused respect. Magazine journalists have to sum things up rather directly so, as it was baseball season, Johnston projected his subject's lifetime batting average on his major crusades:

Against prudishness 1.000
Against medicine .000
Against corsets .890
Against muscular inactivity .333
Against alcohol .250
Against cigarettes .000
Against white bread 1.000[11]

Johnston marveled at Macfadden's profound belief in himself and his willingness to treat every known disease without fee: "The treatment was fundamentally the same for oily skin, locomotor ataxia, fits, weak eyes, weak mind, creaking knees, heart disease, writer's cramp, telegrapher's wrist, baseball player's glass arm, lover's broken heart, red nose and others."[12]

In preparation for his interview Johnston talked to some of the publisher's associates, including editor Fulton Oursler who confided that the boss had once doubted Shakespeare's importance. Macfadden thought it scandalous that Oursler read Shakespeare every day when he might have been building muscles or doing something else worthwhile. "Breaking young men of their weaknesses had been Macfadden's lifelong specialty, and he struggled to induce Oursler to brace up and be a man."[13] After years of nagging Oursler hit on the perfect rebuttal. At the time several New York theatres were playing the Bard's works and Oursler suggested a calculation of his royalties income from around the world had the author been alive. That thought put the matter in a different light as Macfadden respected success. After pondering awhile he assured Oursler that "to have accomplished all that, he must have kept himself in wonderful physical condition. Shakespeare was a great physical culturist."

Johnston gathered other anecdotes talking to other Macfadden staffers. One said that while Horace Greeley's message to young men was "go west," Macfadden's was "find your mate."[14] Another repeated an old office joke—the response to any query about the time of day: "It's always sex o'clock here." But Johnston, not content to repeat dubious jokes, answered significant questions about his subject: "The great proof of Macfadden's sincerity is the harsh doctrine which he preached. He was the fierce evangelist of the hellfire-and-damnation theology of health; he called on his flock to make life a horrid grind at the exercising machines and through painful periods of fasting."[15] Most cult leaders make things easier for disciples but Macfadden never backed away from his rigorous doctrines. No scheming popularity seeker would have shown his followers such a steep and thorny way to the physical-culture heaven."

Macfadden was not in the news during the war years as much as earlier but he still managed to keep his name before the public. Sometimes newspapers made fun of him as when the *Detroit News* commented upon Macfadden's demonstration of standing on his head for a news reporter: "Now let's see him walk."[16] The *Chicago Tribune* thought this jibe funny enough to reprint the Detroit paper's story. It was hard for Macfadden to avoid trouble with the law because he wanted to help people gain good health. In 1943 he established the Macfadden Health Service Bureau in New York to give medical advice but the doctors induced the law to pounce on him and levy a $500 fine. When he had done the same thing years before through the offices of the *Graphic* no one had dared to protest. These days he was not so powerful as he had once been.

Some forty years after Macfadden stormed New York with his provocative physical culture show at Madison Square Garden he put on a spiritual show at Carnegie Hall. Advance advertisements had announced his presentation of a new religion, one "which tries to bring some of heaven down to earth."[17] The old fellow, with his great shock of white, untameable hair, heavily seamed face, corded neck, and rumpled suit, could still fill a house: 2,200 showed up at Carnegie Hall to hear about Cosmotarianism. *Newsweek* enjoyed the new adventure of the 77-year old health crank: "To the affiliated devout of New York it was just another evening of unorthodoxy, but to the curious, the hopeful, and the habituated disciples of Bernarr Macfadden, it was a chance to sit in the Dynamic Presence and hear new truths."

The truths, of course, were not new at all. It was the same old Macfadden message incorporated into an organized religion for those who might prefer such formalization. "Cosmotarianism serves up 'religion through happiness' on a whole-wheat basis,"[18] as *Newsweek* saw it. Macfadden expounded the theme he had expressed in thousands of editorials: man must cherish his God-given body and the Kingdom of Heaven will automatically follow.

Some of Macfadden's activities during this time vexed him. The proceedings over the divorce from Mary in 1945-46 were not pleasant interludes. He had to sit in court listening to the woman he had once rescued from poverty and obscurity brag that "when I met Bernarr he was standing on his head and I put him on his feet."[19] But he was glad to conclude a relationship that had kept him involved with the courts for thirteen years. And around the time of the final divorce he even got a rather nice mention in *Time*. The magazine summarized Macfadden's plans for various new magazines, noting that the publisher intended to labor without salary, depending upon his $2,000 monthly annuity, and generally approved of him: "He still leaps over chairs, does somersaults to prove his agility, and scoffs at retiring. Says he: 'The only place to retire to is the cemetery.' "[20]

Even a busy, old man could recognize when something was missing from his life—particularly one who believed himself as vigorous as a 20-year old. Thus, two years after his divorce from Mary, he was ripe for marriage when he met a most suitable woman. Johnnie Lee, a tall, attractive blonde from Fort Worth, Texas, had been married at age 19 to W.C. Holt, a rich oil man many years older. Soon after the birth of a second child the couple was divorced. Johnnie Lee moved to Hollywood, then Chicago, and finally New York, trying her hand at this and that before becoming a lecturer on health and sex when not consulting as an interior decorator. She had found that "both men and women were eager to learn my formulas for health, youth, love, money, and peace of mind."[21] It had been in California where, after failing as an actress, she had evolved, single-handedly, the science of Cosmo-Dynamics, a way of attaining personal magnetism, everlasting youth, and anything else an individual might wish to have.

It was after hearing Johnnie Lee lecture in New York that Macfadden was introduced by a friend. Sparks flew immediately. Bernarr, 79 years old in 1948, was smitten by the 42-year old beauty. She also experienced electrifying sensations. Macfadden knew nothing of Cosmo-Dynamics but his personal magnetism had not faded over the years even if his once powerful body had diminished somewhat. One could always imagine of the physical culturist that his intensity and energy radiated sparks; he could probably light a dark room.

When Macfadden wanted something he went all-out. He wooed Johnnie Lee with great spirit and even summoned her to Florida where he was campaigning for governor. At times he behaved with great vulgarity and arrogant disregard of Johnnie's finer feelings which caused her to recall rumors about him: "his glorification of sex, his carryings-on with his good-looking young secretaries, his several marriages, his sensational escapades, his unconventional dress, his habit of walking barefoot through the heart of the city."[22] But Macfadden, masterly, persistent, rich, famous, and so ardent he could not forebear pinching her bum and kissing her in public, could not be denied.

At his appearance for their first dinner date Bernarr cut short her polite formalities and called for her admission that she loved him. "Really, Mr. Macfadden," she said. "Oh, come off it, Johnnie Lee," he growled. "Let's not stand on ceremony. I'm serving notice right now on all the wolves that must be after you to keep their distance. I've staked my claim, and don't you forget it. Come on, let's eat!"[23]

Initially, she resisted his macho ways. The age disparity in such a December-June relationship made marriage seem preposterous. At one point, angry ears aflame at his crudities, she had boldly asked, "what could you possibly have to offer me?"[24] Answering was easy for the old showman: "I have everything to offer you, my dear—everything in the world. I have my love and my virility; I am a young man—younger than any man you ever knew, and stronger. I can give you new strength, and mental stimulation, and a whole new world of happiness beyond your wildest dreams."

Soon the couple married in Miami Beach before 500 invited guests and the "Goat Lady." The "Goat Lady," a local character who led a goat around the streets while loudly denouncing smokers, dashed about in the church denouncing the wedding: "This marriage is against the Holy Word. It is illegal."[25] Eventually she was removed by three ushers, who doubled as bellboys at the Macfadden Deauville Hotel, and the ceremony was concluded without further uproar.

Around the nation newspapers found space for mention of the wedding. Many thoughtful men and women, reflecting on the wirephotos picturing the somewhat mismatched couple, wondered if old Bernarr could please his glowing, robust bride. They need not have worried.

For many years Macfadden had advocated sex exercises and a healthy way of life that promoted vitality. Sexual intercourse was not only pleasurable but it was a very healthy exercise. He had never felt very safe in discussing these verities in print but, over the years, the public had shaken off most of the shackles imposed by prudes. Thus, when Johnnie Lee Macfadden was ready to write about her marriage she was free to describe the raptures of her love-making. Bernarr had promised her that he would prove to be "a better man" than any she had known— and he had fulfilled his boast repeatedly. The 38-year age differential became meaningless when Bernarr griped her in his still powerful arms.

The Florida days were a whirlwind of political campaigning and frolic for the newlyweds. They lived at the Macfadden Deauville (during the fall 1948 campaign), a lovely resort hotel in Miami Beach, fronting on the sandy ocean shore in the midst of a tropical garden. Johnnie Lee enjoyed the hotel and enjoyed campaigning too. Often Bernarr piloted his own plane, taking her along for speeches and meetings around the state. Her presence at his side generated much publicity—which may have had something to do with his eagerness for a quick marriage. It was thrilling to be greeted in various towns by supporters' friendly cries as they waved placards expressing the candidate's campaign promises that had been provided by his headquarters:

"LIVE AND LOVE WITH MACFADDEN!"
"SUPERMAN FOR GOVERNOR!"
"MACFADDEN'S MASTER FORMULA WILL CHANGE THE WORLD!"
"SEX, SUN AND FUN WITH MACFADDEN FOR GOVERNOR!"
"MAKE FLORIDA THE GARDEN OF EDEN WITH MACFADDEN!"

As a husband Bernarr was on the whole, considerate, loving, full of fun, and quick to praise his bride. He admitted that he enjoyed shocking people and hoped she could overcome her embarrassment at his public antics. He assured her that she was his special dish, the apple of his eye: "Thank God, Johnnie Lee, you're built like a woman. You know, when men get together and talk about women, the way men always do, they agree that the most desirable women are the ones with rounded, voluptuous hips. That's the view of the real, virile he-man, my dear, and you may congratulate yourself that you measure up where measurements count the most."[26] Such appraisals gave immense comfort to Johnnie Lee because she worried about her hips a lot. Sweets were almost irresistible to her so the temptations were an enormous burden. It helped that Bernarr threw out any candy she smuggled into their suite and loudly denounced her signs of weakness. But he never accused her of being too stout. Indeed, he was constantly booming out his denunciations of the dieting craze, then intensifying in the nation: "Lot of nonsense," he cried. "Look at the Greek ideal of love and beauty, the Venus de Milo—did she have underdeveloped hips? Look at the masterpieces of art—did any of the great masters bother to paint hipless females? You're darn tootin' they didn't."[27]

As ever the octogenarian not only knew who the best women were he also knew how they should present themselves. He had long since vanquished the perfidious corset but he still worried about dictates of fashion calling for the confinement of womens' curves in stiff girdles and tight brassieres. "The most beautiful lines in the world are the curves of a woman's breasts and hips," he argued. "They should be free and unrestrained. Any woman who conceals her natural charms is a damn fool. There should be a law against it."[28] When Macfadden called for a law against something you knew that the matter was a crucial one because generally he opposed restrictive laws.

It was a good thing for their marriage that Johnnie Lee had made a career out of counseling women against too much assertiveness and competition with men, because her husband could be outrageous. She loved shoes and owned dozens of pairs until Bernarr, in a draconian reform, threw them all out. In exchange he offered her the same kind of health shoes he wore himself, sturdy space shoes, half open for ventilation, with thick platform soles to cushion the foot (and make a short man taller). She was furious but wore the cloddish footwear in his presence. Soon she retaliated by throwing out his entire wardrobe of ancient, ill-fitting suits, including some that did not show too much wear after almost thirty years of service. He had to concede that his familiar clothes had felt a little loose lately but she did not make an issue of his obvious shrinkage. Cheerfully he went along with her on a tour of the most fashionable men's clothing stores for a complete outfitting. Johnnie Lee thought that he was a millionaire—a mistake that she never did get straight—and did not wish him to dress like a pauper. For a time Bernarr looked spiffy but eventually the wrinkles and rumples, so characteristic of the man, triumphed.

The voters of Florida decided against Macfadden as governor. His emphasis on making the state a fountain of youth for folks seeking health and long life did not appeal to everyone. Too many people came to Florida now, grumbled some voters who worried about the influx of poor people seeking social services. Macfadden had spent $50,000 of his own money on the campaign and got nothing in return except for the exhilaration of appearing before crowds who admired him and the young wife standing beside him.[29]

The Macfaddens moved back to New York where each had an apartment. Macfadden's, on Central Park West, was in an old, dingy building and unlovely neighborhood. He thought it was fine because he had lived there since 1933 when he had separated from Mary and it was located conveniently for his needs. Johnnie Lee had to have a bed moved in because he had taken up sleeping on a mat on the floor some years earlier. His floor sleeping was healthy for the spine and also put one in closer contact with the magnetic forces of the earth which could be stultified by mattresses. She spent most nights with him until she talked him into leasing an expensive penthouse apartment that seemed suitable to their affluence and her taste. She would have been smarter to leave things as they were because time was putting a sharp edge on Bernarr's geniality.

Aside from her youth, admirable hips, and concern for health and beauty regimes, Johnnie Lee's life-style did not match Bernarr's. Some unkind Macfadden disciples had even written to *Health Review* protesting the match and accusing Johnnie Lee of marrying the publisher for his money. This pained her because she believed ardently "that our marriage was predestined for the purpose of bringing together not only two people made to complete each other, but two theories of life—one physical, one spiritual—which together produced a new and invincible doctrine of health, long-lasting youth, beauty, and peace of mind."[30] She believed that Bernarr's great shortcoming was his lack of faith in a divine power, but when she brought her own faith into their combination it became an unbeatable one for doing good for other people.

Alas, it was true that Johnnie Lee, like most Americans, never walked when she could ride and considered exercise an evil necessity against the ravages of bulging flesh. But she was game and did join Bernarr on walks in Central Park and even learned to enjoy going barefoot when no one was looking. Yet walking did lead to the first major disruption in their happy union. While they were visiting in California she had inadvertently discovered one of his secrets while looking for him along a mountain trail. He was busy burying a metal box full of money and very disturbed that she had seen him do it. He accused her of spying and demanded to know whether she could wait for his death before getting her hands on his money. In time she learned all about his practice of burying money. He had caches near every sanitarium and hotel that he visited often, in Florida, California, New Jersey, and Long Island, New York. She figured that he had buried about $4,000,000, although she did not explain how she arrived at this sum. When he was in a good mood he promised to give her a map showing his caches, but he never did. Burying money was not as bizarre a thing as one might think. Many misers and/or folks who distrusted banks tried to keep their money at hand in this fashion. Someone who had been haunted and terrorized over the years by the ease with which authorities grasped at bank accounts after civil damage actions and divorce suits looked with particular favor at holes in the ground.

At first such manifestations of eccentric behavior and rage were only rare disturbances in a wonderful marriage. Yes, Johnnie Lee thought, her husband was different, but he was wonderful, "quixotic, fanatic, unpredictable, sometimes shocking but always fascinating."[31] It was like being married "to a mixture of Romeo, Huckleberry Finn, Solomon and Captain Kidd," because he switched roles so instantly from "ardent lover to mischievous, small boy to wise patriarch to adventurous buccaneer." They laughed together, sunbathed in the nude, made love at all hours, and enjoyed a rich harmony—for a time. Bernarr's insistence on laughing gave her pleasure but he had long been an advocate of laughing for physical and psychological reasons. He encouraged his disciples to make laughing a habit, to force it until it came naturally. The stretching did wonders for the muscles of the face although some thought that Macfadden's face work left him with unusually deep lines and wrinkles.

Bernarr was not a perfect husband. He could not bring himself to buy Johnnie Lee the gifts of furs and jewelry she naturally yearned for, or to give her more than a few dollars of spending money at a time. Once, in California, he gave her flowers, a small, straggly bunch gathered on a walk. Her wedding ring, a beautiful and imposing one of rubies and diamonds, had been purchased at a pawnshop.

Johnnie Lee understood her husband's tenacity and intensity but she did not sense his focus of them during the first years of their marriage. The old rebel had not abandoned any of his established crusades but had shifted much of his energy to carrying through the fight of his life. One cause, one battle seemed surpassingly important now. One more foe had to be thrown and pinned to the mat. But how to do it when the foe was oneself—one's own advancing years—inevitable death?

Chapter 13
Too Many Wives

Unfortunately, nothing can be written about Bernarr Macfadden without shedding garments.

Mary Macfadden

A tribute to Macfadden's place in American culture was signified in 1950 by a two-part profile by Robert Lewis Taylor in the *New Yorker*. Taylor did not venerate his subject but he acknowledged that Macfadden had "awakened half the world to the sagging state of its muscles."[1] Taylor summed up Macfadden as "the liveliest, and most contentious, American of his century," and believed that he would achieve his goal of living 125 years. "He is one of that tiny, inexplicable band of evangels—the John Browns, the Huey Longs, the Rasputins, the Aimee McPhersons— who have extra-human wellsprings of force. As a whole, their temporal stay is tempestuous."[2]

Taylor reviewed Macfadden's career with the usual journalistic delight in colorful anecdotes and also reported on his current views. At age 82 he was still unhappy with doctors and still believed that he had all the answers to health. Recently he had become very alarmed about the methods doctors were using to treat cancer and, after long research, had come up with a natural remedy of surpassing effectiveness: an exclusive diet of grapes. Oh, he knew that the doctors would start yowling immediately against so simple and healthful a solution to a severe national problem so he challenged them. Advertisements in his *Health Review* formerly *National Hygiene,* held his wager of $10,000 that the grape diet would relieve pain and advance incurable patients towards recovery. Anyone who could prove him wrong could collect the $10,000.[3]

Pursuing rumors that the old health reformer was not happy with his children, Taylor asked about the condition of America's most perfect family. "They've slacked on their bodies,"[4] said Macfadden. "They should have kept on." But a friend of Macfadden's, who knew all about the tough training programs he had set up for the family in Englewood, thought maybe they were still resting up from their youthful exertions.

Johnnie Lee told Taylor how receptive she was to Bernarr's whims. She even encouraged his flying although she was not too keen to go along with him. Lately her great thrust had been to encourage him in more social outings. People were certainly impressed when they met Macfadden at parties even though he refused offers of drinks and was likely to burst into song without reference to programmed events. He had been taking singing lessons; "I Love Life" was his favorite song and he rendered it with great spirit.

Mary Macfadden was one interested reader of the *New Yorker* profiles. She noticed that Bernarr had admitted to only three marriages and figured he would continue to re-write his marital history in subsequent interviews. Her only other correction concerned the number of years Bernarr claimed to have been sleeping on the floor. It was certainly far less than sixty and she had never shared any space with him on the floor. All these little details were important to Mary because Bernarr was much on her mind. She was writing a biography of him and also thinking about suing him again as she was dissatisfied with the divorce settlement made in 1946.

Meanwhile, on Bernarr's current marriage front the idyl had ended with great abruptness. According to Johnnie Lee Bernarr had become rather difficult: "his irrational jealousy, temper and suspicion...grew with the years."[5] He became obsessed with the notion that she was "carrying on flirtations or worse with other and younger men." He even accused her of leaving a window open to admit a secret lover even though their penthouse was on the 15th floor. What little reading he did, mostly in *True Detective* magazine, encouraged his other paranoid delusion that someone, probably the AMA, was trying to poison his food. Once when they returned home to find the door had been left unlocked Bernarr rushed to the kitchen and threw out all the food, even the cans. He was not sure who he could trust: "Don't you ever think you can fool Macfadden! You hear me, Johnnie Lee? Don't you try to put anything over on Macfadden! He's too smart for all of you."[6] She declared her love and he accused her of wanting his money. Finally, she brought him to his senses by giving him a vigorous shake. He covered his confusion by trying to laugh the incident off, pretending that he had just been fooling.

Bernarr tried to distract her with a new scheme—a second honeymoon in Paris. Of course, there was a catch as with most of Macfadden's holidays. He had celebrated his latest birthdays by parachuting from an airplane and gotten generous publicity. But the stunt showed signs of wear in New York so Macfadden decided to jump into the Seine River at Paris. The French, an excitable people, would love it, and world-wide newspaper coverage would follow. He remained suspicious about the French nation and still responded to behavior of which he disapproved as of old ("A man who would do that has been to Paris"), but the French did love spectacles. "This time you jump too!"[7] Bernarr said. "That'll make them sit up and take notice, I bet! See the headlines now! Superman Macfadden and beautiful young wife jump from plane together!"

For once Johnnie Lee was not a good sport. She was afraid of parachuting and indignant that Bernarr planned a degrading gimmick. "You'll look gorgeous in red tights to match mine," he told her. "And across the seat you'll have one word, MACFADDEN, in big white letters! The world will then see that you're all mine. What d'ye say?"[8] She said no and no again. Having his name "written across my fanny" was just too much. All his cajoling, all his lavish praise of her figure did not work this time. Then he got furious and stomped out. The sun-kissed marriage of kindred souls was effectively ended. Whether Johnnie Lee's version of events can be relied upon is not too significant. It appears plausible enough and Bernarr did like his own way.

Bernarr did his parachuting as a solo act. He had to forebear publicizing the time and place of his jump because the French police planned to arrest him and charge him for their costs in crowd control. As he was not too rich he restricted his announcements to the news media. For one reason or another he missed the Seine on his jump but otherwise it went well. "I'm still a young guy!"[9] he crowed to the press.

Perhaps, in the exhilaration of the moment, he did feel young but, overall, the Superman became rather normal in the last stretch of his life. One could sorrow more for his trials—as painful as Job's boils— had he not insisted so strongly that he would "not go quiet into that long night." All his life he had led with his chin—and usually he scored well. But in his mid-eighties, while still asking for trouble, he was not in very good shape to handle the blows.

Some attacks were not so important. The post office, his old nemesis, made a fuss about the Mininberg Oscillator, a device the Macfadden Foundation was allegedly selling "to prevent disease, reduce over-weight, and cure rheumatism."[10] Macfadden succeeded in pointing out that the advertisement in his health magazine did not name the foundation as seller of the device so prosecution was dropped. In a separate proceeding, however, the post office forced him to discontinue exaggerated magazine advertisements for his book on treatments for deafness.

The publication of *Dumbbells and Carrot Strips* in 1953 was aggravating to its subject. This was the first biography of Macfadden published since that banner year of 1929 when three worshipful books appeared. Authors Mary Macfadden and Emile Gauvreau treated him scornfully although they tried to maintain a light tone. The *New York Times* reviewer found the book a "hilarious, uninhibited and merciless" portrait of the "elderly apostle of 'the form divine.' " Macfadden, the reviewer noted, had deserved his notoriety since he "out-Hearsted Hearst in lurid journalism, out-Barnumed Barnum in showmanship, and his eccentricities make Lord Timothy Dexter, Newburyport's eccentric of long ago, seem as staid as the late George Apley."[11]

Mary could not have written *Dumbbells* without professional help. It is entirely possible that Bernarr had exaggerated her educational deficiencies just a few years earlier in divorce proceedings: "I tried to teach her the rudiments of grammar but she still doesn't know the difference between a noun and a verb."[12] He did not knock her out of random churlishness but to counter her story of long years of editorial labors on his magazines. But, whatever Mary lacked in grammar, she made up for in a retentive memory and avenging spirit.

Her co-author was a highly skilled journalist who knew Bernarr very well. It is not clear if Gauvreau's willingness to join in Mary's hatchet job on his old boss had anything to do with bitter feelings for the publisher. In his memoir, *My Last Million Readers,* Gauvreau said that he resigned from editorial management of the *Graphic* in 1929 because he needed a rest after five years of frantic work. Part of his remuneration was paid in company stock and he sold out for $60,000 when he quit. "I liked the Macfaddens but I had to tell the fighting publisher that I was through and I left with regret because I understood him. His muscles did not permit him to pull his punches in the newspaper business."[13] Soon after Gauvreau quit W.R. Hearst hired him as managing editor of the *New York Mirror.* Perhaps Gauvreau just wanted to help Mary out or was paid by her for his work. They had been good friends and had a common antagonist in Fulton Oursler. Mary had been very grateful for Gauvreau's sympathy during the *Graphic* years because she believed that between Oursler and Susie Wood, Macfadden's longtime business associate, she was being frozen out.

Other family woes for Macfadden included an unfortunate fight with his son, Berwyn, age 30.[14] Bernarr charged his son with assault after taking a punch in the head. Berwyn claimed that his father was responsible for his loss of a job with a dance studio and had hit him first. What really went on between Bernarr and his children cannot be defined by a single, scandalous incident. Their relationships did not flower after Bernarr left home in 1933 although he continued to see his children and one daughter even testified for him in the divorce proceedings. Of course, broken marriages are not likely to draw the absent parent closer to his offspring. And, when he was at home, father liked to be the center of attention and of authority. He did not believe in pampering children and insisted that they seek employment once their home-secondary education lessons were concluded.

Over the winter of 1954-55 Macfadden's misfortunes mounted. Johnnie Lee sued for a legal separation and was awarded $1,500 monthly. Neither she nor her lawyers believed that the former millionaire had been reduced to a monthly annuity stipend of $2,000. She retained visions of money buried in caches placed all over the country while he insisted that no such treasure troves existed. When he fell behind on alimony payments and could not raise any cash, he was forced to flee to avoid jail. A newspaper reported that he was hiding out in Niagara Falls, Canada to avoid pursuing officers of the law. The *Chicago Tribune* had reported earlier that he had been begging for loans to avoid going to jail, and had asked boxer Jack Dempsey, an old friend, to help him.[15] Fulton Oursler had recently died or he surely would have come to the rescue. These were tough months for an 87-year old man. He dashed away from the law's clutches in Canada and returned to New Jersey. Rather quickly his hide-out was discovered and he was arrested. He languished in jail for several days before his foundation made bail.[16] On release he told reporters that "New York courts refuse to believe that back taxes and alimony to two wives have depleted my finances. I must raise $10,000 in ten days or go to jail."[17]

His last Christmas was, he told a friend, "my worst Christmas in 86 years."[18] And conditions did not improve. In April Johnnie Lee again complained to the court that she had not been paid and the old man was jailed again briefly. In October he fell ill with jaundice and was taken to the Jersey City Medical Center on October 12, 1955.

Johnnie Lee had returned to her lecturing on health and happiness. Later she expressed her sorrow that she could not share Bernarr's last days and blamed his lawyers and other advisers for their continued separation. She was in California when someone wired news of Bernarr's illness and his request to see her. By the time she reached New York Bernarr had died. His attempt to combat an attack of jaundice with a fast had failed. His last words, if Johnnie Lee and the friend who was at the bedside can be believed, were "Forgive me, Johnnie Lee."

Johnnie Lee wanted to believe in a renewal of romance after such tawdry events, particularly as she identified herself as Bernarr's closest associate and disciple. Bernarr's last words were probably something more characteristic of his life and drive, something like—"weakness is a sin," or "don't call the doctor." His last words of record to Johnnie Lee were in the will he executed on March 13, 1953, denying her any benefits "for the reason that she has unjustifiably abandoned me and has left my home without my consent, and has failed and refused to return to me and my home."

At the hospital Bernarr received the last rites of the Catholic Church, perhaps at the urging of Fulton Oursler's widow. The Ourslers had converted to Catholicism some years earlier. Funeral services were conducted by a Presbyterian minister and a Jewish rabbi with some assistance from the deceased's Masonic order. The rabbi recalled that he had fought "against prudery and tight corsets," which seemed to some relatives to be an inappropriate reminder. Mary and Johnnie Lee were in attendance with their children.

Once he had been a millionaire but his estate did not amount to much of anything. Johnnie Lee persisted in believing in buried millions but no one else did.

Newspaper obituaries were not too generous. The *Chicago Daily News* observed the passing of a faddist "inclined to crackpot notions."[19] He was given credit for pioneering in popular sex education and helping reduce venereal disease. The financial failure of the *Graphic* was deserved: "It was not a true newspaper but a lurid scandal sheet which reflected nothing but discredit on respectable member of the journalistic profession."

The *New York Herald-Tribune* recalled that Macfadden's publishing fortune had been based on "his happy discovery that moral and dietary sermons told in a frank manner and bountifully illustrated with figures of handsome women constituted popular reading matter."[20] Even the New York Public Library had refused to subscribe to the *Graphic*.

Chapter 14
Flamboyance

Queer and puffy, the success of Macfadden has been compounded of odd proportions of hysteria and sound Scotch-Irish business sense.

Allene Talmey

Where are the monuments to Bernarr Macfadden? Can it be that he is less deserving than those dull warriors and politicians who are the conventional subjects of commemoration in bronze? Well, it is disgraceful to forget a man who entertained, outraged, and instructed his countrymen for over fifty years. He should be romping still in New York's Central Park, impressed in some new metal alloy of dramatic quality, showing his strength and inspiring the lazy to exercise.

What can be said against him? Surely it is no crime to be something of an enigma. If we list separately the propositions he would have us believe they are not so hard to swallow one at a time:

1. I know what causes bad health.
2. I know the way to make everyone better.
3. Natures cures through proper diet and exercise.
4. Doctors are bad.
5. Prudes are bad.
6. Sex education is good.
7. My motives are philanthropic.
8. Weakness is a sin.

Macfadden's sillier theories of health treatment cannot be easily dismissed as mere warts since harmful results can follow bad advice. Yet, his voice was only one among many advising on health and, unlike many others, he did not pretend to be an accredited M.D.

What bothered H.L. Mencken about Macfadden was his overriding arrogance, a towering sense of self-importance resting securely on a conviction of his physical, moral, and intellectual superiority over his peers. That he could assume such a posture as easily as he flexed a muscle puzzled Mencken who saw a scarcely-educated hillbilly, a truly shallow man composed of muscle, gall, and flatulence. Mencken, a devoted student of characters, was awed: "His chief intellectual possession, one gathers, is a vast and cocksure ignorance."[1]

As an individual Macfadden is easier to accept if we accept him as he was described by his old friend Fulton Oursler. After leaving *Liberty* Fulton Oursler became a *Reader's Digest* editor and in 1951 did a biographical sketch of his former boss in the magazine's popular feature, "The Most Unforgettable Character I've Met." Oursler admired a man strong enough to start life anew in business and marriage at age 80 and wished to define his friend's essential qualities: "The keynote to Bernarr Macfadden is that he does love life, enjoys it, and seeks to prolong it. In strange ways he keeps himself vigorous, meanwhile scolding and imploring the rest of mankind to take care of themselves, that their days, too, may be long and strong and joyous."[2] Perhaps, while writing this, Oursler wondered if he would wish to prolong his life were he Macfadden's age. Oursler had become wealthy through his books, particularly with his retellings of the Old and New Testaments in *The Greatest Story Ever Told* and *The Greatest Book Ever Written*, but he had experienced a full measure of personal and professional woes in the 1940s. Oursler, whose energy had been comparable to Macfadden's, had never taken very good care of his health. A few months after writing about his friend he died from a heart attack; he was only 59.

After Oursler read his manuscript of the "Most Unforgettable Character" article to Macfadden over the phone the old man expressed his delight and appreciation. Most octogenarians do not hand out inscribed self-portraits but Macfadden always had a current 8 x 10 glossy on hand for news releases and personal uses. Oursler got one inscribed, "Yours for gorgeous health."[3] The men had talked about a rapidly expanding hotel chain as a possible subject for an Oursler article and Macfadden thought it would be a good topic: "Hilton's record in the hotel field is almost as astonishing as I have in the health field."[4]

Historians are not always sure about the meaning of an age or of key figures representing an age. In the 1960s journalism professor William H. Taft considered writing a biography of Macfadden. Unfortunately, he asked the opinion of Allan Nevins, a famous historian and biographer of presidents and business tycoons, who pooh-poohed the idea. Macfadden was not worth it, Nevins said; no serious historian should waste his time researching the subject. Taft settled for a couple of articles. It may be that Nevins thought that characters of dubious or mixed repute could not or should not lend meaning to our past.[5]

The last item in the AMA's Bureau of Investigation file on Macfadden is a copy of a letter written in 1969 to someone inquiring about the physical culturist: "It seems to us that his interest in health was primarily that of someone with something to sell, whether it was a publication, treatment, or idea."[6] This harsh judgment should not stand alone, any more than Oursler's gushing admiration of the great man's life and work should stand alone. A final assessment is not that easy.

Notes

Unless otherwise indicated the correspondence cited in these chapter notes is located in the Bernarr Macfadden file of the AMA's Bureau of Investigation collection.

Chapter 1

[1]*New York Times,* October 6, 1905.

[2]*Ibid.,* October 10, 1905.

[3]*Ibid.,* October 6, 1905.

[4]*Ibid.,* October 7, 1905.

[5]Arrest Record, NY Society for the Suppression of Vice, v. 4, p. 180. NYSSV collection, Library of Congress, Manuscript Division.

Chapter 2

[1]Wood, *Bernarr Macfadden,* p. 35.

[2]*Ibid.,* p. 61.

[3]*Ibid.,* p. 85.

[4]*Ibid.,* p. 86.

Chapter 3

[1]Macfadden, *Encyclopedia,* v. 5, p. 1248.

[2]Whorton, *Crusaders for Fitness,* p. 93.

[3]Carson, *Cornflake Crusade,* p. 52.

[4]Whorton, *Crusaders for Fitness,* p. 78.

[5]*Ibid.,* p. 79.

[6]*Ibid.,* p. 134.

[7]*Ibid.,* p. 274.

[8]*Ibid.,* p. 6.

Chapter 4

[1]Oursler, *True Story,* p. 81.

[2]Whorton, *Crusaders for Fitness,* p. 281.

[3]Oursler, *True Story,* pp. 92-93.

[4]*Ibid.,* p. 81.

[5]Taylor, "Physical Culture," *New Yorker,* October 21, 1950, p. 52.

[6]Wood, *Bernarr Macfadden,* pp. 95-96.

[7]Pringle, *Big Frogs,* pp. 125-26.

[8]*Physical Culture,* January 1913, p. 6; p. ii.

[9]*Ibid.*

[10]Whorton, *Crusaders for Fitness,* p. 205.

[11]*Physical Culture,* January 1913, pp. 85-86.

[12]*Ibid.,* p. 6; p. 11.

[13]*Ibid.,* p. 5.

[14]Various advertisements are discussed by Fishbein,*Medical Follies,* pp. 184-203; and by the same author in *Hygeia* (November, 1924), "Exploiting the Health Interest," pp. 678-83.

Chapter 5

[1]Taylor, "Physical Culture," *New Yorker,* October 28, 1950, p. 37.

[2]*Ibid.,* October 21, 1950, pp. 52-53.

[3]Dowie, *Zion's Holy War,* p. 11.

[4]*Ibid.,* p. 19.

[5]Mark Sullivan, *Our Times,* v. 3. p. 478.

[6]Kemp, *Tramping on Life,* p. 164.

[7]*Ibid.,* p. 165.

[8]*Ibid.,* p. 166.

[9]*Ibid.,* p. 167.

[10]*Ibid.*

[11]Taylor, "Physical Culture," *New Yorker,* October 28, 1950, p. 38.

[12]*Wild Oats* is summarized by Wood, *Bernarr Macfadden,* p. 8.

[13]Oursler, *True Story,* p. 192.

[14]*Ibid.,* p. 195.

[15]A news account of the pardon is in the*New York Times,* November 8, 1909.

[16]Kellogg, *Colon Hygiene,* p. 9.

[17]*Ibid.,* p. 12.

[18]*Ibid.,* p. 47.

[19]There is a colorful summary of Post's career in Carson, *Cornflake Crusade,* pp. 142-75. On the *Collier's* controversy see "C.W. Post, Faker," *Collier's,* December 24, 1910, pp. 13-14 and December 31, 1910, p. 21.

[20]Kellogg's advertisement is from *Collier's,* January 7, 1911, p. 23.

[21]Sinclair, *Autobiography,* p. 158.

[22]*Ibid.,* p. 159; see also Jon Yoder, *Upton Sinclair,* pp. 159-60.

[23]Macfadden, *Encyclopedia,* v. 3, p. 1298.

[24]*Ibid.,* p. 1318.

[25]*Ibid.,* p. 1298.

[26]On the persistence of Sinclair's defense of Abrams see Leon Harris, *Upton Sinclair,* pp. 193-94.

[27]Mencken, *Prejudices: Third Series,* p. 214.

Chapter 6

[1]Mary Macfadden and Emil Gauvreau, *Dumbbells and Carrot Strips,* p. 21, p. 23, p. 38.

[2]*Ibid.,* p. 70.

[3]*Ibid.,* pp. 153-55.

[4]*Ibid.,* p. 125.

[5]*Ibid.,* pp. 171-72.

[6]Macfadden, *Encyclopedia,* v. 1, p. 88.

[7]*Ibid.,* p. xxxi.

[8]*Ibid.,* p. 41.

[9]Schwartz, *Never Satisfied,* p. 9.

[10]Macfadden, *Encyclopedia,* v. 3, p. 1306.

[11]*Ibid.,* p. 1308.

[12]*Town Crier,* March 30, 1912, p. 5; and see Linda Burfield Hazzard, *Fasting In the Cure of Disease.* Seattle: Privately printed, 1908, *passim.*

[13]Asbury, *All Around the Town,* p. 18.

[14]*Ibid.*

[15]*Ibid.,* p. 20.

[16]*Ibid.,* p. 22.

[17]*Seattle Star,* March 20, 1912.

[18]*Ibid.*, April 1, 1912.

[19]*Ibid.*, March 20, 1912.

[20]*Ibid.*, April 1, 1912.

[21]Macfadden, *Encyclopedia*, v. 1, p. 275. For Harris' amazing career see Malone, *Dictionary of American Biography*, VII, 322-23; Webber, *Escape to Utopia*, pp. 320-43; Melton, *Biographical Dictionary of American Cult and Sect Leaders*, pp. 105-106.

[22]*Ibid.*, v. 1, p. 275.

[23]*Ibid.*, p. 16.

[24]*Ibid.*, v. 3, p. 1642.

[25]*Ibid.*

[26]Jameson, *Natural History of Quackery*, p. 206.

[27]*Ibid.*, p. 207.

[28]For biographical data on Still see Malone, *Dictionary of American Biography*, XVII, pp. 21-22 and Furnas, *Great Times*, pp. 176-78.

[29]Jameson, *Natural History of Quackery*, p. 207.

[30]*Ibid.*, p. 208.

[31]Macfadden, *Encyclopedia*, v. 1, p. 485.

[32]*Ibid.*, p. 490.

[33]*Ibid.*, p. 537.

[34]*Ibid.*, v. 3, p. 1180.

[35]*Ibid.*

[36]*Ibid.*, p. 1183.

[37]*Ibid.*, p. 1224; pp. 1221-22.

[38]*Ibid.*, v. 1, p. 45.

[39]*Ibid.*, p. 47.

[40]*Ibid.*, p. 49.

[41]*Ibid.*, p. 51.

[42]*Ibid.*, p. 52.

[43]*Ibid.*, p. 54.

[44]*Ibid.*, v. 5, p. 2493.

[45]*Ibid.*, p. 2445.

[46]*Ibid.*, p. 2446.

[47]*Ibid.*, p. 2447.

[48]*Ibid.*

[49]*Ibid.*, p. 2447.

[50]*Ibid.*, p. 2453.

[51]*Ibid.*, pp. 2466-67.

[52]*Ibid.*, p. 2781.

[53]*Ibid.*, p. 2782.

[54]Haller, *The Physician and Sexuality in Victorian America*, p. 97.

[55]Haller, "From Maidenhood to Menopause," p. 51.

[56]*Ibid.*, p. 52.

[57]*Ibid.*, p. 53.

[58]Macfadden, *Encyclopedia*, v. 5, p. 2716.

[59]On *Onania* see MacDonald, "History of a Delusion," p. 424ff.

[60]*Ibid.*, p. 429.

[61]*Ibid.*

[62]Gilbert, "Doctor, Patient, and Onanist Diseases in the Nineteenth Century," p. 217.

[63]*Ibid.*, p. 218.

[64]Macfadden, *Encyclopedia*, v. 5, p. 2770.

[65]*Ibid.*, p. 2772.

66*Ibid.*, p. 2718.
67*Ibid.*, p. 2719.
68*Ibid.*, p. 2477.
69*Ibid.*, p. 2478.
70*Ibid.*, p. 2479.
71*Ibid.*, p. 2483.

Chapter 7

1Manchester, "True Stories," p. 25.
2Oursler, *True Story of Bernarr Macfadden*, p. 126.
3Oursler, *Behold This Dreamer*, p. 176.
4Pringle, *Big Frogs*, p. 120.
5The argument that Macfadden only rediscovered an old formula for success is in Peterson, *Magazine in the Twentieth Century*, p. 296.
6Oursler, *True Story*, p. 130.
7Mary Macfadden and Gauvreau, *Dumbbells and Carrot Strips*, pp. 218-19.
8*Ibid.*, p. 220.
9Villard, "Sex, Art, Truth, and Magazines," pp. 388-89.
10Repplier, "American Magazines," p. 273.
11Hersey, *Pulpwood Editor*, pp. 212-13.
12*Ibid.*, p. 220.

Chapter 8

1Holbrook, *Golden Age of Quackery*, p. 15.
2*Ibid.*, p. 18.
3*Ibid.*, p. 18-19.
4*Ibid.*, p. 19.
5*Ibid.*, p. 25.
6Red, *Medicine Man in Texas*, p. 6.
7Fishbein, *Medical Follies*, pp. 99-118.
8Radam, *Microbes and the Microbe Killer*, p. 97, p. 99.
9*Ibid.*, p. 108.
10Young, *Toadstool Millionaires*, p. 149.
11Cramp needed no reminder as he had a copy of *Physical Culture* for September 1906 in his Macfadden file—the issue that contained the editor's warning about quacks.
12A reprint (undated) of the editorial with Cramp's annotations is in the Macfadden file.
13Cramp to George H. Simmons, December 28, 1920.
14D.O. Hall to Cramp, December 12, 1912.
15Cramp to Grayson, December 20, 1920; Grayson to Simmons, December 28, 1920; Elder to Grayson, January 13, 1921.
16Undated advertisement, clipping from unidentified magazine, Macfadden file, AMA, Bureau of Investigation.
17Orr to Editor of *Hygeia*, November 28, 1923.
18Macfadden to Dear Doctor, September 29, 1927.
19Cramp to G.B. Roth, September 7, 1927.
20E.O. Harrold to Macfadden, August 4, 1927.
21M.A. Moore to Macfadden, September 1, 1927.
22Cramp to Dr. Edward Wolfe, January 26, 1923.
23Cramp to Eugene Fisk, January 25, 1922.
24Undated cartoon (1924), *New York Graphic*, Macfadden file, AMA Bureau of Investigation collection.
25Cramp memo, August 20, 1924.

[26]Fishbein's two part article, "Exploiting the Health Interest," appeared in *Hygeia*, November and December 1924. Quotes are from p. 745, p. 747, p. 748 (December), and p. 678 (November).

[27]Hale, *These Cults*, p. 137.

[28]*Ibid.*, pp. 143-44.

[29]*Ibid.*, p. 145.

[30]*Ibid.*, pp. 146-47.

[31]*Ibid.*, p. 148.

[32]Bowen, "Macfadden, the Bare Torso King," *Detroit Saturday Night*, May 3, 1924. Clipping in Macfadden file, AMA Bureau of Investigation collection.

[33]Gehman to *Hygeia* editor, January 9, 1926.

[34]Leslie to AMA, November 21, 1926.

[35]Macfadden to Fishbein, June 29, 1946.

Chapter 9

[1]Bessie, *Jazz Journalism*, p. 188.

[2]Tebbel, *Compact History of the American Newspaper*, p. 224.

[3]*Ibid.*, p. 225; see also Walker, *City Editor*, pp. 70-71.

[4]Cohen, *New York Graphic*, p. 6.

[5]*Ibid.*, p. 7.

[6]*Ibid.*

[7]Bessie, *Jazz Journalism*, p. 187.

[8]*Ibid.*, p. 188.

[9]*Ibid.*, pp. 190-91.

[10]*Ibid.*, p. 189.

[11]Cohen, *New York Graphic*, p. 7.

[12]*Ibid.*, p. 107.

[13]Cohen, *New York Graphic*, p. 135.

[14]Gauvreau, *My Last Million Readers*, p. 106.

[15]*Ibid*, p. 124.

[16]*Ibid.*, p. 135.

[17]*Graphic* clipping in Macfadden file, AMA Bureau of Investigation.

[18]Gauvreau, *My Last Million Readers*, p. 102.

[19]*Ibid.*, p. 101.

[20]Cohen, *New York Graphic*, p. 14.

[21]Gauvreau, *My Last Million Readers*, pp. 112-13.

[22]*Ibid.*, p. 114.

[23]Bessie, *Jazz Journalism*, p. 193.

[24]*Ibid.*, p. 195.

[25]Gauvreau, *My Last Million Readers*, p. 118.

[26]*Ibid.*, pp. 118-19.

[27]Klurfeld, *Winchell*, pp. 28-53.

[28]Oursler, *True Story*, p. 242.

[29]Gauvreau, *My Last Million Readers*, p. 105.

[30]Oursler, *Behold This Dreamer!*, p. 225.

[31]Biographical notes, Oursler Collection, Georgetown University.

[32]Bessie, *Jazz Journalism*, p. 199.

[33]*Ibid.*, p. 200; *New York Times*, November 28, 1925; Cohen, *New York Graphic*, pp. 132-35.

[34]Johnston, "The Great Macfadden," *Saturday Evening Post*, June 21, 1941, p. 98.

[35]Cohen, *New York Graphic*, p. 133.

[36]*Ibid.*, p. 121.

[37]*Ibid.*

[38]Gauvreau, *My Last Million Readers,* p. 111.

[39]*Ibid.,* p. 112.

[40]*Time,* February 14, 1927, p. 30-32; see also the magazine's review of a stage revue spoofing the newspaper, *Time,* April 18, 1927.

[41]Wood, *Bernarr Macfadden,* p. 161.

[42]*Ibid.*

[43]Gauvreau, *My Last Million Readers,* p. 112.

[44]Oursler, *Behold This Dreamer!,* p. 268.

Chapter 10

[1]See *Physical Culture* editorials, *passim.*

[2]Mary Macfaddena and Gauvreau, *Dumbbells and Carrot Strips,* p. 228.

[3]Larsen, *The Good Fight,* p. 153.

[4]Macfadden's disagreement with Lindsey are in Macfadden, "10 Deadly Flaws in Companionate Marriage," *Physical Culture,* v. 1xi, July 1928, pp. 29, 88-89. Macfadden and Lindsey held a public debate on what Macfadden termed "trial marriage" and condemned for a variety of reasons.

[5]Macfadden and Gauvreau, *Dumbbells and Carrot Strips,* p. 238.

[6]Sann, *Fads, Follies and Delusions,* p. 107.

[7]*Ibid.*

[8]Macfadden and Gauvreau, *Dumbbells and Carrot Strips,* p. 239.

[9]*Ibid.,* p. 242.

[10]*Ibid.*

[11]*Ibid.,* p. 246.

[12]*Ibid.,* p. 201.

[13]*Ibid.,* p. 202.

[14]*Ibid.,* p. 258.

[15]*Ibid.,* p. 276.

[16]Biographical notes, July 15, 1924, Oursler Collection, Georgetown University.

[17]Macfadden and Gauvreau, *Dumbbells and Carrot Strips,* p. 144.

[18]Oursler, biographical notes, 1928, Oursler Collection, Georgetown University.

[19]*Ibid.*

[20]Talmey, "Millions from Dumbbells," *Outlook,* June 4, 1930, p. 196.

[21]Mencken, "An American Idealist," *American Mercury,* v. 20, no. 77, May 1930, p. 124.

[22]Wood, *Bernarr Macfadden,* p. 4, p. 5.

[23]Oursler, *True Story,* p. 12.

[24]Perkins, *Chats with the Macfadden Family,* p. 158.

Chapter 11

[1]*JAMA,* August 9, 1930, p. 430.

[2]Macfadden, *Encyclopedia,* v. 5, p. 2460.

[3]Macfadden and Gauvreau, *Dumbbells and Carrot Strips,* p. 405.

[4]*Ibid.,* p. 331.

[5]*Ibid.,* p. 332.

[6]*Ibid.,* p. 343.

[7]*Ibid.*

[8]Oursler, *Behold This Dreamer!,* p. 173.

[9]Macfadden and Gauvreau, *Dumbbells and Carrot Strips,* p. 404.

[10]Oursler, *Behold This Dreamer!,* p. 262.

[11]Wood, *Bernarr Macfadden,* p. 251.

[12]*Ibid.*

[13]*Ibid.*, p. 254.

[14]*Ibid.*

[15]*Ibid.*, p. 194, p. 195.

[16]*Ibid.* p. 256.

[17]Taylor, "Physical Culture," *New Yorker*, October 28, 1950, p. 48.

[18]*New York Times*, February 15, 1936; April 9, 1936.

[19]Macfadden and Gauvreau, *Dumbbells and Carrot Strips*, p. 312.

[20]*Ibid.*, p. 313.

[21]A magazine called Macfadden's foundation "a really noble example of eating one's cake and having it" and ridiculed the notion that philanthropy was a motivation, *The Survey*, v. 67, no. 2, October 15, 1931, p. 69.

[22]*Time*, July 11, 1932, p. 25.

[23]*New York Times*, June 9, 1937.

[24]*Bridgeport Herald*, November 26, 1936? Clipping in Macfadden file, AMA Bureau of Investigation.

[25]Oursler Collection, Georgetown University.

[26]Oursler, *Behold This Dreamer!*, p. 271.

[27]Churchill, *The Liberty Years*, p. 258.

[28]*Ibid.*, p. 260.

[29]*Ibid.*

[30]Macfadden and Gauvreau, *Dumbbells and Carrot Strips*, p. 304.

Chapter 12

[1]*New York Times*, April 24, 1940.

[2]*Ibid.*, February 28, 1941.

[3]*Newsweek*, March 10, 1941, p. 59.

[4]*Ibid.*

[5]*JAMA*, v. 115, no. 22, November 30, 1940, p. 1890.

[6]*JAMA*, December 27, 1941.

[7]*Ibid.*, October 11, 1941.

[8]Gardner, *Fads and Fallacies*, pp. 230-41.

[9]Clipping in Macfadden file, AMA Bureau of Investigation.

[10]*Ibid.*

[11]*Saturday Evening Post* press release, no date, Macfadden file, AMA Bureau of Investigation.

[12]Johnston, "The Great Macfadden," *Saturday Evening Post*, June 21, 1941, p. 98.

[13]*Ibid.*, p. 93.

[14]*Ibid.*, June 28, 1941, p. 90.

[15]*Ibid.*, June 21, 1941, p. 99.

[16]Clipping, Macfadden file, AMA Bureau of Investigation.

[17]*Newsweek*, August 12, 1946, p. 69.

[18]*Ibid.*

[19]*New York Times*, February 8, 1945.

[20]*Time*, August 12, 1946, p. 69.

[21]Johnnie Lee Macfadden, *Barefoot in Eden*, p. 12.

[22]*Ibid.*, p. 20.

[23]*Ibid.*, pp. 21-22.

[24]*Ibid.*, p. 39.

[25]*New York Times*, April 24, 1948.

[26]*Ibid.*, p. 26.

[27]*Ibid.*, p. 27.

[28]*Ibid.*

[29]Macfadden liked to tell others later that the Florida vote was very close and he might have won but for some cheating on the tally. In fact, he did not come close to the two leading candidates who led the field to become eligible for the run-off after the primary. Florida then was solidly Democratic so the Democratic primary and its run-off were the important races. In 1940 when he ran for senator from Florida he only missed the run-off by a thousand votes or so but the leader, a Democrat had a huge two-to-one margin over the second place man and won the final election without difficulty.

[30]Macfadden, *Barefoot in Eden*, p. 72.

[31]*Ibid.*, p. 56.

Chapter 13

[1]Taylor, "Physical Culture," *New Yorker*, October 21, 1950, p. 39.

[2]*Ibid.*, October 28, 1950, p. 50.

[3]*Health Review* was the successor to *Physical Culture.*

[4]Taylor, "Physical Culture," *New Yorker*, October 21, 1950, p. 48.

[5]Johnny Lee Macfadden, *Barefoot in Eden*, p. 208.

[6]*Ibid.*, p. 209.

[7]*Ibid.*, p. 211.

[8]*Ibid.*

[9]*New York Times*, August 30, 1952.

[10]Fraud and Lottery Docket, Post Office Department, Inspec. case 8153-F, RG 28, National Archives.

[11]*New York Times Book Review*, April 26, 1953.

[12]*New York Times*, May 5, 1936.

[13]Gauvreau, *My Last Million Readers*, p. 135.

[14]Unidentified newspaper clipping of October 10, 1954 in AMA Bureau of Investigation Macfadden file.

[15]*Chicago Tribune*, December 26, 1954.

[16]*Racine Journal-Times*, January 26, 1955, clipping in the Macfadden file of the AMA Bureau of Investigation.

[17]*New York Times*, April 19, 1955.

[18]*Ibid.*

[19]*Chicago Daily News*, October 14, 1955.

[20]*New York Herald-Tribune*, October 14, 1955.

Chapter 14

[1]Mencken, "An American Idealist," *American Mercury*, May 1930, p. 12.

[2]Oursler, "The Most Unforgettable Character I've Met," *Readers Digest*, v. 53, July 1951, p. 82.

[3]Inscribed photograph in Oursler collection, Georgetown University Library.

[4]Macfadden to Oursler, February 3, 1951, Oursler Collection, Georgetown University Library.

[5]Taft, "Bernarr Macfadden: One of a Kind," *Journalism Quarterly*, Winter 1968, p. 627.

[6]M.J. Manghan to Diane Stences, July 14, 1969, Macfadden file, AMA Bureau of Investigation.

Bibliography

Archival Sources

American Medical Association. Bureau of Investigation files on Bernarr Macfadden, John Brinkley, Norman Baker, Harry Hoxsey, Albert Abrams, and others.

Georgetown University. Fulton Oursler Collection.

Library of Congress. New York Society for the Suppression of Vice Collection.

National Archives. Post Office. RG 28. Fraud and Lottery Docket, no. 21, case no. 75. Mininberg Oscillator and Bernarr Macfadden Foundation (Insp. case no. 81533-F).

Books

Allen, Frederick Lewis. *Only Yesterday*. New York: Harper and Bros., 1931.

Ashbury, Herbert. *All Around the Town*. New York: Alfred A. Knopf, 1934.

Bessie, Simon M. *Jazz Journalism*. New York: E.P. Dutton, 1938.

Brevda, William. *Harry Kemp*. Lewisburg: Bucknell University Press, 1986.

Broun, Heywood and Margaret Leach. *Anthony Comstock*. New York: Albert and Charles Boni, 1927.

Calhoun, Mary. *Medicine Show*. New York: Harper and Row, 1976.

Carson, Gerald. *Cornflake Crusade*. New York: Arno Press, 1976.

_____ *The Roguish World of Doctor Brinkley*. New York: Holt, Rinehart and Winston, 1960.

Churchill, Allen. *The Liberty Years 1924-1950*. Englewood Cliffs, NJ: Prentice-Hall, Inc., 1968.

_____ *The Year the World Went Mad*. New York: Thomas Y. Crowell, 1960.

Cohen, Lester. *The New York Graphic: The World's Zaniest Newspaper*. Philadelphia: Chilton Books, 1964.

Comstock, Anthony. *Frauds Exposed*. Montclair, NJ: Patterson Smith, 1969.

_____ *Traps for the Young*. Cambridge: Harvard University Press, 1967.

Cramp, Arthur J. *Nostrums and Quackery and Pseudo-Medicine*. Chicago: American Medical Association, three volumes, 1912, 1921, 1936.

Deutsch, Ronald M. *The Nuts among the Berries*. New York: Ballantine Books, 1961.

Dowie, John Alexander. *Zion's First Feast*. Chicago: Press of Zion Printing Works, 1901.

_____ *Zion's Holy War Against the Hosts of Hell in Chicago*. Chicago: Zion Publishing House, 1900.

Emery, Edwin and Michael. *The Press and America*. Englewood Cliffs, NJ: Prentice-Hall, Inc., 1978.

Fishbein, Morris. *A History of the American Medical Association 1847 to 1947*. Philadelphia: W.B. Saunders Company, 1948.

_____ *The New Medical Follies*. New York: Boni and Liveright, 1927.

_____ *The Medical Follies*. New York: Boni and Liveright, 1925.

Furnas, J.C. *Great Times*. New York: G.P. Putnam's Sons, 1974.

Gardner, Martin. *Fads and Fallacies in the Name of Science.* New York: Dover Publications, 1957.

Gauvreau, Emile. *Hot News,* New York: Macaulay Co., 1931.

———. *My Last Million Readers.* New York: Arno Press, 1974.

Green, Harvey. *Fit for America.* New York: Pantheon, 1986.

Hale, Annie. *These Cults.* New York: National Health Foods, 1926.

Haller, John S. and Robin M. *The Physician and Sexuality in Victorian America.* Urbana: University of Illinois Press, 1974.

Harris, Leon. *Upton Sinclair. American Rebel.* New York: Thomas Y. Crowell, 1975.

Hersey, Harold B. *Pulpwood Editor.* New York: Frederick A. Stokes Company, 1977.

James, Merice M. *Book Review Digest.* New York: H.W. Wilson Co., 1954.

Jameson, Eric. *The Natural History of Quackery.* Springfield: Thomas, 1951.

Johnson, Allen and Dumas Malone. *Dictionary of American Biography.* vol. 4. New York: Charles Scribner's Sons, 1930.

Johnson, Neil M. *George Sylvester Viereck.* Urbana: University of Illinois Press, 1972.

Kellogg, John Harvey. *Colon Hygiene.* Battle Creek: Good Health Publishing Co., 1916.

Kemp, Harry. *Tramping on Life.* New York: Boni and Liveright, 1922.

Klurfeld, Herman. *Winchell.* New York: Praeger, 1976.

Larson, Charles. *The Good Fight.* Chicago: Quadrangle, 1972.

Lee, Alfred McCluny. *Daily News in America.* New York: Farrar, Straus and Giroux, 1973.

Macfadden, Bernarr. See separate list.

Macfadden, Johnnie Lee. *Barefoot in Eden: The Macfadden Plan for Health, Charm, and Long-Lasting Youth.* Englewood Cliffs, NJ: Prentice-Hall, 1962.

Macfadden, Mary and Emile Gauvreau. *Dumbbells and Carrot Strips. The Story of Bernarr Macfadden.* New York: Henry Holt, 1953.

Mallen, Frank. *Sauce For The Gander.* White Plains: Baldwin Books, 1954.

Malone, Dumas. *Dictionary of American Biography.* Various years. New York: Charles Scribner's Sons.

Melton, J. Gordon. *Biographical Dictionary of American Cult and Sect Leaders.* New York: Garland, 1986.

Mencken, H.L. *Prejudices: Third Series.* New York: Alfred A. Knopf, 1922.

Nissenbaum, Stephen. *Sex, Diet, and Debility in Jacksonian America.* Westport, Conn.: Greenwood Press, 1980.

Oursler, Fulton. *Behold This Dreamer! An Autobiography by Fulton Oursler.* Edited and with commentary by Fulton Oursler, Jr. Boston: Little, Brown and Company, 1964.

———. *The Greatest Book Ever Written.* New York: Doubleday Co., 1951.

———. *The Greatest Story Ever Told.* New York: Farrar and Rinehart, 1949.

———. *The True Story of Bernarr Macfadden.* New York: Bernarr Macfadden Foundation, 1930.

Oursler, Will. *Family Story.* New York: Funk and Wangalls, 1963.

Perkins, Grace. *Chats with the Macfadden Family.* New York: Lewis Copeland Company, 1929.

Peterson, Theodore. *Magazines in the Twentieth Century.* Urbana: University of Illinois Press, 1964.

Phillips, Cabell. *The New York Times Chronicle of American Life From the Crash to the Blitz 1929-1939.* New York: Macmillan Publishing Co., 1975.

Radam, William. *Microbes and the Microbe Killer.* New York: Knickerbocker Press, 1890.

Red, George P. *The Medical Man in Texas.* Houston: Standard Printing, 1930.

Rugoff, Milton. *Prudery and Passion.* New York: G.P. Putnam's Sons, 1971.

Sann, Paul. *Fads, Follies and Delusions of the American People.* New York: Crown Publishers, 1967.

Schwartz, Hillel. *Never Satisfied. A Cultural History of Diet, Fantasies and Fat.* New York: Free Press, 1986.

Schwarz, Richard W. *John Harvey Kellogg, M.D.* Nashville: Southern Publication Association, 1970.

Spivak, John. *Man in His Time.* New York: Horizon Press, 1967.

Sinclair, Upton. *The Autobiography of Upton Sinclair.* New York: Harcourt, Brace and World, 1962.

––––––. *The Jungle.* Urbana: University of Illinois Press, 1988.

Sullivan, Mark. *Our Times* Vol. 3. New York: Charles Scribner's Sons, 1936.

Tebbel, John. *Compact History of American Newspapers.* New York: Hawthorn Books, 1963.

Walker, Stanley. *City Editor.* New York: Frederick A. Stokes, 1934.

Whorton, James C. *Crusaders for Fitness.* Princeton: Princeton University Press, 1982.

Winston, Alvin. *The Throttle. A Fact Story of Norman Baker.* Muscatine, Iowa: Baker Sales, 1934.

Wood, Clement. *Bernarr Macfadden. A Study in Success.* New York: Lewis Copeland Co., 1929.

Yoder, Jon A. *Upton Sinclair.* New York: Frederick Ungar, 1975.

Young, James. *The Medical Messiahs.* Princeton: Princeton University Press, 1967.

––––––. *The Toadstool Millionaires.* Princeton: Princeton University Press, 1961.

Articles

Bowen, N.H. "Macfadden, the Bare Torso King, and His Shoddy Sex Magazines," *Detroit Saturday Night,* May 3, 1924, p. 87, p. 188.

Fishbein, Morris. "Exploiting the Health Interest," *Hygeia,* part 1, November, 1924, pp. 678-83; part 11, December, 1924, pp. 744-48.

Anon. Editorials on "C.W. Post, Faker," *Collier's,* December 24 and 31, 1910; January 21, 1911.

––––––. Anon. "Mr. Macfadden Discusses Army Medical Service," *Journal of the American Medical Association* (JAMA), v. 115, no. 122, November 30, 1940, p. 1890.

Coryell, Russell M. "The Birth of Nick Carter," *Bookman,* v. lxix, no. 5, July 1929, pp. 495-502.

"False Hypocrites," *Time,* February 14, 1927, p. 30.

"For Ever and Ever," *The Survey,* v. 67, no. 2, October 15, 1931, p. 69.

Johnston, Alva. "Contented Crusader: John S. Sumner," *New Yorker,* February 20, 1937, pp. 22-27.

––––––. "The Great Macfadden" *Saturday Evening Post,* June 21, 1941, pp. 9-11, 97-100; June 28, 1941, p. 28, pp. 91-93.

"Macfadden Steps Down," *Newsweek,* March 10, 1941, p. 59.

"Macfadden's New Religion," *Time,* June 4, 1945, p. 93.

MacMullen, Margaret, "Pulps and Confessions," *Harper's Magazine,* v. 175, June 1937, pp. 94-102.

Manchester, Harland. "True Stories," *Scribner's*, v. 104, no. 2, August 1938, pp. 25-29, p. 60

Mencken, H.L. "An American Idealist: Three Macfadden Biographies," *American Mercury*, v. 20, no. 77, pp. 124-25.

Oursler, Fulton. "The Most Unforgettable Character I Have Ever Met: Bernarr Macfadden," *Readers Digest*, October, 1951.

"Porno-Petard," *Time*, April 18, 1927, p. 23.

Pringle, Henry F. "Another American Phenomenon: Bernarr Macfadden—Publisher and Physical Culturist," *The World's Work*, v. lvi, no. 6, October 1928, pp. 659-66.

Repplier, Agnes, "American Magazines," *Yale Review*, v. xvi, no. 2, January 1927, pp. 261-74.

Talmey, Allene. "Millions from Dumb-bells," *Outlook*, June 4, 1930, pp. 163-66, pp. 196-97.

Sonenschein, David. "Love and Sex in the Romance Magazines," *Journal of Popular Culture*, v. 4, Fall 1970, pp. 398-409.

Taft, William H. "Bernarr Macfadden," in *Dictionary of Literary Biography*, v. 25. Edited by P.J. Ashley. Detroit: Gale Research, 1984.

———. "Bernarr Macfadden," *Missouri Historical Review*, v. lxiii, no. 1, October 1968, pp. 71-89.

———. "Bernarr Macfadden: One of a Kind," *Journalism Quarterly*, v. 45, Winter 1968, pp. 627-33.

Taylor, Robert Lewis. "I Was Once a 97-Pound Weakling: Profile of Charles Atlas," *New Yorker*, January 3, 1942, pp. 21-27.

———. "Physical Culture: Profile of Bernarr Macfadden," *New Yorker*, October 14, 1950, pp. 39-51; October 21, 1950, pp. 39-54; October 28, 1950, pp. 37-50.

Villard, Oswald Garrison. "Sex, Art, Truth, and Magazines," *Atlantic Monthly*, v. 137, no. 3, March 1926, pp. 388-98.

Wiggam, Albert Edward. "The Most Remarkable Man I Have Ever Known: Dr. John Harvey Kellogg," *American Magazine*, v. 100, December 1925, pp. 14-15, pp. 117-22.

Yagoda, Ben. "Bernarr Macfadden," *American Heritage*, v. 33, no. 1, December, 1981, pp. 22-29.

Books by Bernarr Macfadden

The Athlete's Conquest. New York & St. Louis: Brown, 1892; revised edition, New York: Physical Culture Publishing Co., 1901.

Macfadden's *System of Physical Training*. New York: Hulbert, 1895.

Physical Training. New York: Macfadden, 1900.

Fasting, Hydropathy, and Exercise, by Macfadden and Felix Oswald. New York: Physical Culture Publishing Co., 1900.

Virile Powers of Superb Manhood: How Developed, How Lost, How Regained. New York: Physical Culture Publishing Co., 1900.

New Cookery Book, by Macfadden, Mary Richardson, and George Propheter. London: 1901.

Power and Beauty of Superb Womanhood. New York: Physical Culture Publishing Co., 1901.

Strength from Eating. New York: Physical Culture Publishing Co., 1901.

Strong Eyes. New York: Physical Culture Publishing Co., 1901.

Natural Cure for Rupture. New York & London: Physical Culture Publishing Co., 1902.

Vaccination Superstition. New York: Macfadden, 1902.

What a Young Husband Ought to Know. New York: Macfadden, 1902.

What a Young Woman Ought to Know. New York: Macfadden, 1902.

Marriage a Lifelong Honeymoon: Life's Greatest Pleasures Secured by Observing the Highest Human Instincts. New York & London: Physical Culture Publishing Co., 1903.

Building of Vital Power. New York & London: Physical Culture Publishing Co., 1904.

Creative and Sexual Science. New York: Macfadden, 1904.

Diseases of Men. New York & London: Physical Culture Publishing Co., 1904.

Health, Beauty, and Sexuality, by Macfadden and Marion Malcolm. New York & London: Physical Culture Publishing Co., 1904.

How Success Is Won. New York & London: Physical Culture Publishing Co., 1904.

How to Box. New York: Macfadden, 1904.

A Perfect Beauty, by Macfadden and Barbara Howard. New York: Macfadden, 1904.

Physical Culture for Babies, by Macfadden and Marguerite Macfadden. New York & London: Physical Culture Publishing Co., 1904.

Strenuous Lover. New York: Physical Culture Publishing Co., 1904.

Muscular Power and Beauty. New York: Physical Culture Publishing Co., 1906.

Macfadden Prosecution—A Curious Story of Wrong and Oppression under the Postal Laws. New York: Macfadden, 1908.

Vitality Supreme. New York: Macfadden, 1915.

Brain Energy-Building and Nerve-Vitalizing Course. New York: Physical Culture Publishing Co., 1916.

Manhood and Marriage. New York: Physical Culture Publishing Co., 1916.

Womanhood and Marriage. New York: Macfadden, 1918.

Strengthening the Eyes. New York: Physical Culture Publishing Co., 1918.

Making Old Bodies Young. New York: Physical Culture Publishing Co., 1919.

Eating for Health and Strength. New York: Physical Culture Corp., 1921.

Truth about Tobacco. New York: Physical Culture Corp., 1921.

The Miracle of Milk. New York: Macfadden, 1923.

Fasting for Health. New York: Macfadden, 1923.

How to Keep Fit. New York: Macfadden, 1923.

Keeping Fit. New York: Macfadden, 1923.

Preparing for Motherhood. New York: Macfadden, 1923.

Constipation, Its Cause, Effect and Treatment. New York: Macfadden, 1924.

How to Raise A Strong Baby. New York: Macfadden, 1924.

Physical Culture Cook Book, by Macfadden and Milo Hastings. New York: Macfadden, 1924.

Physical Culture Food Directory. New York: Macfadden, 1924.

Walking Cure, Pep and Power from Walking—How to Cure Disease from Walking. New York: Macfadden, 1924.

Hair Culture. New York: Macfadden, 1924.

Diabetes, Its Cause, Nature and Treatment. New York: Macfadden, 1925.

Headaches, How Caused and How Cured. New York: Macfadden, 1925.

Strengthening the Nerves. New York: Macfadden, 1925.

Strengthening the Spine. New York: Macfadden, 1925.

Tooth Troubles: Their Prevention, Cause and Cure. New York: Macfadden, 1925.

Asthma and Hay Fever. New York: Macfadden, 1926.
The Book of Health. New York: Macfadden, 1926.
Colds, Coughs, and Catarrh. New York: Macfadden, 1926.
Foot Troubles. New York: Macfadden, 1926.
How to Raise the Baby. New York: Macfadden, 1926.
Plain Speech on a Public Insult: Bernarr Macfadden Replies to Atlantic Monthly. New York: Macfadden, 1926.
Predetermine Your Baby's Sex. New York: Macfadden, 1926.
Rheumatism, Its Cause, Nature and Treatment. New York: Macfadden, 1926.
Skin Troubles, Their Nature and Treatment. New York: Macfadden, 1927.
Digestive Troubles, How Caused and Cured. New York: Macfadden, 1928.
Good Health, How to Get It and Keep It. New York: Macfadden, 1928.
Talks to a Young Man about Sex. New York: Macfadden, 1928.
Exercising for Health. New York: Macfadden, 1929.
Health for the Family. New York: Macfadden, 1929.
Tuberculosis. New York: Macfadden, 1929.
Home Health Manual. New York: Macfadden, 1930.
Home Health Library. 5 volumes, New York: Macfadden, 1933.
After 40-What?, by Macfadden and Charles A. Clinton. New York: Macfadden, 1935.
Man's Sex Life. New York: Macfadden, 1935.
Practical Birth Control and Sex Predetermination, by Macfadden and Clinton. New York: Macfadden, 1935.
Woman's Sex Life. New York: Macfadden, 1935.
How to Gain Weight. New York: Macfadden, 1936.
How to Reduce Weight. New York: Macfadden, 1936.
Be Married and Like It. New York: Macfadden, 1937.
Exercise and Like It. New York: Macfadden, 1937.
Handbook of Health. New York: Macfadden, 1938.
More Power to Your Nerves. New York: Macfadden, 1938
New Handbook of Health with First Aid. New York: Macfadden, 1940.
Stomach and Digestive Disorders. New York: Macfadden, 1946.
Confessions of an Amateur Politician. New York: Macfadden, 1948.
Other: *Mary and Bob's True Story Book,* compiled by Macfadden. New York: Macfadden, 1930.

Index

Abrams, Albert 53, 97-98, 106
Acton, William 72, 75
Adams, A.C. 177
Adams, Samuel Hopkins 93
Adventists 20
Albizu, L.W. 32
Alcott, Bronson 19
Alcott, William 8, 17-18, 28
American Medical Association (AMA) 24, 27, 66, 92-110, 141, 172, 185-86, 188, 196, 197, 203
American Protective League 103
Applegate, Joseph 140
Athlete's Conquest 9, 25
Atlantic Monthly 88
Atlas, Charles 31-32
Austin, Harriet 19
Automotive Daily News 177
Babies, Just Babies 179
Baker, Norman 103
Ballard, Mary 27
Bates, William H. 186-88
Beecher, Henry Ward 3
Bennett Medical College 106
Bennett, Sanford 155-56
Bernard, Pierre 156-57
Bernarr Macfadden's Detective Magazine 185
Blackwell, Elizabeth 72
Blakie, William 8
Bloomer, Amelia 19
Bowen, N.H. 108-109
Bowers, Edwin C. 106
Brach, Leon S. 184
Brain Power 165
Breibart, Mr. 33
Brennan, John 84-85
Brinkler, G.H. 35
Brinkley, John 96-97, 98
Brisbane, Arthur 24
Broun, Heywood 145

Browning, Edward W. 146, 150-51
Bunker Hill Academy 9
Bureau of Investigation: see American Medical Association
Carroll, Earl 147-48
Carroll, Norman 147
Castle Heights Military Academy 176
Chicago World's Fair 10
Chiropractors 64, 66
Christian Scientists 67
Claflin, Tennessee 3
Cohen, Leslie 136-40
Collier's 35, 47, 93, 170, 180, 182
Collins, Frederick 106
Comstock, Anthony 2-5, 42, 81, 105, 151
Cornaro, Luigi 59
Coryell, John 43-44, 85, 162-63
Cosmopolitan 81
Cramp, Arthur J. 92, 98, 103-105, 109-110
Crane, Frank 106
Creel, George 155
Croy, Homer 107
Dance, The 164
Dansville Health Hotel 176
Darrow, Clarence 143
Dempsey, Jack 200
Desbrow, G.W. 105
Desgrey, Charles 54
Detroit Daily 179
Dierker, Hugh 158
Doherty, Edward 181-82
Dowie, John Alexander 37-39, 63, 157
Dream World 164
Elder, O.J. 34, 103

219

Ellis, Havelock 107
Evans, Wainwright 155
Federal Trade Commission
   100, 186
Ferber, Edna 81
Fiction Lovers 164
Fields, W.C. 174
Fishbein, Morris 33, 103-110
Fisk, Eugene A. 105
Fletcher, Horace 28-29
Food and Drug Act 100
Ford, Henry 88, 152, 154
Fowler, Orson 75, 77
Gauvreau, Emil 84, 140-46,
   150-52, 199
Gehman, Jesse Mercer 109
Ghost Stories 164
Graham, Slyvester 8, 13-17,
   71, 77
Gray, Edmund C. 104, 105-106
Gray, Judd 148
Grayson, Cary T. 102-103
Grey, Zane 81
Hainer, Lee M. 81
Hale, Annie 107-108
Hall, Edward 148
Harris, Thomas Lake 63-64,
   157
Harrold, E.O. 104
Hartford Courant 140
Hauser, Gaylord 187-88
Hazzard, Linda 59, 61-63
Health Review 194, 196
Hearst, William Randolph
   24, 81, 88, 136
Hecht, Ben 179
Hedden, H.G. 101-102
Heenan, Peaches 146
Hershey, Harold 90—91
Holbrook, Martin 28
Homeopaths 186
Hoover, J. Edgar 180
Howard, Tom 149
Hubbard, Elbert 39-40
Hunter, Robert 7
Hurst, Fannie 81, 179
Huxley, Aldous 187
Hygeia 103, 105
I Confess 86
Intimate Stories 86

Isham, Mr. 94
Jackson, James Caleb 19
James, Henry 29
Jennings, Ella A. 23
Jerome, William Travis 151
Johnston, Alva 188
Jungle, The 94-95
*Journal of the American
   Medical Association (JAMA)*
   92, 100
Kellogg, John Harvey 16, 19,
   20, 29, 45-53, 73, 75, 77, 94
Kellogg, Will 48
Kemp, Harry 39-41, 52
Kent, Frank 88
Kimbrough, Mary Craig 52
Kinistherapist 9
LaGuardia, Fiorello 172
Lane, William Arbuthnot 46
Lardner, Ring 179
Leopold-Loeb 180
Lee, Johnnie: see Macfadden,
   Bernarr—wives
Leeds, Homer Stansbury 156
Lent, Gwendoline 27
Lewis, Dioclesian 18-19
Liberty 179-83, 185
Lincoln, Abraham 159
Lindsey, Ben 142-43, 155
London, Jack 27
London Daily Mirror 135
Love and Romance 86
Ludlow, Alice 27
Lust, Benedict 34
McCormick, Robert 179
McFadden, Alma and Mary 6
McFadden, Michael 33
McFadden, William 6
Macfadden, Bernarr: airplanes
   176, 197; attacks on doctors
   68-69, 92-110; Bernarr
   Macfadden Foundation 176,
   178; Castle Heights Military
   Academy 176; censorship
   fights 1-5, 42-44, 154-55,
   167; Christianity 7, 76-77;
   corsets 24-26, 154, 200;
   Dansville Health Hotel
   176, 181; death 200;
   depression 183;

Encyclopedia 13, 24, 34, 57-79; England (first trip), 11-12; England (second trip) 54-56; European trip (1930), 168-69; evaluation 79, 160, 189, 202-203; expressions 55, 56, 159; exhibitionist 154; first New York studio 11; family and home life 157-58, 168-71, 178-79, 196-97, 199; films 158-59; flat chested women 67-68, 192-93; health theories 19, 22-35, 57-79, 160, 185-88, 189 and *passim*; Healthatorium 31, 102, 104; inventions 159-60, 203; magazine ideas 83-85, 89-90; misc. opinions 56, 154; mother 6; name change 6; *New York Graphic* 135-52, and see main index listing; novel 9, 25, Penny restaurant 44-45, 177; perfect family 88; personal appearance 193; Physcultopathy 57, 66; Physical Culture City 37-45, 51, 54; *Physical Culture* magazine 3, 9, 22-35, 50, 52, 54, 55, 57, 82, 87, 98, 101, 106, 146, 153, 154, 163, 178, 185; Physical Culture Press: 165; physical therapy 9; politics 168-83, 184; prudery 76-77, 167, 200; publication 22-35, 43-44, 80-91; and *passim*; resigns from Macfadden Publishing Co. 184; sanitariums 31, 36-37, 47-48, 54, 102, 104, 168, 172, 176, 181; sex ex-ploitation 5; sex theories 5, 13, 26-27, 69-79, 154-55, 167; *True Story* 80-91, 137; youth 6-12; war 181; wives (Johnnie Lee) 190-95 (Marguerite) 41, 54; (Mary)—see Macfadden, Mary; Wrestling 9;

Macfadden, Mary: 157; courtship 54; divorce 178, 190; *Dumbbells and Carrot Strips* 55, 198-99; loss of baby 169-71; opinions on Bernarr 159, 190; opinions on Fulton Oursler 161; politics 175-76; *True Story* idea 87-88 family life 87-88; marriage crisis 168-71

Macfadden Deauville Hotel: 191, 192

Macfadden Peak 168

McPherson, Aimee 148-49

Madison Square Garden 1

Marriage Manuals 73

Mencken, H.L. 20, 53, 165-66, 202

Miller, William 20

Mills, Eleanor 148

Modern Marriage 164

Modern Romances 87

Moore, M.A. 104

Morrow, Prince Albert 27

Mussolini, Benito 168, 171-72

Muscle Builder 164

National Hygiene 185, 196

Naturopaths 66-67, 106, 186

New Haven Times 177

Newsweek 185, 190

New York Daily Investment News 165, 177

New York Daily News 135, 136, 149, 152

New York Graphic 105, 110, 135-52, 153, 163, 165, 172, 177

New York Journal 141

New York Mirror 136, 142, 152

New York Times 3-4, 198-99

New York World 42

New Yorker 31, 83, 196-97

Oakes, June 63

Oliphant, Laurence 64

Oom the Omnipotent 156-57

Osteopaths 64-66, 186
Oursler, Fulton 53, 91, 163,
  171, 179, 183, 203;
  biography of Macfadden 166;
  career 161, editing 161-62;
  Liberty 179-82; *New
  York Graphic* 140, 142, 144,
  146, 147; *True Story*
  81, 84; *True Romances*
  86; Walter Winchell, 144-45
Own Your Own Home 164
Palmer, Daniel David 66
Pasteur, Louis 58
Patterson, Joseph 179
Perkins, Grace (Oursler)
  166-67, 180
Pegler, Westbrook 179
Personal Romances 86
Phelps, Niel S. 48, 50
Philadelphia Daily News 177
Pool, Magistrate 4
Post, C.W. 19, 45-53
Radam, William 99-100
Rapp, William Jordan 85,
  89
Readers Digest 83
Restell, Madame 3
Repplier, Agnes 88
Revealing Romances 86
Rhinelander, Kip 150
Rockwell, Norman 95
Roosevelt, Eleanor 179, 181
Roosevelt, Franklin D. 172-73,
  175, 180, 181, 188
Roosevelt, Teddy 44
Runyon, Damon 145
St. Augustine 14
Sandow, Eugene 10, 12
Saturday Evening Post
  (SEP) 179, 180, 182,
  188-89
Scarberry, Alma Sioux 142
Seattle Star 62
Senator, Herrmann 46
Seventh Day Adventists 17,
  45, 48
Shakespeare, William 189
Shaw, George Bernard 2, 27,
  54, 55
Shuttleworth, John 164

Siciliano, Angelo: see Atlas
  Charles
Sinclair, Meta 51-52
Sinclair, Mary Craig
  Kimbrough 52
Sinclair, Upton 28, 29-30,
  50-53, 59, 94, 98
Snyder, Ruth 148-49
Society for the Suppression
  of Vice 2-5
Spivak, John 142, 147
Sterling, Nana 30
Steur, Max 151
Still, Andrew Taylor
  65-66
Storm, John 4
Strongfort, Lionel 32
Sturgis, Frederick R. 72
Sullivan, Ed 139
Sumner, John S. 81, 135, 151
Sunday, Billy 38, 88
Taft, President William
  Howard 44
Talmey, Allene 165
Taylor, Robert Lewis 196-97
Thaw, Harry 151
Time 83, 151, 159, 177, 190
Tanner, H.S. 59-61
Thacher, L.C. 93-94
Tissot, S.A. 6, 74
True Confessions 87
True Love Stories 86
True Detective 164, 197
True Experiences 86
True Marriage Stories 86
True Romances 86
True Story 80-91; cf
  publications Mark 20, 69,
  158, 163, 188
Turner, Terry 143
Tyler, Moses Coit 22
U.S. Post Office 198
Vaca, Cabeza de 96
Valentino, Rudolph 105, 150
Vandercook, John W. 141-42
Viereck, George Slyvester 182
Villard, Oscar Garrison 88
Walker, Jimmy 88, 90
Walker, John Brisbane 161
Walter, Dr. 34

Washington, Booker T. 49
Washington, George 69
White, Ellen 19-20, 45, 49
White, James 20
Wickersham, George 44
Winesap, George 18
Williamson, Clair and
 Dorothea 61-62
Williamson, Mary 54—see
 Macfadden, Mary
Whitley, Alexander 11
Wiggam, Albert Edward 30,
 107

Williams, Carl 107
Wilson, President Woodrow
 102
Winchell, Walter 139, 144-45
Woodhill, Victoria 3
Wood, Clement 151-52,
 163, 174
Woollcott, Alexander 145
Young Men's Christian
 Association 2